MINISTERING ANGELS

MINISTERING ANGELS

Stella Bingham

Medical Economics Company Book Division
Oradell, New Jersey

Published in 1979 by Medical Economics Company, a division
of Litton Industries, Inc., 680 Kinderkamack Road, Oradell,
New Jersey 07649 U.S.A.

ISBN 0-87489-237-6

Printed in Great Britain

10 9 8 7 6 5 4 3 2 1

CONTENTS

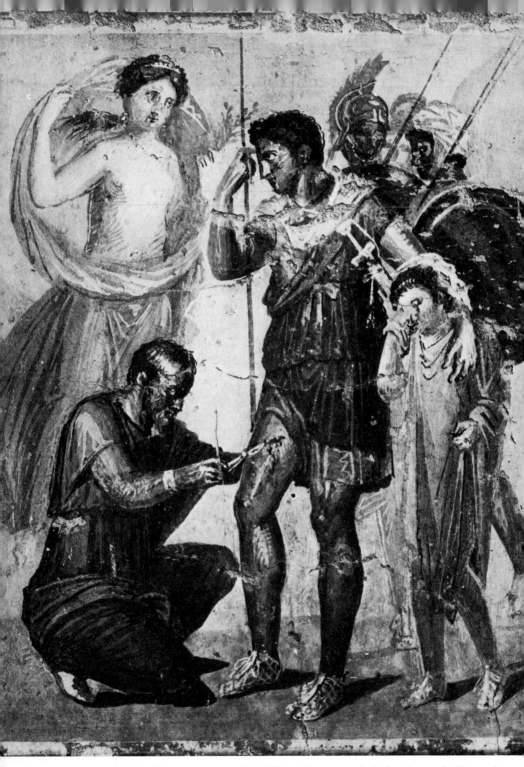

A physician treats a wounded soldier with a sympathetic female muse looking on in this fresco from Pompeii, dating from the 1st century AD. With the coming of Christianity, women took on a more active role; the first hospital in Rome was founded by a woman in AD 390

In the Beginning 1

Women have nursed since the first mother gave birth to the first baby. Nursing has always been a woman's duty, as much her responsibility as cooking, sewing and sweeping the floors: a domestic chore. Christianity made caring for the sick poor a work of charity, a penance, one of the most unpleasant jobs women (and men) could do to show their love of God. Even with the introduction of paid nurses – one of the consequences of the Protestant Reformation, particularly in England—things did not improve. The work was unpleasant, the hours killing, food and accommodation often poor, and wages low, and the sick poor got the sort of care they might have expected in such circumstances. Only in the last century did it begin to dawn on a few of the more enlightened doctors and social reformers that, with a little training, nurses might do more than care for a patient: they might help to cure. Woman's oldest duty became her first profession.

While many ancient civilizations developed quite advanced systems of medicine and surgery and, particularly, of public hygiene and sanitation, women had only a small part to play in them. In the earliest days, medicine was inseparable from religion and superstition: medicine was magic, the priests were physicians and disease was the work of evil spirits. The functions of priest and doctor gradually separated but women's work was generally confined to midwifery and nursing at home.

Christianity made a sacred duty of loving your neighbour and caring for the sick, the old and the afflicted. Deaconesses, ordained by the laying on of hands, achieved a particularly important position in the Eastern Church. They had the same role as

7

consecrated virgins and widows, who undertook specific functions within the church and devoted their lives to charitable work, which included sick visiting. In the early centuries such women lived and worked freely in society, but gradually they formed themselves into communities and hence their spheres of activity were limited and curtailed. Care of the sick was a particular responsibility of the bishops who, from the 4th century AD, built separate hospitals for their care. One of the earliest and most magnificent was built by Basil, Bishop of Caesarea, in AD 370. The Basilias, like such later foundations as the Hôtel Dieu at Lyons (542) and the Hôtel Dieu, Paris (about 650), combined the functions of hospital, almshouse, orphanage and hostel, as it was not thought necessary to make a distinction between the various objects of charity. The first hospital in Rome was founded in 390 by Fabiola, a wealthy widow who was converted to Christianity, and, in expiation of her former life and an unhappy second marriage, lavished her fortune on the sick and the poor.

In 817, the Council of Aix declared the care of the poor to be the chief duty of monastic communities. However, a gradual transfer of part of this responsibility had been taking place since St. Benedict (born 480) had declared in his monastic Rule, 'Before all things and above all things care must be taken of the sick.' The monastic life was particularly attractive to women as an alternative to marriage. The early nuns led free lives, most of them not even wearing distinctive dress. They were given the opportunity to develop their own interests, and many nunneries became centres of learning. The great double communities of monks and nuns were usually led by an abbess, often of the highest rank and ability. Hilda, Abbess of Whitby in the 7th century, was a kinswoman of the King of Northumbria. She trained many eminent monks and was a woman of national importance. The monasteries had wards for their own sick and many, particularly those belonging to the Benedictine rule, had separate buildings for travellers and the needy. Well-born ladies visited the hospitals to help care for the sick. The quality of medical care was low, but the spiritual tone was excellent.

By the 12th century, hospitals specifically for the sick were emerging as separate institutions. At the same time a number of religious orders were founded with the principal duty of nursing. In about 1050 a group of merchants from Amalfi, moved by the plight of the pilgrims pouring into Jerusalem, founded two hospitals in the Holy City. The one for men was under the protection of St. John the Almoner, the women's, St. Mary Magdalene. After the capture of Jerusalem by the Crusaders in 1099, the Order of St. John, which had devotedly nursed the soldiers during the Crusades, was endowed with generous gifts and lands from all over Europe. Under the second Grand Master of the Order the members took the Augustinian Rule and added military duties to their nursing work. The Hospitallers were divided into three grades: the knights who bore arms and held the important positions, the priests, and the serving brothers who probably did most of the nursing. The Order was rich and glamorous and membership eagerly sought after. Their hospitals were well equipped and run with a military discipline which strongly influenced later hospital management. When Jerusalem fell to the Saracens in 1187 and Acre followed in 1291 the Knights lost all their possessions in Palestine and the few left alive escaped to Cyprus. They took and held Rhodes from 1310 to 1522 and then the Holy Roman Emperor Charles V gave them Malta, where they remained until the island was captured by Napoleon Bonaparte in 1798. The female branch of the Order, however, apparently gave up nursing after fleeing from Jerusalem.

The German Teutonic Knights were formed to serve the sick and poor and defend the holy places. Their first hospital was destroyed when Jerusalem fell in 1187, but they re-formed and nursed wounded Christian soldiers during the siege of Acre in 1190. After Acre's capture, they built a church and hospital there – but retreated to Venice and then Marienbad when the city fell finally into Moslem hands. Many hospitals in Germany were given to them. The Knights of St. Lazarus undertook military duties as well as the care of lepers in Jerusalem, and elsewhere.

The oldest purely nursing order of nuns were the Augustinian Sisters of the Hôtel Dieu in Paris. By the 13th century they were completely enclosed under the control of the clergy, and only allowed to leave the hospital for visiting nursing. In 1212 a decree by the Bishops in Council instructed hospitals in France to use as few nursing sisters as possible in order to economize on the expenditure of charitable gifts, so the hospital was understaffed, the Sisters untrained, ill-fed and dreadfully overworked. The standard of nursing was fairly low, though some visitors commented on the Sisters' cheerful loving manner. Periods of overcrowding saw as many as five or six patients in one large bed.

For centuries the clerical and civil powers fought over the administration of the hospital. Investigations led to reforms, and then to decline. In the 14th century there were reports of insubordination, insolence and moral scandal. In the 17th century the Sisters were accused of disobeying orders, neglecting the sick in favour of religious meditation, and selling drugs. Visitors at the end of the 18th century reported overcrowding, bed bugs, filth and insanitary conditions. Throughout, the Sisters, with justification, pleaded overwork. With the French Revolution came suppression of the Augustinian Order, though conditions were improved and the Sisters were allowed to remain as lay nurses.

The increasing decadence of the monastic orders led to the growth of secular equivalents, many of whom devoted themselves to nursing. The most interesting of the women's orders were the Béguines of Flanders, founded in 1180 as a protest against the more restrictive and artificial aspects of monastic life. They were vowed to chastity and obedience but could keep their own property and were free to leave the order and marry. The women lived together in threes and fours in small houses, grouped in a precinct, and nursed in hospitals and in the homes of the sick poor. The order spread to Germany, Switzerland and France and by 1300 it had about 200,000 members. Its independence made it unpopular with the Church, but the civil authorities and the people both gave it their support.

It was not until the 16th, 17th and 18th centuries that a further flowering of religious and secular nursing orders took place, many doing noble and self-sacrificing work. The members of one sisterhood, the Camellines, all died nursing in the last great plague of Barcelona, for instance. The most important of these later orders were the Sisters of Charity, founded by St. Vincent de Paul in 1630. St. Vincent was convinced that the work of visiting nurses was incompatible with enclosure and was determined that his Sisters should not become religious in the monastic sense. 'My daughters,' he said, 'you are not nuns . . . for whoever says the word *nun* says *cloister* and the Sisters should go everywhere.' He enlisted simple country girls with a basic education, clothed them in grey-blue rough gowns and handed them over to his associate Mlle. le Gras for practical nursing training. The girls were instructed to obey the doctors but also to watch and learn, so that they could be of use when no doctor was within call. They were to be willing and ready helpers, able to go anywhere and do anything. In 1639 they took over the nursing of a hospital in Angers. In 1642 the first four Sisters took vows, which were to be renewed annually. In 1654, at Sedan, they undertook for the first time the military nursing for which they were to become well-known.

When St. Vincent and Mlle. le Gras both died in 1660 there were 350 Sisters in seventy establishments in France and Poland and the Order continued to grow rapidly. However, the early 19th century saw its decline. While nursing education broadened generally, its own narrowed. Sisters were not allowed to be present during childbirth or at gynaecological examinations and they were forbidden to nurse venereal cases or take full charge of men patients. For these reasons, they were not suited to the demands of general hospital work.

The early hospitals in England, as in the rest of Europe, were religious foundations. In 936, Athelstan established a hospital in York, nursed by eight Sisters. Archbishop Lanfranc opened two hospitals in Canterbury in the 11th century. In 1101, Queen Mathilda founded St. Giles in the Fields for lepers, served by Poor Clares, and, in 1148, St. Katharine's, where noblewomen undertook nursing duties, was founded. St. Bartholomew's – nowadays known as Barts – was founded in 1123, the Holy Cross, Winchester, in 1132 and in 1215 St. Thomas's, founded as the infirmary of the Priory of St. Mary Overie, became a separate hospital. Brothers and Sisters of the Augustinian Order nursed at Bart's and St. Thomas's.

By the time of the Reformation, the care of patients at St. Thomas's had fallen to an extremely low standard. In 1536, the parishioners complained that a woman in childbirth was turned away to die at the church door; that infant baptism was refused until the Master received half a noble; that religious services were not held; that the Master kept a concubine within the hospital; and that he was in the habit of selling church plate and claiming it had been stolen. But any care was better than none. England had no secular nursing orders and no public hospital system so, with the dissolution of the monasteries in the 1530s, the plight of the sick poor became desperate. St. Bartholomew's, however, was reconstituted by Henry VIII in 1544, and in 1547 the mayor and aldermen of the City of London petitioned Edward VI for leave to take over St. Thomas's, St. Bartholomew's, Bethlehem and other lesser institutions.

Stripped of its religious elements of loving care and self-sacrificing duty, nursing was revealed as little more than domestic work. The matron was in charge of all the women in the hospital and was responsible for seeing 'that the said washers and nurses of this howse be alwaies well occupied and not idle', but it was not felt necessary that she should have any nursing experience and her duties were mainly concerned with housekeeping: 'You shal also in every quarter of the yeare examine the inventorie which shal be delivered unto you, of the implements of the howse; as of beddes, bolsters, mattrasses, blanquets, coverlets, shets, pallads, shirts, hosen, and such other.' Nurses were instructed: 'Ye shall also

A drawing of a 16th century hospital ward. By the 1500s, women – particularly nuns – had nursed the sick for centuries, though in many cases social and religious custom limited their involvement

faithfully and charitably serve and help the poor in all their griefs and diseases as well as by keeping them sweet and clean as in giving them their meats and drinks after the most honest and comfortable manner.' Their duties were to keep the wards and the patients clean, to distribute food and drink, and to administer any medicines and special food ordered by the doctor.

The monastic term Sister was retained and applied to the nurse in charge of a ward. Sometimes Sisters were appointed from among the nurses or attendants, sometimes from the upper domestic classes outside. At St. Bartholomew's, each Sister had sole charge of nine or ten patients and was expected to use her free time to spin. In 1550, twenty-one pairs of sheets were delivered to the matron, cut from cloth woven and spun by the Sisters. Earliest staffing lists also include a 'foole' or 'innocent', presumably employed to keep the

Sisters amused. A cosy picture emerges of the earliest lay nurses serenely weaving, laughing at the antics of the fool, and stopping occasionally to comfort a patient, shoo the hens into the yard or consume a substantial meal. Unfortunately this happy picture is marred by the evidence of the surviving hospital records. At St. Thomas's the matron was brought before the court three times from 1572 to 1580 for drunkenness. In 1559, the matron of St. Bartholomew's was forbidden to sell ale in her house. In 1563, a St. Thomas's Sister was reported by the matron as 'she wolde not do her dutie in the office but ronne to the taverne.' In 1650, a Sister at Bart's was rebuked for entertaining men all night and letting them play cards in her ward; six years later three Sisters who had disturbed patients by fighting were dismissed. The nursing itself was probably quite adequate though, and the matron of St. Bartholomew's, for example, distinguished herself during the plague of 1665, when some of the physicians had fled, and was commended and rewarded by the governors.

With the secularization of nursing, however, ladies almost ceased to regard the sick poor in hospitals as worthy objects of Christian charity, though nursing, and even a little surgery, continued to be numbered among the domestic arts. Women collected recipes for medicines as eagerly as those for potting meat, and wealthier ladies accepted responsibility for the health of their households and their less fortunate neighbours as one of their domestic duties. The diary of Lady Hoby (1599–1605) contains many entries like the following: 'After I praied, then I dined, then I walked and did see a sicke man,' and, 'I dressed the hand of one of the servants that was verie sore Cutte.' Lady Mildmay (died 1620) recorded in her journal: 'Also every day I spent some time in the Herball and books of phisicking, and in ministering to one or other by directions of the best phisitions of myne acquaintance.'

In the 18th century, wealthy British philanthropists set an example to the rest of the world by throwing themselves into an orgy of hospital building: the London opened in 1740; the Middlesex in 1745; the Westminster in 1719; St. George's in 1728; and Guy's in 1725. Outside London, Manchester Royal Infirmary opened in 1753; Liverpool Royal Infirmary in 1749; Leeds General Infirmary in 1767; and Edinburgh Royal Infirmary in 1729. Towards the end of the century, public fever hospitals were set up, and, in a first glimmering of organized sanitation and preventative medicine, whitewash was applied to hospital walls. Iron bedsteads replaced bug-infested wooden ones. The forceful criticisms of John Howard, a prison reformer who also investigated hospitals, stung many hospital managements into spring-cleaning. Yet, during this period, the status of nurses and the standard of nursing actually declined.

The London Hospital opened with a man and wife to act as caretakers and look after the patients. A nurse was not appointed until a year or two later when it was decided that 'Squire be contracted with by the Chairman of the Committee as Nurse for the Women's wards at the rate of £14 a year.' A night nurse was appointed at £9, but when both nurses became resident in 1743, their salaries were reduced to £6 and £4 respectively. The nurses slept off the wards and the watches (night nurses) in the attic. Day duty began at 6 am in summer and 7 am in winter and lasted until supper at 10 pm. Nurses had to be in bed by 11 pm, had no holidays, no days off and no pension. In 1756, the list of their duties included the following: 'To make the beds of the officers and servants, to clean the rooms, passages and stairs and the Court and Committee rooms.' Records of most hospitals of the time report, with dreary regularity, nurses rebuked or dismissed for drinking, insolence, lack of discipline, absenteeism, thieving, or soliciting payment from the patients. One visitor recorded seeing an in-coming patient stopped at the door by a loud-mouthed virago – the Sister – who demanded her fee before he could enter.

The nurses seldom wore uniform, usually cooked their own food and ate it in the ward kitchens or sculleries. Their hours were long, their accommodation inadequate and insanitary, and night nurses often had to sleep in lobbies next to the racket of the wards. Most of the actual nursing was done by medical students. It was almost impossible to get respectable women to work in such conditions. One doctor reported, 'We always take them without a character because no respectable woman would take such work.' Another wrote, 'I know that a respectable woman was declined the other day, as being too good for the situation. The only conditions that are made are . . . that they are not confirmed drunkards . . . In general they are not educated at all.' The London Hospital decided to appoint only women who could read and write, but was forced to compromise when insufficient numbers of suitable candidates

The luxurious looking infirmary of the Hospital of Charity, Paris, in about 1660. In France, the Sisters of Charity, a religious order devoted to nursing, was founded in 1630. By 1660 there were 350 nursing sisters at work in hospitals in France and Poland, the order's two main centres

presented themselves. Instead, the hospital ordered 'that only those nurses who could read and write were to administer medicine.' In 1844 the Board of Leeds Infirmary rejected a proposal that 'no nurse be engaged in the domestic duties of the House'. Guy's finally relieved nurses of scrubbing floors as late as 1857, but ordered that, as a consequence, each nurse was to care for twice as many patients.

Standards were not uniformly bad. Edinburgh Royal Infirmary maintained a reasonable level of nursing care and operated an excellent set of nursing regulations. Although formally untrained, some Sisters who worked for years on the same ward under the same physician picked up a useful amount of practical skill. In 1885, Sir James Paget spoke in their defence: 'It is true that even fifty years ago there were some excellent nurses, especially among the Sisters on the medical wards, where everything was more gentle and orderly than in the surgical. They had none of the modern art: they could not have kept a chart or skilfully taken a temperature, but they had an admirable sagacity and a sort of rough practical knowledge which were nearly as good as an acquired skill.' A correspondent to *The Times* in 1857 wrote with more understanding of the nurses' position than was then usual, 'Hospital nurses have been much abused; – they have their faults, but most of them are due to the want of proper treatment. Lectured by committees, preached at by chaplains, scowled on by treasurers and stewards, scolded by matrons, sworn at by surgeons, bullied by dressers, grumbled at and abused by patients, insulted if old and ill-favoured, talked flippantly to if middle-aged and good humoured, tempted and seduced if young and well-looking – they are what any woman might be under the same circumstances.'

Efforts to improve the quality of nursing were generally limited to pious hopes, stern injunctions and envious glances across the English Channel to the religious orders who at least gave loving care (though by then most of the nursing in the major public institutions was done by lay attendants, as much practical nursing was banned to the Sisters on the grounds of impropriety). It did not seem to have occurred to hospital managers and doctors that they got what they paid for and that respectable, even educated, women might be drawn to nursing by higher salaries and improved conditions. Unable to visualize good nursing outside the confines of a sisterhood, all they could do was to vainly ask, 'Where are our Sisters of Charity?'

The conditions in the great voluntary hospitals affected only a minority of the sick. The rich employed private nurses at home, though as most of these were of the Mrs. Gamp stamp vividly described by Charles Dickens, the quality of care was no better than in hospital. The remainder of the population stayed at home for as long as their family and friends could cope with them. Most who were forced to seek institutional care ended up in the workhouse infirmaries, either because there was no voluntary hospital in their area or because the voluntary hospitals would not accept them. When the great union workhouses were built following the Poor Law Amendment Act of 1834, they undertook to provide medical attention and in-patient facilities to all who were both destitute and in need of them. But, such was the deterrent effect of the grim buildings, the penal restrictions and the comfortless diet and accommodation, that the able-bodied preferred almost any fate to incarceration within their walls. Most workhouse inmates were incapacitated in some way – by age or youth, chronic illness or disability, pregnancy or idiocy, drunkenness or madness. As little or no distinction was made between the grades of inmates; the sick had to face the same punishing regime as the so-called idle or evil. Sadly, it was only too easy for a respectable and hard-working man or woman to end their days in the workhouse simply because they had nowhere else to go.

Some workhouses were, within the restrictions of the Act, admirable institutions. In 1841, the retiring Board of Guardians of Manchester Workhouse described with justifiable pride their 'ample and convenient' sick wards, a lying-in ward, and the 'commodious and conveniently situated' surgery. Unfortunately, in most cases, the guardians were uninterested and neglectful, or even corrupt, while the matron and master could be at best uncaring and at worst, unkind to the point of cruelty. The outside world, supposing all inmates to be getting no more than they deserved, were pleased by a system which, they believed, kept the cost down. Only when the early lady visitors and the more sensitive medical officers and chaplains started investigating and, shocked, published what they discovered, did the real picture emerge.

Dr. Joseph Rogers, medical officer at the Strand Workhouse, one of the worst in London, described conditions as he first found them in 1855. The Guardians received £400 a year from carpet beating which the inmates carried out just outside the male wards, so that the noise deprived the sick of sleep and the dust made it impossible to open the windows. The 'foul' ward was separated from the tinker's shop only by an eight-foot partition. The female insane ward was just under the lying-in ward. But the worst scandal was the nursing. 'There was no paid nurse. Such nursing as we had and continued to have for the first nine years I was there, was performed

A German engraving of hospital inmates receiving food and medicine from a woman visitor. The religious implications have been formalized by the artist in the halo surrounding the woman's head

by more or less infirm paupers, with the occasional aid of some strong woman who had been admitted temporarily and was on pass.' In the 1850s, there were only seventy paid nurses (all untrained) in the whole of London, compared with 500 pauper nurses of whom half were over 50, a quarter over 60, many over 70 and some over 80. 'The responsible duties they had to perform were remunerated by an amended dietary and a pint of beer,' Dr. Rogers wrote. He continued '. . . I had not been the medical officer for many months before I found that my pauper nurses were frequently under the influence of drink, and that, too, in the forenoon. On inquiring, I heard to my surprise that the master was in the habit of giving out the stimulants at 7 a.m., and, as many of the inmates sold their allowances, the nurses had become partly or wholly intoxicated when I reached the House in the morning.' Not the least of the deterrents to good medical care was the fact that the doctors had to pay for medicines and drugs out of their own salaries – which, in Dr. Rogers's case, amounted to £50 a year.

Louisa Twining, who devoted her life to the cause of workhouse reform, had her interest in infirmaries aroused by a visit to an old crossing sweeper in St. Giles Workhouse in 1856. 'He was in the basement ward, nearly dark, and with a stone floor; beds, sheets, and shirts were all equally grey with dirt . . . The sick in the so-called infirmary, a miserable building, long since destroyed, were indeed a sad sight, with their wretched pauper nurses in black caps and workhouse dress. One poor young man there, who had lain on a miserable flock bed for fourteen years with a spine complaint, was blind, and his case would have moved a heart of stone; yet no alleviation of food or comforts were ever granted him.' In 1858 she outlined her findings in a letter to *The Times* and appealed for improvements in the nursing. 'There is generally one nurse and a helper to each ward, sometimes containing twenty or thirty patients. The nurse sleeps in it and lives in it, whether the patients are men or women, in cases under my own knowledge. She may be said to be at work almost equally during the twenty-four hours for who else is to tend the sick and dying sufferers by night?' In the wards, 'Here are all those, in short, both young and old . . . who have no homes where they can be nursed. I have known such sufferers who never left their beds for years, I have known them tended at their deaths by drunken nurses. The women who are set over wards full of helpless sufferers drink whenever they can obtain the means, for they came not to this, the lowest office which a worn out woman can fill, till all other chances of subsistence are gone.'

Frances Power Cobbe, who was particularly interested in improving conditions for 'destitute incurables', started workhouse visiting in 1859, 'and *this* is what I saw. The sick lay on wretched beds, fit only for able-bodied tramps, and were nursed mainly by old pauper women of the very lowest class. The infirm wards were very frequently placed in the worst possible positions. I remember one (in London) which resounded all day long with din from the iron-foundry just beneath. . . . On one occasion I visited an enormous workhouse in a provincial town where there were nearly 500 sick and infirm patients. The Matron told me she had but lately been appointed to her post. I said, "It is a tremendously heavy charge for you, especially with only these pauper nurses. No doubt

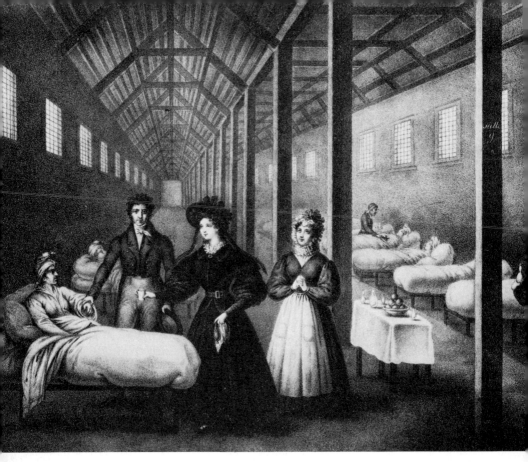

An unknown Countess visits the sick in another scene from a Paris hospital. Though noblewomen counted knowledge of nursing among the domestic virtues, the public nursing of the sick was usually left to other, inferior, hands

you have gone through a course of Hospital training, and know how to direct everything?" "O, dear No! Madam!" replied the lady with a toss of her cap-strings; "I never nursed anybody I can assure you, except my 'usband, before I came here. It was misfortune brought me to this!"'

Conditions in American hospitals rivalled those in Britain. Most big cities had almshouses which, like British workhouses, included infirmaries for the sick poor, and where the nursing, such as it was, was undertaken by other inmates. The origins of Bellevue Hospital, New York, lay in a small hospital built by the West India Company in 1658. In 1736, the new building was called the 'Publick Workhouse and House of Correction of New York' and by 1816 it contained almshouse quarters, a penitentiary and wards for the sick and insane. There was shocking overcrowding, insanitary conditions, and constant epidemics, while the doctors were cruelly overworked and the nurses detailed from the prison. In 1837, a committee of investigation reported filth, no ventilation, no clothing, patients with high fever lying naked under coarse blankets, jail fever rife, overcrowding, no supplies, putrefaction and vermin. As a result of the report, male and female prisoners were removed and smallpox cases and the insane were taken to separate infirmaries.

Blockley Hospital, Philadelphia, started life as an almshouse in 1731. An investigation in 1793 found shocking abuses and spoke of 'an abandoned, profligate set of nurses and attendants'. All work, including the nursing, was done by the inmates. In the cholera epidemic of 1832, the attendants demanded and received more wages which they at once spent on drink, then fought each other or lay in a drunken stupor in the wards. Sisters of Charity were summoned from Emmitsburgh. They restored order, but refused to stay. In 1856, a further report revealed scandalous conditions.

Not all hospitals were as bad. The Pennsylvania Hospital, which opened in 1751 and was the first in the United States devoted solely to the curative care of the sick, had a better history, and its records mention 'experienced and trustworthy persons' who did the nursing. New York Hospital, which was granted its charter in 1771, was, like the Pennsylvania, a wealthy foundation and probably employed a superior class of attendants. It was these standards that the reformers were determined to achieve for all.

2 Where are our Sisters of Charity?

By the early 19th century a number of compassionate and humanitarian ladies and gentlemen had woken up to the fact that care for the poor and the sick left much to be desired. Inspired with charitable zeal, they led a crusade to alleviate the lot of these, the least of God's creatures. At the same time the germ of a revolutionary idea was born in medical minds. Concerned at the shocking state of nursing and hospital conditions generally, it occurred to doctors that good nursing might actually contribute to the cure of patients. These two trends led eventually to the establishment of the nursing profession.

The first attempt to train hospital attendants was made by Dr. Valentine Seaman of the New York Hospital. In 1798, he organized a course of twenty-four lectures which included the outlines of anatomy, physiology and child care, the course being run in connection with the maternity department. But most early attempts at nursing reform centred naturally on the idea of nursing sisterhoods. In Germany the deaconess movement had never wholly died out and after several false starts elsewhere it was successfully revived at Kaiserswerth on the Rhine. The village pastor, Theodor Fliedner, had been impressed, during his travels through Europe, with the need for better nurses. 'Would not our young Christian women be able and willing to do Christian nursing?' he wrote. '. . . Ought we to delay in bringing back consecrated women into the service of the Lord?'

Fliedner's hospital opened in 1836. The deaconesses, with Pastor Fliedner's wife, Friederike, as superintendent, led simple and frugal lives, undertaking the cooking and cleaning as well as the nursing of the sick poor both in the hospital and at home. They were given theoretical and clinical instruction and studied for the state examination in pharmacy. A probationary period was introduced, and after five years of service the deaconesses were free to leave and marry. The cheerful loving spirit which inspired their work impressed many visitors, including the British reformer Elizabeth Fry on her visit in 1840.

Gradually the work and influence of the deaconesses expanded. They were invited to take over the nursing in other hospitals. New motherhouses were established and in 1849 Pastor Fliedner took a party of deaconesses across the Atlantic to Pittsburgh to start a house there.

Visitors came to Germany from many other countries to learn from Fliedner's example. Among them was Florence Nightingale, who spent three months there in 1851. Looking back on her time at Kaiserswerth, she wrote: 'The nursing there was nil, the hygiene horrible. The hospital was certainly the worst part of Kaiserswerth.' However, Miss Nightingale continued: 'But never have I met with a higher tone, a purer devotion than there. There was no neglect. It was the more remarkable because many of the Deaconesses had been only peasants – none were gentlewomen (when I was there).' Although far from ideal, the nursing at Kaiserswerth was far in advance of all other nursing at the time. The deaconesses served bravely and devotedly in epidemics and wars – they worked in sixty military hospitals in the Franco-Prussian War.

During the latter part of the 19th century the institution went into a decline. The freshness and reforming zeal melted away. Pastor Fliedner had placed a great emphasis on the movement's inde- pendence from church or state control, but gradually the pastors took over the control of the nurses from the matrons and restricted their intellectual freedom and spheres of work. The need to earn money meant that nurses were sent out to take on hospital work with little or no training, probationers were accepted at younger and younger ages, and the deaconesses were often cruelly overworked.

The movement's influence was widespread, however. In England the cry went up, 'Let all serious Christians join, and found an order of women like the Sisters of Charity.' Good nurses must be 'animated by religion,' the men insisted, 'science and mere humanity cannot be relied on' – though no one seems to have suggested that doctors should be similarly hemmed in by a religious Rule. Elizabeth Fry, fresh from Kaiserswerth, was the first to answer the appeal, though the secular nature of her Institute of Nursing, founded in 1840, roused suspicions in some clerical

" 'Sairey Gamp' – a nurse of sixty years ago." This illustration was produced for the Wellcome Trustees' Professional Nurse's Diary *for 1907–8 and gives a vivid impression of how nurses were regarded in Britain before the Nightingale era*

quarters. Her Sisters were carefully chosen, mainly from the higher domestic or small farm and trading classes, and they had to be able to read and write. They received a limited practical training at Guy's Hospital in London, wore plain clothes, were maintained by the Institute and were forbidden to accept money and gifts. They were employed mainly in private nursing, but, between jobs, they lived in the Home and undertook nursing the poor. The Institute had limited influence – by 1857 only ninety nurses had been trained – but it proved that such an experiment could work. It was also popular with its customers. William Thackeray wrote to the Lady Superintendent in 1860, 'I have the pleasure of sending you ten guineas for the five weeks service of the excellent nurse I had from your institution, and beg it to accept the other five pounds.'

A similar body to Mrs. Fry's Institute was founded in Philadelphia in 1839. There, a group of young ladies banded together to organize the Nurse Society for the purpose of 'providing, sustaining, and causing to be instructed as far as possible, pious and prudent women' to nurse poor females during and after childbirth. The nurses were given lectures, and practised on a manikin. After attending six cases satisfactorily they were awarded a certificate and could work as home nurses. In 1850 a Home and School were opened and teaching improved, even though the course's duration was not extended to a year until 1897.

The first Church of England Sisterhood, the Park Village Community, opened under Dr. Pusey's guidance in 1845. The Sisters of Mercy had no hospital training and devoted themselves chiefly to welfare visits to the sick and poor. A similar group, also known as the Sisters of Mercy, was founded by Miss Sellon in Devonport in 1848. In the beginning, they also had no hospital experience but worked energetically through several cholera epidemics. By 1866 the two communities had merged.

St. John's House, founded in 1848 by an eminent group of clergymen and physicians, was the first purely nursing order sponsored by the Church of England. The 'Training Institution for Nurses in Hospitals, Families, and for the Poor' had three classes of members. Probationers had to be at least eighteen and to be able to read and write. They paid a fee of £15 a year in return for their training and board, lodging, and laundry. After two years, if they were satisfactory, the probationers became nurses and received board and lodging and wages. After a further five years, if they were competent, they were awarded a certificate. Better educated women could start as nurses, without going through the pro-bationary period. Sisters could live in the Home, where they paid

£50 for their keep, with a clergyman as 'Master' of the establishment, or with their families. The rules were strict on the styles of
dress and hair permitted.

In 1849 King's College Hospital undertook the six months'
training and in 1856 St. John's House took over the nursing in the
hospital. 'Many are the stories told of the day the Sisters took
possession;' the *St. John's House League News* recalled in 1904.
'Nearly all the old staff, who resented the change, waited bonneted
and cloaked in the hall for their arrival, and then left at once,
leaving them "to find out the bad cases for themselves"; and by the
end of the day the new-comers, who had arrived in clean and dainty
uniforms, were more like a set of sweeps or char-women, in such an
appalling state of disorder had they found their wards.'

St. John's House was reorganized to take on the new hospital
work. The staff consisted of a lady Superior, Sisters, Associate
Sisters, lady pupils, nurses, assistant nurses, probationers and
candidates on trial. The Sisters were ladies who received no pay and
paid for their keep. They entered on three months' trial, when they
became lady pupils, and then assistant Sisters and Sisters. The
probationers were of the servant class and were paid. After three
months they became assistant nurses for nine months and then
nurses. The training period was increased to one year, all spent in
the hospital. The standard of nursing was high; Florence
Nightingale described it as the most 'homelike' she had ever seen.

St. John's House provided the nursing at King's College Hospital
until 1885, though in 1883, as a result of an internal quarrel, most of
the nurses formed a breakaway group and the organization was
placed under the control of the All Saints Sisterhood. St. John's also
nursed at Charing Cross Hospital from 1866 to 1889, the
Metropolitan Hospital from 1888 to 1896 and at several other
institutions. As the leading hospitals established their own training
schools, St. John's House withdrew increasingly from the public
service. Finally, in 1919 the institution was taken over by St.
Thomas's Hospital to provide totally private nursing.

Throughout the period, St. John's maintained their original
hierarchy, which, towards the end, became completely outdated.
In her autobiography, the writer Carola Oman told of encounters
with the two different traditions. In 1897, a St. John's nurse was
called to Carola Oman's Oxford home to nurse her mother through
typhoid fever. Her mother 'always attributed her recovery to her
excellent trained nurse, but there is a twist to this story. Nurse
told mother that her case reminded her so much of that of another
lady she attended – "Just like you, madam. There was such a nice-

looking gentleman, and two little ones in the nursery, just like you. Well, after the poor lady died, you should have seen the husband's mourning!...." She settled my mother for a nice little sleep and said as she stole out, "Of course, he married within the year." Mother decided to live.' Four years later, her brother, Charles, was born. 'We heard with awe that the St. John's nurse this time was something very special. She was a lady-nurse. What that was supposed to mean we knew not but she was certainly no nurse. She left my poor mother on a hot June night lying on a rubber sheet. "Let me see, where is that kitchen?" It was too much trouble to go down two flights to collect a clean draw-sheet.'

The All Saints Sisterhood, which had taken over the direction of the St. John's House nurses at King's College Hospital, dated from 1851, when they had established a home for incurable women and children. In 1857, they took over the nursing in some of the wards of University College Hospital; from 1862 they were in charge of the nursing of the whole of that hospital, as well as doing private nursing. The hospital authorities were at first delighted with the vastly improved standard of nursing, but the Sisters failed to keep up with new methods and knowledge. The result was that in 1899 the hospital established its own training school. All Saints Sisters also undertook nursing in other hospitals and were active in India.

The women of America also responded to the question: 'Where are our Sisters of Charity?', greatly to the benefit of early 19th-century nursing. The St. Joseph's Sisterhood of Emmitsburgh, founded in 1809, adopted the Rule of St. Vincent de Paul's Sisters of Charity. The Sisters of Mercy reached the United States in 1843 and founded hospitals in Pennsylvania, Illinois and Missouri. The first Protestant sisterhood – 'of the Holy Communion' – was established in 1845. From 1853 they worked in a New York parish infirmary and transferred to St. Luke's Hospital, New York, when it opened in 1859. Lay nurses did most of the actual nursing, but the Sisters stayed in charge until a secular nursing school was opened in 1888.

Outside the hospitals, the chief field of activity for the reformers – both in Europe and the USA – was the workhouse, or similar institutions. The ladies, who had begun workhouse visiting with the admirable and modest intention of cheering the poor inmates' lives with flowers, readings and such little comforts as good tea and bedjackets, were shocked at the conditions they found and astonished at the resistance they encountered in many cases from the responsible authorities. Finding that improvements were impossible to achieve within the system, they set about rousing public opinion. Committees were formed, governing bodies harried, pamphlets distributed, statistics collected, letters and articles published, questions asked in Parliament. The tireless reformer Louisa Twining claimed, in *Workhouses and Women's Work* (1857), that the poor felt it more of a disgrace to go into the workhouse than to go to prison. The authorities seem to have felt the same as they employed larger and better paid staffs in prisons: a jail for 900 inmates paid its surgeon £220, while the surgeon in a workhouse for 500 or 600 received only £78 15s.

The Workhouse Visiting Society was formed in 1858, with Miss Twining as honorary secretary, to try to help the inmates and to enlighten public opinion. In the same year *The Times* published Louisa Twining's letter on workhouse infirmary nursing and the Poor Law Board sanctioned a plan to train able-bodied women in the infirmaries and send them out as nurses. This economical proposal received little support from the reformers: '. . . we think that little could have been known of the real character of this class of women by those who made the suggestion,' Miss Twining commented with restraint, 'or of the fact that the greater number of them were brought to the workhouse by some loss of character, the chief cause of which was certainly intemperance.' Florence Nightingale poured scorn on the idea in typically robust style: 'Are we to expect that we shall find suitable women for an occupation which requires, perhaps above every other occupation, sobriety, honesty, trustworthiness, truthfulness, orderliness, cleanliness, good character, and good health, among those who, nearly all, at least in the workhouses of the large towns, are there because they have *not* been sober, *not* been honest, *not* been trustworthy or truthful, *not* been orderly or cleanly, *not* had good character or good health, because they have *not* been one or other of these things, because they have failed in one or all of these.' The plan came to nothing.

Miss Frances Power Cobbe launched her 'Plea for Destitute Incurables' in 1860. Her proposals, circulated through letters, papers and pamphlets, were that the case of these inmates (80,000 of whom passed through the workhouse each year) should be considered apart from the general residents, that they should be placed in special wards and that benevolent individuals should be allowed to provide comforts for them. A petition to this effect was signed by ninety influential doctors and surgeons and sent to every Board of Guardians.

The scandal which most captured the British public's attention was the death of Timothy Daly at Holborn Workhouse, London, from what was obviously appalling neglect. Although an enquiry exonerated the workhouse, it exposed the shocking conditions that prevailed there to the ratepayers who were, as electors, in some way responsible. 'I was so very much obliged to that poor man for dying,' Miss Nightingale wrote. A few months later, in April 1865, the *Lancet* announced that it was setting up a Sanitary Commission for Investigating the State of the Infirmaries of Workhouses. The three-man commission visited thirty-eight of the thirty-nine London workhouses. They found that only eleven had more than one paid nurse, fourteen others had one each, while the rest relied on pauper nurses. They concluded that six workhouses were unsuitable for the sick, or even the able-bodied, that ten needed major structural alterations, but that the rest could be made satisfactory. The Commission also reported that the workhouses cared for more sick people than did the voluntary hospitals. The eighteen London voluntary hospitals provided 3,738 beds, the metropolitan work-houses had 7,463 beds for the 'sick' and, nominally, about 7,000 for 'infirm' inmates, though, in fact, they cared for many more of the latter.

Investigating pauper nurses, the Commissioners found: 'It is notorious that the majority of them are aged and feeble and past work, or have strong tendencies to drink and in many cases have otherwise led vicious lives.' Workhouse visitors had found, 'in the great majority of cases, pauper nurses can only manage their patients by inspiring fear, and that their conduct is consequently brutish'.

The investigators came across shockingly insanitary conditions. 'In several infirmaries the nurses of one or more wards admitted that the bedridden patients habitually washed their hands and faces *in their chamber utensils.*' Sometimes they could scarcely believe their own ears. 'At one infirmary, the nurse of the syphilitic women's ward distinctly stated to us . . . that there was but one round-towel a week for the use of the eight inmates.' The number of medical officers was found to be inadequate: in one case one surgeon assisted by a resident junior was expected to look after 300 acutely sick and 600 chronic cases. In another, one medical officer cared for 130 acute and 200 chronic patients in intervals of private practice. The commissioners also condemned the custom whereby doctors had to pay for medicines out of their own pockets.

The *Lancet's* Commission inspired newspapers outside London to undertake their own investigations. The Association for the Improvement of Workhouse Infirmaries was formed. There were angry debates in Parliament. The same year Mr. Farnall, the Metropolitan Poor Law Inspector and an enthusiast for reform,

*The interior of Rahere's Ward, St Bartholomew's Hospital, London, in 1844.
Even before Florence Nightingale revolutionized nursing, improvements were being
made in many countries as part of the general mood of social reform*

made an official investigation into workhouse infirmaries. He
reported that the London workhouses housed annually 23,000
people of whom 6,000 were temporarily disabled, 10,300 were old
and infirm, 1,800 were imbeciles and idiots, 1,850 were able-bodied
and 3,000 were children. Amongst these classes there was little or no
classification. In 1866, Dr. Rogers formed the Poor Law Medical
Officers' Association to protect the character and interests of these
officials and to supply information to the public on how their best
efforts were hampered and thwarted.

Parliament could hold out no longer. In 1867, the Metropolitan
Poor Act was passed. The Act gave London unions power, alone or
in groups, to set up separate infirmaries detached from the
workhouse and under independent Boards of Management. The
Metropolitan Asylums Board was established to provide fever
hospitals for patients with infectious diseases. Thanks largely to Dr.
Rogers's campaigning, the Act made the Guardians, not the doctors,
responsible for providing medicines and medical appliances. Some
of the infirmaries built as a result of the Act became leading London

hospitals which, by 1875, were admitting all types of patient. Other districts, though under no legal obligation to do so, were inspired by London's example to build their own separate infirmaries.

The Act also recommended the employment of paid nurses and the use of asylums as nursing training schools, but progress here was slow. The Workhouse Nursing Association was started in 1879 to 'promote the employment of paid and efficiently trained nurses in all workhouse infirmaries and sick asylums'. But typical of the times even then was the election of a nurse for a Norfolk workhouse infirmary. The only candidate was the cook of one of the Guardians who felt like a change. She would have been elected if the Workhouse Nursing Association had not stepped in and secured the introduction of a trained nurse from the Liverpool Infirmary.

3 | Nurses go to War

fter the Crimean War, nursing could never be the same again. For the first time, lay women, organized and disciplined, were officially employed in the medical services of an army at war. Never after this would women accept that battle was a male preserve – as the men of America were the first to discover during the Civil War. Like the common soldier, nurses earned a new image. How could they be drunken, ignorant and promiscuous when Miss Nightingale was so fearless, pure and compassionate? How could nursing be fit work only for the most depraved classes when the 'Lady with the Lamp' did not hesitate to shoulder the most menial and sickening tasks?

Nursing was the last thing on anyone's mind (and, unfortunately, on the British Army's agenda) when Great Britain and France declared war on Russia on March 27, 1854. In June troops landed at Varna in Bulgaria where cholera broke out in the camp. The London crowds who had cheered the soldiers on their way confidently expected victory. Nobody then realized what thirty-nine years of peacetime economies and penny pinching, petty regulations and inefficiency had done to the British army. The system successfully created and utilized by the Duke of Wellington in the Napoleonic Wars had rotted under the twin savings on men and money. On September 14 an allied force landed in the Crimea and advanced on Sebastapol. Because there were not enough transports for the crossing of the Black Sea, tents, medical supplies, bedding and cooking equipment were left behind. A week later the battle of the Alma was won. The surgeons performed operations and amputations without anaesthetics, without lights, without even bandages, all of which had been abandoned as inessential.

At home, joy at victory turned to outrage as the news came in of how the sick and wounded were being treated. On October 9 *The Times* special correspondent William Howard Russell exposed the absurdity of sending out Chelsea pensioners to form an ambulance corps, who were found 'rather to require nurses themselves than to be able to nurse others'. Three days later, Russell reported: 'It is with feelings of surprise and anger that the public will learn that no sufficient preparations have been made for the proper care of the wounded. Not only are there not sufficient surgeons – that, it might be judged, was unavoidable; not only are there no dressers and nurses – that might be a defect of the system for which no one is to blame; but what will be said when it is known that there is not even linen to make bandages for the wounded? . . . Not only are the men kept, in some cases, for a week without the hand of a medical man coming near their wounds – not only are they left to expire in agony, unheeded and shaken off, though catching desperately at the surgeon whenever he makes his rounds through the fetid ship, but now, when they are placed in the spacious building . . . it is found that the commonest appliances of a workhouse sick ward are wanting . . .'

A fund was launched by *The Times* to send comforts to the sick and wounded which Sir Robert Peel opened with £200, and Russell, describing the treatment of the casualties as 'worthy only of the savages of Dahomey', went on in his next report: 'Here the French are greatly our superiors. Their medical arrangements are extremely good, their surgeons more numerous, and they have also the help of the Sisters of Charity, who have accompanied the expedition in incredible numbers.' In fact there were only fifty of 'these devoted women', but the next day 'A Sufferer by the Present War' demanded, 'Why have we no Sisters of Charity?'

The man responsible for the financial administration of the army was the Secretary at War, Sidney Herbert. He found it hard to credit Russell's reports as he knew that the stores the army thought necessary for the campaign had left England. Nonetheless, he instructed the British Ambassador at Constantinople, Lord Stratford de Redcliffe, to buy anything necessary for the hospitals. He appointed a 'Commission of Enquiry into the State of the Hospitals and the Condition of the Sick and Wounded' to go to the East and report back to him. And he decided to send female nurses to the hospitals at Scutari.

This novel idea had been mooted earlier but had been dropped because, according to the Duke of Newcastle, Secretary for War, the man to whom the Commander-in-Chief and the forces were responsible, 'it is not liked by the military authorities'. Never before had women, except for a few soldiers' wives, quite untrained and inexperienced, been allowed abroad to tend the casualties of war. There was, in fact, some doubt as to whether the Secretary at War or the Secretary for War directed the army medical services, but Mr. Herbert bravely shouldered the responsibility. He understood the delicacy of the task and the prejudices that would have to be overcome if the scheme was to succeed. 'There is but one person in England that I know of who would be capable of organising and superintending such a scheme . . .' he wrote to Florence Nightingale. 'Would you listen to the request to go and superintend the whole thing?'

Florence Nightingale was then thirty-four and already impatient with the restricted scope of her first job, as Superintendent of the Institution for the Care of Sick Gentlewomen in Distressed Circumstances, in Harley Street. She was making plans for a nurses' training school at the newly rebuilt King's College Hospital when she was called to save the health of the British Army.

Florence Nightingale was born with every advantage that a 19th-century woman could desire; wit, intelligence, beauty, money and excellent social connections. Family life was a settled routine of summer at Lea Hurst, Derbyshire, a portion of the 'season' in London and the rest of the year at Embley Park in Hampshire (where Lord and Lady Palmerston were neighbours). She led the life of a squire's daughter but, unusually for the time, was educated by her father in Greek, Latin, Italian, German, French, history and philosophy (later she learned mathematics). From her socially ambitious mother, Fanny, she acquired social graces and womanly skills. When, with her parents and sister Parthenope, she made an eighteen-month tour of Europe, she was welcomed into the highest intellectual and social circles and enjoyed herself enormously. On their return the girls were presented at Court. Florence was popular and courted. She was clever and amusing and she danced beautifully. Fanny was delighted with her. No one doubted that she was destined for a conventionally dazzling future – except Florence herself.

When she was nearly seventeen Florence had received a 'call'. She wrote, 'God spoke to me and called me to His service.' She strove to make herself worthy of God and became increasingly frustrated by life in her gilded cage: 'O weary days – oh evenings that seem never to end – for how many years have I watched that drawing-room clock and thought it never would reach the ten!' In 1844, she

A characteristically thoughtful study of Florence Nightingale. Born into the British upper classes, Florence Nightingale's determined belief that God had called her to become a nurse overcame all the obstacles that convention put in her path

realized that her vocation lay in nursing. She told no one of her hopes, knowing that her family would be appalled, and was kept busy for the next year looking after her grandmother, her old nurse, and cases of sickness in the village. These experiences made her aware that training was essential for good nursing. She wrote to her cousin Hilary Bonham Carter, 'I saw a poor woman die before my eyes this summer because there was no one but fools to sit up with her, who poisoned her as much as if they had given her arsenic.'

In December 1845 she put forward a bold plan to her family. 'It was,' she wrote to Hilary, 'to go to be a nurse at Salisbury Hospital for these few months to learn the "prax".' Her father was disgusted, Parthenope had hysterics, and Fanny was terrified – 'I do not mean the physically revolting parts of a hospital, but things about the surgeons and nurses which you may guess . . .' Florence was an obedient and dutiful daugher but, after the rejection of her plan, she wrote, 'my misery and vacuity afterwards were indescribable.' She sought escape in secretly studying government reports on public health, and hospital reports, and collected a vast quantity of information on sanitary conditions throughout Europe. But in 1847 her health broke down.

At this crucial time, two new friends, Charles and Selina Bracebridge, whom she had met a year earlier, came to her aid. The Bracebridges understood Florence's state of mind, and, at this crisis in her life, whisked her off to Rome for the winter. 'I never enjoyed any time in my life as much as my time in Rome,' she wrote later. There she met Sidney and Liz Herbert, Archdeacon Manning and Mary Stanley – all High Church Anglicans and all flirting with Roman Catholicism. At home again, however, she fell into the withdrawn day-dreaming state which increasingly worried her.

Once again the Bracebridges rescued Florence and took her to Egypt and Greece. Travelling home through Germany she visited Kaiserswerth for the first time and left after two weeks, 'feeling so brave as if nothing could ever vex me again'.

In spite of continued opposition from Fanny and Parthenope, Florence managed to spend three months at Kaiserswerth in 1850. Following this, she had arranged to go to Paris to work with the Sisters of Charity there, when negotiations began instead for her to take over the Institution for Sick Gentlewomen, which was moving to new premises. At the end of May 1853, Florence indeed went to Paris, but caught measles and had to return home. Her father made her an allowance of £500, but, determined to break with her mother and sister, she took rooms in Pall Mall until she could move to Harley Street on August 12.

This was her first experience of committees and administration and she managed both beautifully. She sent committee members all over London searching for inventions that would save nurses' time and effort. She insisted that all religious denominations be admitted to the wards, and visited by their respective priests. She made sure that the new house surgeon should also be a dispenser, to save on druggists' bills. She achieved a revolution in the diet, introduced a series of 'House Rules', reorganized the system of ordering, checked wastage, managed the nurses, assisted at operations and won praise everywhere for producing order out of chaos. She also managed to keep up an active social life. In August she went briefly to the Middlesex Hospital to superintend the nursing of cholera victims.

Mrs. Gaskell, the celebrated author and a guest at Lea Hurst, wrote a description of Florence at this time. 'She is tall; very slight and willowy in figure; thick shortish rich brown hair, very delicate pretty complexion . . . grey eyes which are generally pensive and drooping, but when they choose can be the merriest eyes I ever saw; and perfect teeth making her smile the sweetest I ever saw . . . She is like a saint.' But, under that charming exterior, Mrs. Gaskell discovered the hardness and singleness of purpose which Florence had developed in her years of frustration. 'She has no friend – and she wants none. She stands perfectly alone, half-way between God and His creatures. She used to go a great deal among the villagers here, who dote upon her . . . She will not go among the villagers now because her heart and soul are absorbed by her hospital plans, and she says she can only attend to one thing at once. She is so excessively soft and gentle in voice, manner, and movement that one never feels the unbendableness of her character when one is near her.'

As early as January 1854 Florence had begun to look beyond the confines of Harley Street and had turned her attention again to hospital nursing. The King's College Hospital plan seemed to be just what she was looking for, but, before it could come to anything, the country called her to service. After reading the revelations in *The Times* she immediately planned to take out a small party of nurses to the hospitals at Scutari. On October 14 she wrote to Liz Herbert to tell her of her plans, and to ask her, as a committee member, to get her released from her Harley Street contract, and to write to Lady Stratford de Redcliffe in Constantinople to say, 'This is not a lady but a real Hospital Nurse.' Her letter crossed in the post with the one from Sidney Herbert, officially asking her to undertake the momentous task.

Herbert did not underestimate the difficulties Miss Nightingale would face. He knew that selecting nurses would be hard, 'the task of ruling them and introducing system among them, great; and not the least will be the difficulty of making the whole work smoothly with the medical and military authorities out there.' He hoped that the scheme would have a far-reaching and long-term influence: 'If this succeeds, an enormous amount of good will be done now, and to persons deserving everything at our hands; and a prejudice will have been broken through, and a precedent established, which will multiply the good to all time.'

Miss Nightingale's parents, who had reluctantly given their consent to her going to the Crimea as a volunteer, dropped all resistance at the news that she was going in response to an appeal from the Government itself. Liz Herbert smoothed her path at Harley Street, while both the Bracebridges agreed to accompany her. On October 19, Mr. Herbert sent her the official letter of appointment. She was to be 'Superintendent of the female nursing establishment in the English General Military Hospitals in Turkey'. He continued: 'Everything relating to the distribution of the nurses, the hours of their attendance, their allotment to particular duties, is placed in your hands, subject, of course, to the sanction and approval of the Chief Medical Officer; but the selection of the nurses in the first instance is placed solely under your control.' The powers of discharge and dismissal were also entirely vested in her.

The news made Florence a popular heroine. A lady, the *Examiner* journal enthused, 'young, graceful, feminine, rich, and popular,' was setting out to render 'the holiest of women's charities to the sick, the dying and convalescent.' All that remained was to assemble the party. The War Office was besieged by eager, idealistic ladies, but Miss Nightingale wanted no 'ladies' as such. Only women with nursing experience would do. Five Roman Catholic Sisters of Mercy from Bermondsey, the English branch of an Irish order, had already set out independently. They were stopped at Paris and asked to wait for the official party. These Sisters were to prove among the most useful of the recruits, and Reverend Mother Bermondsey became a close friend of Florence's. Five Catholic Sisters of the Faithful Virgin, who had no nursing experience, were recruited from their Norwood convent.

Margaret Goodman, one of Priscilla Sellon's Sisters of Mercy, had nursed through the cholera epidemic at Plymouth and was recuperating and teaching at a small school in a Devon village when she received the message: 'Let nothing prevent your reaching London by to-morrow morning.' Eight Sellonites joined the party. It was essential for the success of the experiment that Miss

Nightingale should have complete authority over all her nurses, including those from secular orders. They had to take their nursing orders from her, and not from their religious superiors. The Catholic nuns and the Sellonites accepted these terms, but, unfortunately for religious balance, Mrs. Fry's Institute refused. St. John's House, on the other hand, was persuaded to fall in with Miss Nightingale's plans and sent six sisters. The remaining fourteen of the party of thirty-eight were hospital nurses. Mary Stanley, who helped to select them, wrote: 'Here we sit all day. I wish people who may hereafter complain of the women selected could have seen the set we had to choose from.' Under Miss Nightingale's iron discipline, many of these turned into excellent nurses, however, and she herself was to write after the war, 'Paid nurses are always the most useful.'

No one was entirely happy with the final selection. The high proportion of Catholics and High Church Anglicans outraged the stricter Protestants, while the Catholics were alarmed at nuns being placed under a Protestant lady. The nuns continued to wear their habits. As a distinguishing feature – and also to protect them from the soldiery at Scutari – the luckless nurses were issued with a uniform: a grey tweed dress, grey worsted jacket, white cap, a short grey woollen cloak, a brown straw bonnet and a brown scarf or sash worn over one shoulder with 'Scutari Hospital' embroidered on it in red. It was certainly not a becoming costume.

A strict code of discipline was also enforced. The nurses were not to wear flowers or ribbons or walk out except with the housekeeper or in groups of three. They were allowed a limited amount of liquor and were to be paid 12s to 14s a week with board and lodging, rising to between 16s and 18s after three months of service, and 18s and 20s after a year.

On the evening of October 20, Sidney Herbert addressed the assembled party, giving respective cautions to the nuns and to the nurses. The nuns were particularly instructed to 'forebear teaching' and were called on to give their word that they would not attempt conversions. The next morning the ill-assorted party left London Bridge station on the start of their great adventure.

At Boulogne, the quayside fishwives carried their bags to a hotel, where the landlord refused to accept payment for their dinner. Miss Nightingale intended that no distinction should be made between the Sisters and nurses, but the Sisters refused to sit with the nurses and so she waited on them herself. At Paris the Bermondsey nuns joined the party which then continued on to Marseilles. From there, Miss Nightingale's uncle, who had accompanied the party thus far, wrote: 'The rough hospital nurses, on the third day after breakfasting and dining with us each day, and receiving all her attentions, were quite humanised and civilised, their very manners at table softened. "We never had so much care taken of our comforts before; it is not people's way with *us*." '

Before leaving England, Miss Nightingale had been assured by Dr. Andrew Smith, the director of the Army Medical Service, that it was quite unnecessary for her to take out any stores. Nonetheless at Marseilles she bought a quantity of provisions before the party sailed on a ramshackle vessel, the *Vectis*, on October 27. On November 4, they anchored off Seraglio Point and everyone rushed to take their first look at the Hospital. One nurse said: 'Oh, Miss Nightingale, when we land don't let there be any red tape delays, let us get straight to nursing the poor fellows!' Miss Nightingale replied grimly: 'The strongest will be wanted at the wash tub.'

The nurses had arrived in time to witness the destruction of the British Army – not by war but by mismanagement. The Turks had handed over to the British the barracks and general hospital at Scutari, a village across the Bosphorus from Constantinople. The first thousand cholera victims had filled the general hospital and the senior medical officer, Dr. Menzies, was ordered to turn the barracks into an additional hospital to receive the Alma casualties and more cholera cases. He had barely enough equipment and staff for the general hospital itself, let alone the vast hollow square of the barracks which, at one point, held four miles of beds. Supplies sent out from England often made the journey to and fro several times before they were finally extracted from the ships' holds. Others went into the bottomless pit of the Turkish customs house. The stores which actually arrived were often not unpacked for weeks because they had not been inspected by the right officials. Even when goods were in store, 'they are not issued without forms so cumbrous as to make the issue unavailing through delay', Sidney Herbert wrote.

The already over-taxed system soon faced an even greater crisis. Two battles – Balaclava on October 25 and Inkerman on November 5 – brought a fresh flood of wounded, while, already weakened by disease, the surviving troops now settled down to a bitter winter before Sebastopol without adequate food, shelter, fuel or clothing. Men suffering from scurvy, frostbite, starvation, dysentery and fever poured across the Black Sea to Scutari, crammed into hospital ships for a journey averaging eight and a half days with almost no food or attention. At Scutari, those who were unable to walk to the hospital were carried there by rough and

Transport difficulties in the Crimea are vividly captured in this contemporary illustration. Shortage of medical supplies, food, adequate hospitals and practically all necessary facilities came close to draining the British army of its life blood before Florence Nightingale's arrival on the scene

uncaring Turkish porters. When they finally reached the entrance to the barracks hospital, which Miss Nightingale said should have written over it, 'Abandon hope all ye who enter here', they found no beds, no food – in all nothing for their care and attention.

Not only did the sick and wounded fill the wards, they also lined both sides of the wide corridors. The Hon. and Rev. Sydney Godolphin Osborne, who had come to Scutari shortly after the nurses to offer his services as a chaplain, wrote: 'For some weeks, there were many men lying in bed, with dysentery or with open sores, who had not had a change of linen for months...Is it any wonder that the smell in the wards was at times so offensive as to be scarcely endurable even to the oldest Medical Officers.

'Such articles even as basins to wash the wounded from, towels, cups for drinking out of, had to be provided from *The Times* fund, to say nothing of linen and flannel. By far the greater proportion of the bedsteads were constructed, long after the Hospitals were a great deal too full. There was not, a few days before I left, a single operating table; I have seen a capital operation performed in a ward, amongst the other patients, on a door or something like it, laid on two trestles.' Patients suffering from dysentery 'lay either on the floor, or on the wooden divans which surrounded some of the wards. The boards under the thin chaff beds on which they lay, were rotten, and I have seen them alive with vermin and saturated with everything offensive; the orderlies told me, they could not keep them clean.' One side of the building had been damaged by fire. In the cellars, women camp followers drank and whored, gave birth and died. The lavatories were blocked and overflowed into the wards. The huge wooden tubs put out to replace them were rarely emptied.

The cooking department, Osborne reported, 'would have disgraced the management of an English workhouse.' All the cooking was done in thirteen huge Turkish coppers. The orderlies queued for over an hour for their ward's meat ration, which was then thrown, bones and all, into one of the coppers. When the cook felt time was up the meat was retrieved, either raw or in shreds, and tea was made in the uncleaned coppers. The laundry had managed to produce six clean shirts in a month.

In complete contrast, the French started the war with an efficient ambulance corps, well-ordered hospitals and well-trained and adequately equipped medical officers and orderlies. Osborne reported of the French Military Hospital at Pera: 'I found it difficult to believe that the order, quiet, regularity of service and perfect machinery of this Hospital could be the growth of but a few months, and that too in a foreign land. One element was obvious throughout – system.' But as conditions in British hospitals improved, those in French ones declined, and, by the autumn of 1855, Fanny Taylor found: 'The wards of both officers and men were inferior in cleanliness and general appearance of comfort to those at Koulali and Scutari.'

The British officials were overworked and underpaid. Conditioned by years of peacetime economies and military regulations, these were not the men to shoulder responsibility, to take the sort of decisive action which might have forestalled the calamity. Margaret Goodman wrote, '. . . from time immemorial a prescribed course had been resorted to in order to meet certain exigencies, and if it did not meet them, it was *supposed* to do so.' This was why the men had to eat their meat with their hands. Regulations said that each man came into hospital with his knapsack containing knife, fork, spoon, comb, razor, clean shirt, and so on, even though most of the men had left their kits in the Crimea, often on officers' orders.

The officials took the only way out and denied that the problem existed. 'They had everything – nothing was wanted,' Dr. Menzies told Sydney Godolphin Osborne. He gave the same assurance to

Lord Stratford who, not bothering to check for himself, passed it on to Sidney Herbert with the recommendation that *The Times* Fund be devoted to building a Protestant church at Pera. Mr. Macdonald, arriving to administer the fund, was also assured that his help was not required. He placed himself and his funds at Miss Nightingale's disposal.

Such officials were not likely to welcome a society lady with influential friends, together with a parcel of nurses, come to meddle and spy. Sidney Herbert had instructed Lord Stratford and Dr. Menzies to give Miss Nightingale every assistance and support. The ambassador sent his secretary to welcome her. The party rowed across to Scutari (the Sellonites' departure being delayed by the need to remove a dead Russian general, a prisoner of war, from their room) and were received at the entrance to the hospital by Dr. Menzies and Major Sillery, the military commandant. But the welcome extended no further than the door.

The party were taken to their living quarters. Six rooms, one a kitchen and another a closet, which had previously been occupied by three doctors, were provided for forty people. There was no bedding, almost no furniture or food, and the rooms themselves were filthy. 'Our dinner and tea service consisted of a metal basin for each person, which held about a pint,' Margaret Goodman wrote. 'Out of this we first ate our meat and vegetables, and then after wiping it as clean as paper could make it, we returned for our allowance of porter; we also washed our faces in this hard-worked copper basin . . . We had no cheese, butter nor milk, and the supply of goat's flesh was limited; but there was always sufficient bread.' The water allowance was one pint a day each for all purposes.

The doctors had to allow the nurses into the hospital, but they did not have to employ them. Miss Nightingale's orders gave her power to put the nurses to work only with 'the sanction and approval of the Chief Medical Officer'. She knew that the experiment of female nursing could only succeed if she won the confidence of the doctors. The nurses remained idle for nearly a week while the sick and wounded poured in, 'occupied in our several quarters, in making shirts, pillows, slings, &c. We thought this time very long.' Miss Nightingale allocated ten nurses to the General Hospital and twenty-eight to the barracks, and waited. In the meantime, with the doctors' permission, she set up an extra-diet kitchen in the nurses' kitchen and, on requisition from a doctor, issued invalid food, such as arrowroot, jellies, wines (port was the most common) and eggs. For five months, her kitchen was the only source of invalid food.

On November 9 shiploads of sick and wounded flooded in. The

overwhelmed doctors put aside their prejudices and everyone was pressed into service. The nurses stuffed mattresses with straw and laid them on the bare floors. 'Just as our beds were made up,' a Sellonite, Sarah Terrot, reported, '. . . the patients came in, mostly walking, though their pale faces and severely wounded bodies showed they were scarcely able for this effort . . . Scarcely one was able to undress without assistance; many had lost an arm, others a leg, and all had gunshot wounds. Our task was to get them undressed as quickly as possible . . . the surgeons meanwhile went round examining each wound and giving us directions how to dress them. . . . It seemed a hard rough place to lie down in, this noisy, windy passage on a bundle of straw laid on the cold pavement, but to these poor men these hardships were luxuries and they expressed great delight . . . When all were settled quietly in bed, soup was brought in and administered.'

The nurses worked amid scenes of total horror '. . . we are steeped up to our necks in blood . . .' Miss Nightingale wrote. 'In all our corridor, I think we have not an average of three Limbs per man . . . Then come the operations, and a melancholy, not an encouraging List is this. They are all performed in the wards – no time to move them; one poor fellow exhausted with haemorrhage, has his leg amputated as a last hope, and dies ten minutes after the Surgeon has left him . . . I am getting a Screen for the amputations, for when one poor fellow, who is to be amputated to-morrow, sees his comrade to-day die under the knife, it makes impression and diminishes his chance.'

The men's clothing and hair were verminous and their wounds so offensive that some of them warned the nurses off. 'Sister, you must get away from me; I am so loathsome that even *my own mother* could not approach me,' Margaret Goodman heard. Osborne recorded that '. . . for cleansing the wounds it was extremely difficult, in the first place, to procure water, and secondly, any vessel in which to wash them; so the copper basin was again in requisition.' Nurses and doctors 'did work from morning till night and through the night . . . but the whole thing was a mere matter of excited, almost phrenzied energy', largely because so much that was essential was missing.

The different temperaments and attitudes of the doctors made it impossible to institute a uniform system of nursing in the hospitals. Miss Nightingale reported: 'The number of nurses admitted into each division of a hospital depended upon the medical officer of that division, who sometimes accepted them, sometimes refused them, sometimes accepted them after they had been refused; while the

An idealized Victorian view of Florence Nightingale taking dictation from a wounded man in the Crimea (the hat at the head of the bed suggests that he was a sailor). In reality, however, Florence could be a harsh taskmistress, as some of the more idealistic among her nurses found to their cost

duties they were permitted to perform varied according to the will of each individual medical officer.' As a consequence, the nurses were instructed by Miss Nightingale 'only to attend to those in the divisions of those surgeons who wished for our service . . . and she charged us never to do anything for the patients without the leave of the doctors.'

Some nurses fretted against these restrictions during a crisis which clearly called for all their skill, and thought Miss Nightingale callous and hardhearted. But obedience to regulations was essential. Other nurses were causing her different problems. One, Mrs. Wilson, had to be sent home for being intoxicated almost as soon as she arrived. In December, two more were sent packing for the same reason and another for buying and selling for the patients in the hospital. Four St. John's Sisters proved unable to accept either the discipline or the privations and also returned to England. Another nurse came to Miss Nightingale to complain: 'There is the Caps, Ma'am, that suits one face, and some that suits another. And if I'd known, Ma'am, about the Caps, great as was my desire to come out and nurse at Scutari, I wouldn't have come, Ma'am.' The Norwood Sisters' lack of nursing experience meant that they were not very useful. Fortunately Miss Nightingale was able to report that Mrs. Roberts from St. Thomas's Hospital 'is worth her weight in gold', and that Mrs. Drake from St. John's House (who died of cholera in the Crimea) 'is a treasure'.

Within five or six weeks of their arrival the nurses were not only fully occupied in the wards, but the doctors and officials were also looking to Miss Nightingale to supply everything that was missing. She had a large sum of money at her own disposal and Mr. Macdonald and *The Times* fund at her elbow. She arranged for Mr. Macdonald to buy scrubbing brushes and sacking to clean the floors. She insisted that the wooden tubs be emptied regularly. She rented a house, installed boilers and set soldiers' wives to do the laundry. She employed workmen to repair the burnt-out section of the hospital so that more patients could be received and equipped the new wards herself. Lady Alicia Blackwood, who had come out with her husband after Inkerman to offer what help they could, was set to organizing a lying-in ward for the camp followers and to help the wives and widows.

'I am a kind of General Dealer in socks, shirts, knives and forks, wooden spoons, tin baths, tables and forms, cabbages and carrots, operating tables, towels and soap, small tooth combs, precipitate for destroying lice, scissors, bed pans, and stump pillows,' Miss Nightingale wrote to Sidney Herbert. From her own stores, again on doctors' requisitions, she was supplying the hospital almost single-handed. Fifty thousand shirts alone were eventually issued. She cut red tape, and initiated reform. People began to talk of the 'Nightingale power' – even Queen Victoria, who took a keen interest in the nurses' work. She found out what comforts would be most useful to her 'poor noble wounded and sick men' and asked Miss Nightingale to undertake the distribution of the free gifts. Miss Nightingale's authority seemed beyond challenge.

At home the experiment was regarded as a success. If thirty-eight nurses could do so much good, it was argued, how much more could double that number achieve? In London, Mrs. Herbert, Miss Stanley and Miss Jones, superintendent of St. John's House, had carried on interviewing would-be nurses and sending successful candidates to gain experience in London hospitals. On December 2, a second party, consisting of nine ladies, twenty-two nurses and fifteen Irish Catholic Sisters of Mercy under the superior of the Convent of Kinsale, Reverend Mother Bridgeman, left London for Scutari, with Mary Stanley in charge.

When the news reached Miss Nightingale on December 14 she was furious. Her original instructions had said, 'the selection of nurses in the first instance is placed solely under your control.' In response to the volunteers clamouring to enlist, Mr. Herbert had written to the newspapers on October 21, 'No one can be sent out until we hear from Miss Nightingale that they are required.' 'Had I had the enormous folly to write at the end of eleven days experience to require more women,' Miss Nightingale wrote to Mr. Herbert, 'would it not seem that you, as a Statesman, should have said, "Wait until you see your way better?" But I made no such request.'

The new party was ordered to report to Dr. Cumming, one of the Hospital Commission, and not to her. Accommodating them would be a physical impossibility. The high proportion of Roman Catholics and High Church Anglicans in the first party had caused uproar. Now fifteen more Catholics were to be added to their numbers, and Miss Nightingale knew that Mary Stanley herself was intending to join the Catholic church. At least one of the ladies, Fanny Taylor, was to take the same step. Nine ladies were included in the party. 'You have sacrificed the cause so near to my heart,' Miss Nightingale raged. 'You have sacrificed me – a matter of small importance now – you have sacrificed your own written word.'

By the time these unwelcome reinforcements anchored off Constantinople on December 17, they were already in difficulties. They had travelled in such grand style that their funds were exhausted. The nurses got drunk, Miss Stanley was incapable of imposing discipline and the ladies seemed to have little idea of the hard work required. While Miss Nightingale decided with the military and medical authorities what to do with this unwelcome burden, the nuns were taken in by the French Sisters of Charity and the rest of the party went to a partly furnished house at Therapia, where Miss Stanley had the economical idea of employing the nurses in domestic work. 'But now the evils of the equality system began to appear,' Fanny Taylor wrote. 'The ladies suffered by it through the journey, for having no authority to restrain the hired nurses they were compelled to listen to the worst language, and to be treated not infrequently with coarse insolence. Whispers were heard amongst them that first evening, that they had come out to nurse soldiers not to sweep, wash, and cook.'

Their services were offered to the British naval hospital which declined them on the grounds that they were expecting their own female nurses. The naval hospital was, in fact, always far better run than those at Scutari. Osborne wrote of it: 'Nothing could exceed the cleanliness, comfort, and order which appeared to prevail.' The drunken and thieving orderlies were a problem, though, and the Admiralty appointed Mrs. Mackenzie to take six nurses to Therapia, with the intention of making female nursing general, if it proved successful. 'I am to be the Miss Nightingale there,' Mrs. Mackenzie wrote nervously. She was not, in fact, called on to face challenges on anything like the same scale. Some of the doctors and surgeons were suspicious, but they welcomed the party on January 10, 1855, and even made Mrs. Mackenzie an honorary member of the officers' mess. She found the 'Rules of Service' frustrating but tackled them energetically. Although ill health, brought on by strain, forced her to return home in November, the experiment was judged a success.

Miss Stanley's party was at last absorbed. Dr. Cumming had at first refused to accept this unwelcome contingent but eventually agreed to increase the number of nurses at Scutari to fifty. Miss Nightingale wrote a civil letter to Mother Bridgeman, inviting her to send five of her nuns to take the place of the Norwood Sisters whom she was sending home. Mother Bridgeman refused to allow her nuns into the barracks hospital without her and without their own priest. On New Year's Day, seventeen nurses, who had been going daily to the General Hospital, were accommodated there under the superintendency of Miss Tebbut. The General Hospital, Sarah Terrot wrote, 'had a different aspect from the Barracks; it seemed cleaner, lighter and more cheerful in every way. The wards were in better repair; no broken windows stuffed with rags.'

At the end of January Lord Raglan, the British Commander-in-Chief, requested that eleven nurses be sent to the General Hospital at Balaclava. Miss Nightingale did not like what she had heard of conditions there but, as it was obvious that some of Miss Stanley's party were determined to escape her authority, she sent them there under the superior of the Sellonites. At the same time the Turkish barracks at Koulali, five miles down the coast from Scutari, were to open as a hospital. Mary Stanley, who had originally intended to return as soon as she had seen her party settled, went to Koulali as superintendent, taking with her Mother Bridgeman, ten of her nuns, and six ladies and nurses. These also served the General Hospital which opened a few days after her arrival. Miss Stanley placed herself under Lady Stratford's authority.

Miss Nightingale had almost succeeded in moulding her band of nurses into a disciplined team. Now she was faced with religious squabbles, determined defiance from Mother Bridgeman, whom she called Mother Brickbat, and unruly behaviour from some of the nurses. The nuns, Miss Nightingale wrote, 'wander over the whole Hospital out of nursing hours, not confining themselves to their own wards, or even to patients, but "instructing" (it is their own word) groups of Orderlies and Convalescents in the corridors, doing the work each of ten chaplains.' The Kinsale nuns earnestly believed that spiritual welfare was as important as physical health. Two of the six Presbyterian nurses sent out in the interests of religious balance came home drunk after an evening out with a couple of orderlies and were sent home. One morning six nurses presented themselves to Miss Nightingale and announced that they wanted to get married.

While this internal wrangling was going on, the sufferings of the troops in the Crimea grew even worse. In January, there were more men in hospital than in the camps before Sebastopol. It was, Miss Nightingale said, a 'calamity unparalleled in the history of calamity.' At Scutari, there was no improvement in the supply situation and, increasingly, doctors and officials relied on Miss Nightingale. Fanny Taylor, assigned to the Barrack Hospital, recorded the scene in the nurses' kitchen. 'We used, among ourselves, to call this kitchen the tower of Babel, from the variety of languages spoken in it and the confusion. In fact, in the middle of the day everything and everybody seemed to be there. Boxes, parcels, bundles of sheets, shirts, and old linen and flannels; tubs of butter, sugar, bread, kettles, saucepans, heaps of books, and of all kinds of rubbish, besides the "diets", which were being dispensed; then the people, ladies, nuns, nurses, orderlies, Turks, Greeks, French and Italian servants, officers and others, waiting to see Miss Nightingale.'

Fanny Taylor found the ladies' quarters 'well furnished with fleas' while the rats 'took nightly promenades about the room'. Rats were a common problem in all the hospitals, and healthy and energetic cats were eagerly sought after. Every Tuesday, a Turk passed through the room at sunrise and sunset to raise and lower the Turkish flag – 'he always omitted the ceremony of knocking at the door'. Two days after her arrival Miss Taylor escorted Miss Nightingale on her nightly rounds. 'We went round the whole of the second story, into many of the wards and into one of the upper corridors. It seemed an endless walk, and it is one not easily forgotten. As we slowly passed along, the silence was profound; very seldom did a moan or a cry from those multitudes of deeply suffering

Another view of Florence Nightingale, this time in the main ward of the hospital at Scutari. She carries the famous lamp. Some officers condemned her for meddling, but the men saw her as a 'ministering angel'

ones fall on our ears. A dim light burnt here and there. Miss Nightingale carried her lantern, which she would set down before she bent over any of the patients. I much admired Miss Nightingale's manner to the men – it was so tender and kind.'

Miss Nightingale assisted at the most painful operations, tended the most serious cases, sat through the night with dying men – not only were there insufficient nurses for night duty but she did not trust the paid nurses in the wards after eight at night in any case. 'She is a "ministering angel",' Mr. Macdonald wrote and a legend was born. One patient wrote home: 'What a comfort it was to see her pass even. She would speak to one and nod and smile to as many more; but she could not do it all, you know. We lay there by hundreds, but we could kiss her shadow as it fell, and lay our heads on the pillow again, content.'

Fanny Taylor shared the care of about fifteen hundred men with another lady, a nurse, and the orderlies. She found 'the full horror of the reality' far worse than anything she had imagined. 'When we woke in the morning, our hearts sank down at the thought of the woe we must witness that day. At night we lay down wearied beyond expression . . . On all side prevailed the utmost confusion.' The nurses could not get the doctors to sign the necessary requisitions to obtain the extra diets they ordered from Miss Nightingale. Eventually they persuaded the doctors to requisition a quantity of dry stores which they could make up on the wards when requested, but Dr. Cumming then forbade cooking on the wards and, once again, the men went without. 'Amid all the confusion and distress of Scutari Hospital, military discipline was never lost sight of.' After a fortnight Miss Taylor went to Koulali to join Miss Stanley and her nuns, with whom she felt a spiritual affinity.

Miss Stanley and her party had arrived at Koulali on January 27 and found the hospital in a shocking state, filthy and ill-equipped. Two days later they admitted 300 patients and both hospitals were soon packed with sick and wounded. The nurses misbehaved, and eleven out of twenty-one were sent home in eight months for immorality or drunkenness. The ladies soon gave up wearing uniform to distinguish themselves from the paid colleagues. There was much sickness among the staff – at one time the work of both hospitals fell on one lady and ten sisters – and the mortality rate was the highest of all the hospitals.

The hospital was run on what Miss Nightingale called the lady-plan which, as she said, 'ends in nothing but spiritual flirtation between the ladies and the soldiers'. The set of rules formulated by Miss Stanley made it clear that the menial work was to be done by the nurses. A lady, a Sister and a nurse were appointed to each ward. To the nurses fell the tasks of ensuring cleanliness, order and ventilation, giving diets and medicines as ordered by the doctors, accompanying the surgeons on their rounds, taking their orders, dressing wounds, changing poultices and applying fomentations. The ladies were involved chiefly in supervising (the nurses were never left alone in the wards), administering extra diets and stores, writing letters for the men and procuring books. Dr. Cumming reported that the ladies did little but wander around holding notebooks. The strict system of requisitioning was abandoned with the intention of ensuring that the men got all they needed. Nurses wrote their own requisitions for stores after receiving verbal orders from the doctors. This resulted in considerable extravagance and unaccountability and in November it was ordered that the diet roll be reinstated. The ladies were outraged but Fanny Taylor admitted, 'a regulation once made for a military hospital should not be broken'.

Miss Nightingale, too, had to deal with many complaints of proselytising by the Koulali nuns. In March Mary Stanley, to Lady Stratford's horror, was received into the Roman Catholic church, but the simple fact was that she was not up to the superintendency. As early as January she wrote, 'I *could* not go through the nursing. I cannot stand the fatigue, and therefore I gave it up at once . . . I learned all I wanted in my two days going the round.' After her conversion she went home, and was replaced by Miss Hutton.

The number of casualties at Koulali declined with the coming of spring and the policy of keeping more of the men in Crimean hospitals. In the autumn of 1855 the General Hospital was given up to the Sardinians and on October 8 Mother Bridgeman went with her nuns to take charge of the General Hospital at Balaclava. The remaining ladies and nurses were disbanded and the Barracks hospitals closed by the end of the year.

At Scutari, in spite of improved cleanliness and the benefits responsible and reliable nursing could bring, the deaths continued. An epidemic killed four doctors and three nurses. Patients recovered from their wounds but died of hospital fever. 'At one period, the Scutari hospitals had become so extremely unhealthy, that there were many cases . . . of convalescents being stricken down while waiting merely for the vessel to convey them to England,' Margaret Goodman wrote. At the end of January, Mr. Roebuck MP tabled a motion in the House of Commons for an inquiry into the conditions of the army before Sebastopol. It amounted to a motion of censure. The government resigned and Sidney Herbert was replaced by Lord Panmure, who combined the two offices of Secretary at War and Secretary for War. At the end of February he dispatched a Sanitary Commission to investigate conditions at Scutari and the Crimea and remedy defects.

The Commission, Miss Nightingale said, 'saved the British Army'. They had sewers opened and cleared, removed the dead horses that were contaminating the water supply, got rid of the piles of decaying rubbish and animal carcases which filled the central courtyard, cleaned and limewashed the walls and destroyed the rat- and vermin-infested wooden divans. Spring brought a drop in the number of sick. M. Alexis Soyer, chef at the Reform Club in London, came to Scutari with official blessing, designed new ovens, and taught the orderlies to use the rations to the best advantage. He failed, however, to get the meat ration boned. That would have needed a new regulation. By the summer the mortality rate had fallen from 42 per cent to 2.2 per cent. Now, Miss Nightingale felt, she could visit the Crimea.

Eleven nurses had gone to the General Hospital at Balaclava in January, while nurses had also been sent to the Castle Hospital when it opened in huts above Balaclava in April. At Balaclava, nurses found conditions to rival those that had met the first party at Scutari. One of the nurses, Elizabeth Davis, a Welshwoman given to violent prejudices, who always refused to accept Miss

Nightingale's authority, wrote: 'Not a man there had a bed. They lay upon bunks – having one blanket under, and a blanket and a rug over each patient. Their great-coats were their only pillows, and they had no sheets. The sick and wounded were alike neglected, unclean, and covered with vermin ... The patients in the wards were placed so close together, that I could not put my foot straight down between their beds.' The cooking was so badly managed that the patients went without dinner two days running.

Mrs. Davis was asked to take charge of the extra-diet kitchen. Under her open-handed regime extra diets and free gifts were distributed with reckless generosity. An entire shipload of supplies was distributed without any record of who had received them. The superintendent, Miss Langston, fell ill and was succeeded by Miss Wear, an elderly lady far too weak to control Mrs. Davis's extravagance. One of her first acts was to turn one of the wards over to officers. This was contrary to Miss Nightingale's declared policy. She believed that the officers had the financial resources to help themselves.

The nurses received full backing for their defiance from Dr. John Hall, the chief of medical staff, and, at sixty-three, a veteran of the Peninsular War, veteran in both fact and attitudes. Quite untouched by the humanitarian mood of the times, he was against what he saw as spoiling the troops. He discouraged the use of chloroform as an anaesthetic, for instance, saying: 'The smart use of the knife is a powerful stimulant and it is much better to hear a man bawl lustily than to see him sink silently into the grave.' Fortunately, most doctors at Scutari used chloroform freely. Dr. Hall, too, was the man originally responsible for stating that 'nothing was lacking' at Scutari. The Hospital Commission had reported unfavourably on his hospitals in the Crimea and he was furious. He disputed Miss Nightingale's authority and resented her interference. He was assisted by a flaw in her instructions which named her only as superintendent in Turkey – not in the Crimea as well. This matter was not finally cleared up until March 16, 1856, when General Orders stated: 'Miss Nightingale is recognised by Her Majesty's Government as the General Superintendent of the Female Nursing Establishment of the military hospitals of the Army. No lady, sister, or nurse, is to be transmitted from one hospital to another, or introduced into any hospital without consultation with her.' This was a direct snub to Dr. Hall but a belated triumph for Miss Nightingale (peace was signed on March 30).

Miss Nightingale arrived in the Crimea on May 5, 1855. She visited the General Hospital where Mrs. Davis greeted her with, 'I

Nurses at Work in the Early Dawn after the Battle of Alma, 1854

The Russians lost 5,000 men (including 900 prisoners) and the allies lost 3,400

The restlessness of Russia and the prominence of the woman question give unusual interest to Miss Florence Nightingale, who has recently been honoured by the King and is to be presented with the freedom of the City of London, for she reminds one of both interests. Born in 1829, Miss Nightingale began her famous work in hospitals in 1844, and she departed for the Crimea on October 21, 1854, with thirty-four nurses. When she came home a testimonial fund amounting to £50,000 was subscribed by the public in recognition of her services, and was at her special request devoted to the formation of an institution for the training of nurses. For many years she has lived in complete retirement at 10, South Street, Park Lane.

Miss Nightingale's colleagues are also being remem for the honour recently paid to the men who went t the Mutiny has drawn attention to the services o little band of women who helped Miss Nightingale Crimea. Few of them now remain with us. Miss Emma Faog, who is now nearly eighty-three, ha in the Thanet Union twenty-two years, and is quite in her surroundings. Nurse Langley of Bury St. Ed went out to the Crimea as wife of a sergeant in th Lancers and nursed the Duke of Cambridge; Mrs. who lives at Watford, is now ninety years of age Death, who lives at Plaistow, is in poor circumstances so on the story might be told in many other cases.

Mrs. Death

Over eighty years of a

Mrs. Langley

Aged eighty

Florence Nightingale

As she looked fifty years ago

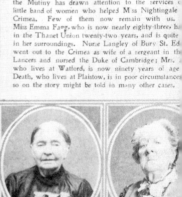

Mrs. Ellen Butler

Over seventy-eight

Mrs. Evans

A soldier w

should as soon have expected to see the Queen here, as you,' and proceeded to ignore all her suggestions. She went to the Castle Hospital where Miss Shaw Stewart, one of Miss Nightingale's staunchest allies, was having a hard time of it with Dr. Hall. Then she collapsed with Crimea fever. For a while her life was feared for. When she recovered friends (and enemies) tried to persuade her to go home but she was afraid that, if she went, the entire experiment would collapse. When she was well enough to travel, she went back to the Bosphorus to convalesce.

She arrived to find staff and patients in good spirits. The first war nurses, like their successors, were deeply impressed by the courage and the stoicism of their patients. The 'scum of the earth', despised and neglected, were heroes to their nurses. 'I fear I should scarcely be credited were I to attempt to describe in detail the noble manner in which the army behaved under their unprecedented trials,' Margaret Goodman wrote. Miss Nightingale, too, paid tribute to the behaviour of patients and orderlies. 'Never was there one word nor one look which a gentleman would not have used . . . amidst scenes of loathsome disease and death, there rose above it all the innate dignity, gentleness and chivalry of the men.'

Without sentimentality but with practical good sense Miss Nightingale looked after the welfare of the men as well as their health. The sick in hospital had 9d a day stopped from their pay, but the wounded had only 4½d removed. At her instigation, the Queen ensured that the sick lost the same amount as the wounded, and also got the military cemeteries at Scutari made over to the British. In the summer of 1855, as the numbers of sick and wounded fell, the numbers of idle convalescents rose. They had only drink to distract them. Miss Nightingale established a coffee house, the Inkerman Café. She organized a Money Order Office through which men could send money home to their families. She opened reading rooms and class rooms and appealed for equipment from home which was sent in large quantities. The officers said, 'You are spoiling the brutes,' but the brutes flocked in. 'I have never seen so teachable and helpful a class as the Army generally,' Miss Nightingale wrote.

On September 8, 1855, Sebastopol fell. In the Crimea, none of the reforms Miss Nightingale had initiated had come to fruition, and there was no course but another visit. Dr. Hall, without her knowledge, had recruited Mother Bridgeman and her nuns for

A full-page tribute from a 1908 issue of The Sphere, *issued to commemorate the award of the Order of Merit to Florence Nightingale by King Edward VII. For forty years after the Crimea, she was a dominant influence on the development of world nursing*

Balaclava. Mother Bridgeman had insisted that her four nuns still at Scutari should join her and, to avoid friction, Miss Nightingale gave way. The nuns arrived to find confusion, dirt and quarrelling nurses, drunken orderlies and shortage of proper cooking and washing facilities. Miss Nightingale visited the General Hospital where Mrs. Davis hospitably offered her brandy or wine. Miss Nightingale asked for Miss Wear to be removed from the General Hospital. Dr. Hall immediately appointed her to the new Monastery Hospital where she managed to cause a scandal. 'She spent most of her time cooking good things, eating, drinking, and gossiping with an old Medical Officer until the small hours of the morning . . .' Miss Nightingale wrote. 'I had to speak to these two old fogies, each of whom was twice as old as myself.' At the end of November, Miss Nightingale went back to Scutari where cholera had broken out.

On publication of the General Order, Mother Bridgeman, who had only gone to the Crimea on the assurance that Miss Nightingale had no authority there, resigned and took her nuns home on April 11. Miss Nightingale went to take over the General Hospital and was kept waiting for hours in the snow until the keys were fetched. The Bermondsey nuns summoned to take over were shocked at the conditions they found and spent days washing wards and men. A party of nurses requested for the Land Transport Corps hospitals in the Crimea were taken out in March 1856 by Miss Nightingale who found, 'The Inspector-General and Purveyors wish to see whether women can live as long as horses without rations.' For ten days she fed the nurses out of her own pocket while they in turn ministered to 260 patients.

Gradually, the nurses began to disperse. Everyone was provided for in some way by Miss Nightingale. She paid tribute to her three most valued colleagues. To Reverend Mother Bermondsey she wrote: 'You were far above me in fitness for the General Superintendency, both in worldly talent of administration, and far more in the spiritual qualifications which God values in a Superior.' Of Miss Shaw Stewart, she wrote: 'Without her our Crimean work would have come to grief – without her judgment, her devotion, her unselfish, consistent looking to the one great end . . . without her untiring zeal, her watchful care of the nurses, her accuracy in all trusts and accounts, her truth, her faithfulness.' Mrs. Roberts had been her loyal support and companion: 'Her total superiority to all the vices of a Hospital Nurse, her faithfulness to the work, her disinterested love of duty and vigilant care of her patients, her power of work equal to that of *ten*, have made her one of the most important persons of the expedition.'

After the last patient had been released from Scutari, Miss Nightingale left Constantinople on July 28. She was worn out, her health was broken and the memory of the thousands of dead men was weighing on her mind. She slipped quietly into England, a national heroine who did not know whether her brave experiment had succeeded. The last year had been plagued by dissensions, disputes and jealousies. Doctors and officials who had relied on her in the crisis of the winter of 1854–55 had been anxious to dissociate themselves from her as conditions improved. Malicious rumours and secret reports circulated accusing her and her nurses of everything from extravagance to immorality. Her very popularity at home told against her. 'I have unbounded admiration for her qualifications,' a naval doctor wrote, 'but dozens of things are placed to her credit that I happen to know that she had nothing to do with.'

Whatever the official verdict on her own work might be, Miss Nightingale and her small band of nurses (125 in all) were an inspiration to women everywhere. No longer would they accept without question that war was a male preserve. Faced with official rebuff or indifference, women would demand, in the words of one would-be Confederate nurse: 'Is the noble example of Miss Nightingale to pass for nothing?' and press on.

When the American Civil War broke out in April 1861, the North had no organized ambulance service, no general army hospitals, no nurses except for convalescent soldiers. The head of the army medical services was an eighty-year-old veteran of the 1812 war who regarded almost any expenditure as unjustified extravagance. It was the Crimea all over again. The most elementary preparations for the care of the sick and wounded had not been made, so that even healthy young recruits sickened in the filthy and insanitary conditions of the camps. And yet, when the Women's Central Association of Relief for Sick and Wounded of the Army, formed to co-ordinate the work of the local aid societies, approached the military medical authorities, they were told: 'The United States Medical Bureau is a well organised, thoroughly tried and hitherto wholly successful department of the United States government and any attempt to interfere with its methods would only cause confusion.'

The Central Association refused to accept these assurances. It combined with two New York medical relief groups in an appeal to President Lincoln. On June 9, an order was issued creating the Sanitary Commission, the forerunner of the Red Cross. Its aim was 'a simple desire and resolute determination to secure for the men

'Our women and the war' – a Northern view of the various roles women played in the US Civil War. In both North and South, women were determined to follow Florence Nightingale's example, though, like her, they had to overcome considerable prejudice

who have enlisted in this war, that care which it is the duty of the nation to give.' One of its first jobs was to inspect the army camps round Washington. It found bad food, overcrowding and filthy conditions and made recommendations for improvement to the authorities, who ignored them. When the North was defeated in July at the Battle of Bull Run it was found that one of the reasons was exactly those conditions exposed by the Sanitary Commission – the men were not fit to fight.

The medical services were eventually forced to accept the aid of the Sanitary Commission which built up a splendid record of humanitarian achievement. Armed with a thorough knowledge of the sanitary history of the Crimean War and with Miss Nightingale's own help and advice, its members inspected and reported on camps and hospitals. They brought about improvements in water supplies, latrines and garbage disposal, introduced moveable pavilion hospitals, tended the wounded, acted as a general relief agency, supplied fresh fruit and vegetables for the

In this extremely rare photograph, Union soldiers wounded at the Battle of Fredericksburg convalesce outside their hospital in the company of a nurse, one of the 3,000 who nursed in the North during the Civil War

troops and equipped hospital trains. They collected and spent over $5 million in cash and $15 million in supplies.

For female nurses the government turned first to the Catholic and Protestant sisterhoods. Nearly 600 sisters of twelve religious orders served in the North and South and the nursing of some of the largest government hospitals was assigned to them. A committee of the Women's Central Relief Association under Dr. Elizabeth Blackwell (a friend of Miss Nightingale and the first woman to receive a degree in medicine) selected about 100 women for a month's training in New York hospitals. Women elsewhere fitted themselves as best they could.

On July 10, Dorothea Dix, who had devoted her life to improving the conditions of the insane, was officially appointed superintendent of women nurses. Four days later she issued her requirements for nurses. Candidates were to be aged between thirty-five and fifty and in good health: 'Matronly persons of experience, good conduct, and superior education and serious disposition will always have preference; habits of neatness, order, sobriety, and industry are

Scenes from the General Hospital at Fortress Monroe, dated 1862. These are probably highly idealized views, as medical services in both the North and the South were of an appallingly low standard until forced to accept intervention by the Sanitary Commission, which had achieved so much in the Crimean War

prerequisites.' Nurses had to enlist for at least three months, and dress soberly in black, brown or grey with no ornaments. An ideal application to Miss Dix read: 'I am in possession of one of your circulars and will comply with all your requirements. I am plain-

looking enough to suit you, and old enough. I have no near relatives in the war, no lover there. I never had a husband, and am not looking for one. Will you take me?' Army regulations allowed one nurse to ten beds and a ratio of two men nurses to one woman nurse.

Miss Dix was nearly sixty when she was appointed. She faced an almost impossible task. The demand for nurses was enormous and the candidates flooded in. Careful selection became impossible and many unsuitable nurses found their way to the army hospitals.

Husband seekers, sentimentalists, ladies too fastidious for much of the work all contrived to alienate doctors already prejudiced against women nurses. But most of the 3,000 women who nursed in the North acquired through experience a considerable practical skill in hospitals where conditions often mirrored the horrors of Scutari. The women were popular with the sick and wounded and many doctors came to appreciate their work.

Louisa May Alcott arrived to nurse at the overcrowded and insanitary Union Hotel Hospital, a former tavern in Washington, expecting 'much humiliation of spirit from the surgeons, and to be treated by them like a doormat ... Great, therefore, was my surprise when I found myself treated with utmost courtesy and kindness.' Her immersion in the work was sudden and total: 'My three days experience had begun with a death and, owing to the defalcation of another nurse, a somewhat abrupt plunge into the superintendence of a ward containing forty beds, where I spent my shining hours washing faces, serving rations, giving medicine, and sitting in a very hard chair, with pneumonia on one side, diphtheria on the other, five typhoids on the opposite, and a dozen dilapidated patriots, hopping, lying, lounging about, all staring more or less at the new "nuss".' In a month Miss Alcott herself succumbed to typhoid and had to give up nursing.

During the Crimean War, hundreds of miles from home, the authorities had been able to exercise some control over the numbers of volunteers heading to help on the battlefields. The Civil War took place in everyone's back yard and such control was therefore impossible. Wives, mothers and sweethearts flocked to care for their menfolk. Other women found that the war came to them. Clara Barton, founder of the American Red Cross, was in Washington on April 9 when a regiment from her home state, the 6th Massachusetts Volunteers, were attacked by a mob as they passed through Baltimore. As they staggered into Washington Miss Barton, entirely on her own authority, distributed food, clothing and bandages to them. After that she became a one-woman relief organization, taking food and medical supplies to battlefields, and feeding and nursing the wounded. At her own expense she conducted searches for missing men on behalf of their relatives.

The most colourful of the unofficial volunteers was Mary Ann Bickerdyke. She was nearly forty-four when war broke out, but she responded to an appeal from her minister, Henry Ward Beecher (brother of Harriet Beecher Stowe), for women to nurse the sick and wounded. She worked without pay and without official authority but her drive, determination and administrative ability made her famous. She brought order to hospitals, set up special diet kitchens, organized laundries so that the men's filthy uniforms could be washed and disinfected instead of being wastefully burnt or buried. She took food and medical supplies to the front and scoured battlefields by lantern light until she was sure that no wounded man remained untended. When she saw that the sick and wounded at Memphis were short of fresh milk and eggs she went north and brought back cattle and hens. General Grant gave her a pass allowing her to move freely anywhere in the army areas. The Sanitary Commission made her an agent and she promptly bought vast quantities of hospital stores, leaving the Commission to worry about how to pay for them.

The men adored her, christening her Mother Bickerdyke. Some of the doctors were less enthusiastic. Armed with no authority, she once dismissed a doctor for arriving late on the wards for the fourth time in a month. The doctor complained to General Sherman who asked who had accused him. When the man said it was Mother Bickerdyke the General replied, 'Ah, then you are indeed out, and I cannot help you. She ranks me. There is nothing left for you to do except to bring your case before President Lincoln.'

The South started the war with its medical services even worse prepared than those in the North, and they also suffered as the war went on from the extra disadvantage of the North's naval blockade. Southern women smuggled quinine and opium through the lines, hidden in their hooped skirts, and threw open their homes as hospitals. Prejudices against women nurses were stronger in the South – bedpans and poultices conflicted with the Southern belle tradition – and women worked in hospitals as volunteers for a year and a half before they were given official status and duties. The Confederate army never did appoint a director of nursing, but President Jefferson Davis made Miss Sally Tompkins a Captain. She took charge of a hospital set up in a friend's house after the Battle of Bull Run. When such private hospitals were ordered to close, Miss Tompkins appealed directly to the President. He let her hospital remain open and made her a Captain of cavalry to comply with the regulations. Only seventy-two of her 1,333 patients died. With practice and dedication the medical services of the South achieved a degree of efficiency which led President Jefferson Davis to pay tribute to them when the war ended in April 1865: 'The only department that was not demoralized was the Hospital Department which was well in hand and doing efficient service until the end of the war.'

4 | The First Nightingales

When in the summer of 1855 the news reached Britain that Miss Nightingale was recovering from the fever that had brought her close to death in the Crimea, the country was swept by an urge to express its gratitude to her in some permanent way. Her friends knew that anything in the nature of statues or gold plate would be unacceptable to her. So, with her consent, they opened a fund to enable her to 'establish and control an institute for the training, sustenance and protection of nurses.' The Nightingale Fund was launched at a glittering and enthusiastic public meeting, chaired by the Duke of Cambridge and held at Willis's Rooms on November 29.

Nursing stood on the threshold of total reform. The leader, the inspiration and the money were at last united to set in motion the scheme which was to revolutionize nursing throughout the British Empire and the United States and influence nursing wherever hospitals existed. But the world had to wait. For nearly five years the £44,000 collected (£9,000 from the troops) lay idly gathering interest. Miss Nightingale, returning from the Crimea as an invalid, devoted her considerable mental powers and the energies of her friends to compiling evidence for the Royal Commission into the health of the army. In 1858, unable to foresee the time when she would be free to establish a training school, she asked the Fund's council to release her. They persuaded her to stay. In 1859, however, she realized that her health would never allow her to take on the superintendency of a new Institution, and asked the council to form a committee to carry out the objects of the Fund. Miss Nightingale believed that only a civil general hospital would serve her purpose, which was nothing less than the world-wide reform of nursing. The committee inspected a number of hospitals and selected St. Thomas's Hospital, London.

'It is not the *best conceivable* way of beginning. But it seems to me to be the *best possible*', Miss Nightingale wrote of the birthplace of modern nursing. On the credit side it had Mrs. Wardroper and Mr. Whitfield. Mrs. Wardroper, the widow of a doctor, became matron in February 1854 and Miss Nightingale first met her when she was searching for nurses to take to the Crimea: 'Training was then unknown; the only nurse worthy of the name that could be given to that expedition, though several were supplied, was a "Sister" who had been pensioned some time before, and who proved invaluable,' Miss Nightingale wrote on Mrs. Wardroper's death in 1892. She continued: ' I saw her [Mrs. Wardroper] next after the conclusion of the Crimean War. She had already made her mark; she had weeded out the inefficient, morally and technically; she had obtained better women as nurses; she had laid her finger on some of the most flagrant blots, such as the night nursing, and where she laid her finger the blot was diminished as far as possible, but no training had yet been thought of . . .' Mrs. Wardroper was a strict disciplinarian, autocratic and hard working, an efficient administrator and excellent teacher.

Mr. Whitfield, the resident medical officer, had appealed to Miss Nightingale for help when a dispute between the hospital governors had ended in deadlock. St. Thomas's lay across the route of a proposed railway line and the governors could not decide whether to sell part of the site to the railway company, or dispose of it all and rebuild elsewhere. Miss Nightingale proved statistically that, as many of the patients came from outside the locality, the hospital would not be abandoning the people it served by moving. A move was decided on, to Mr. Whitfield's satisfaction, and Miss Nightingale acquired another devoted admirer.

At this stage, what the training of nurses would involve was not clearly understood. Many people assumed that nurses would become medical students, but Miss Nightingale was always quite clear about the difference between the functions of medicine and nursing. In *Notes on Nursing*, an excellent practical guide for all women who had to care for the health of their family and household (first published in 1859), she wrote: 'Surgery removes the bullet out of the limb, which is an obstruction to cure, but nature heals the wound. So it is with medicine; the function of an organ becomes obstructed; medicine, as far as we know, assists nature to remove the obstruction, but does nothing more. And what nursing has to do in either case, is to put the patient in the best condition for nature to act upon him.' As late as the 1880s, Miss Nightingale felt obliged to spell out this simple message in even simpler form. 'Nursing is to help the patient to live. Training is to teach the nurse to help the patient to live.'

Many doctors, looking to cure the patient rather than simply care for him, appreciated the advantages skilled nursing might bring. Others agreed with Lady Palmerston who is reported to have said: 'The nurses are very good now; perhaps they do drink a little, but so do the ladies' monthly nurses, and nothing can be better than them; poor people, it must be so tiresome sitting up all night.'

One of the fiercest opponents of the reforms was based in St. Thomas's itself – John Fleet South, the senior consulting surgeon and the President of the College of Surgeons. In 1856, on discovering that Jane Shaw Stewart, one of the Crimean lady nurses, was coming to St. Thomas's to learn to nurse, he wrote agitatedly to the hospital treasurer: '. . . the intention . . . however carefully concealed, is to change entirely the whole nursing establishment of the house and to place it in the hands of persons who will never be content till *they* become the executive of the hospital.' In 1857, on first hearing that a training school was planned, he published a short book, *Facts relating to Hospital Nurses*, in which he defended the present system of nursing: 'As regards the nurses or ward maids, these are in much the same position as housemaids, and require little teaching beyond that of poultice making which is easily acquired, the enforcement of cleanliness and attention to the patients' wants.' Mr. South also took pleasure in pointing out that very few doctors and surgeons were listed as subscribers to the Nightingale Fund. The census, however, gives an indication of how much was achieved in the following forty years. In 1861 nurses were listed under the heading 'Domestic'; by 1901, they appeared under 'Medicine'.

Negotiations began between the Fund council and St. Thomas's Hospital in 1860. The hospital agreed to provide facilities for training fifteen probationers and separate accommodation for them. The resident medical officer, Matron and sisters would participate in the training. In return the Fund would pay the hospital 10s a week for each probationer's board and lodging, the matron would receive £100 a year, the resident medical officer £50 and each instructing sister £10. Candidates were to be aged between twenty-five and thirty-five, in good health and of irreproachable character. Advertisements were placed in the newspapers in May 1860. The Crimean War may have enveloped nursing in a rosy glow of heroism and sentiment but women seemed reluctant to commit themselves to the drudgery of civilian ward work. The romantic attitude to the work was one, anyway, that Miss Nightingale despised. 'It seems a commonly received idea among men and even among women themselves that it requires nothing but a disappointment in love, the want of an object, a general disgust, or incapacity for other things, to turn a woman into a good nurse,' she wrote in *Notes on Nursing*. '. . . The everyday management of a large ward, let alone a hospital . . . are not these matters of sufficient importance and difficulty to require learning by experience and careful inquiry, just as much as any other art?' Religious inspiration was necessary to good nursing, military discipline important (though nurses, unlike soldiers, had to learn to ask the 'reason why') but above all, training was essential. As Miss Nightingale was to fulminate nine years later, '. . . three fourths of the whole mischief in women's lives arises from their excepting themselves from the rules of training considered needful for men.'

The first fifteen probationers entered St. Thomas's on July 9, 1860 – the vanguard of the Nightingale system that was to revolutionize nursing in Britain and spread its influence throughout the world. These were not the first nurses to receive training – St. John's House was training its members at King's College Hospital – but they were the first to be trained on an entirely secular basis for a profession (though Miss Nightingale preferred to think of it as a vocation) that would earn them independence, respect, satisfaction and reasonable, or, in the case of matrons and superintendents, substantial financial rewards. Apart from training, the Nightingale system had two other basic principles. Nurses were to be entirely under the authority of the matron, who alone would have the authority to appoint or dismiss them. Hitherto, the matron had often been little more than a housekeeper. Nurses would, of course, continue to obey the doctors. The character of the nurses was to be at least as important as their technical ability. If the scheme was to succeed, the popular image of the hospital nurse – dirty, drunken, immoral, unreliable, thieving – had to be entirely dispelled. The probationers' quarters at St. Thomas's, where each one of them had their own cubicle and shared a dining room and sitting room, made bright by gifts of flowers, pictures and books from Miss

Florence Nightingale in old age. From 1857 onwards, she lived as an invalid, mainly in London, and entertained her innumerable visitors from a couch or her bed. She continued her work by means of an extensive correspondence.

Nightingale, served a dual purpose. These conditions were better than any provided for nurses before and respectable parents might be persuaded to allow their daughters to live there. And here, too, character could be carefully monitored.

The training period lasted for a year, during which the probationers served as assistant nurses in the wards. They received instruction from the sisters, themselves untrained, and the resident medical officer, and attended lectures given by other doctors. Prayers were said twice daily, there were weekly Bible classes and music classes, and on two days a week the probationers were released from supervision for one and a half or two hours for 'reading and improvement'. They received board and lodging, including tea and sugar, washing and a free uniform, and were paid a salary of £10 a year in four instalments. If, at the end of the year, they proved satisfactory, their names were entered on the Register. For the following three years they were contracted to the Fund and required to accept employment arranged for them at salaries usually of £20 a year plus board and lodging.

The probationers' day started at 6 am. Breakfast was at 6.30 and then they worked in the wards until dinner at 12.45. Duties back on the wards lasted from 1.30 to 5 pm, when there was a break for tea, and then 6 pm till 8.30, when they went to the dormitory. Supper was at 9 pm, followed by bed at 10 pm. There was a daily exercise period – either from 11.30 to 12.45 or 3.30 to 5.00. The carefully selected candidates were watched closely throughout the year – indeed, it must have sometimes seemed to them as if every gesture and sneeze was being recorded somewhere by someone. Probationers were required to be 'sober, honest, truthful, trustworthy, punctual, quiet and orderly, cleanly and neat, patient, cheerful and kindly'. They were also expected to become skilful at dressing wounds, the application of leeches, bandaging, the management of helpless patients, watching over and recording the course of an illness, understanding ventilation, bed making and changing sheets while the patient was in bed, and cooking for invalids. They were required in addition to attend operations.

A monthly record was kept of their Personal Character – summed up under the headings of punctuality, quietness, trustworthiness, personal neatness and cleanliness – while the Acquirement of Nurse table, a day-to-day record of nursing proficiency, had fourteen subheadings, including skill in dressings, invalid cooking, and keeping the ward clean. In the top right-hand corner of each record sheet there was a special box. Headed 'Moral Character During Probation – First dereliction causes dismissal', it was divided into three sections for 'Sobriety', 'Honesty' (designed particularly to stamp out the practice of taking petty bribes from patients) and 'Truthfulness'. This box was scrupulously filled in for the first few years but, presumably as standards rose, the habit grew of simply scrawling 'satisfactory' across all three sections, or even leaving it blank. The probationers were also required to take case notes and, at Miss Nightingale's suggestion, to keep diaries which would be open for inspection.

Discipline, of course, was strict and Mrs. Wardroper supplemented the official records with private notes to Miss Nightingale on each probationer: 'Although I have not the smallest reason to doubt the correctness of her moral character, her manner, nonetheless, is objectionable, and she uses her eyes unpleasantly; as her years increase, this failing – an unfortunate one – may possibly decrease.' Of the first batch of probationers, one was dismissed for drunkenness, one for failing to carry out the resident medical officer's orders, and a third for refusing to comply with the regulations. Another resigned because of ill health.

The first year was regarded as a success. In August 1860, Dr. Bowman, a member of the Fund committee who had been surgeon at the Harley Street Institution, wrote to Miss Nightingale, '. . . everything seemed perfect as to order, cleanliness and simplicity of demeanour – home costume I particularly liked . . . they seemed earnest and simpleminded, intelligent and nice mannered. Altogether the experiment seemed to be working well . . . Mrs. Wardroper I was much pleased with.'

The following year, a further step was taken. In October 1861 the Nightingale Fund made an arrangement with King's College Hospital, London, for training midwives. The plan was that women, six at a time, would be sent from country parishes to the hospital for six months of practical training, taught by physician accoucheurs (the Victorian term for obstetricians) and return home to put their knowledge into practice. The scheme had to be abandoned in 1887 because of an epidemic of puerperal fever.

The course at St. Thomas's was of a practical, rather than theoretical, nature, designed to be easily absorbed by women of limited education. The application form, which asked, 'Can you read and write well?' made it clear that Miss Nightingale expected most recruits to come from lower down the social scale. Middleclass gentlewomen, however, were not excluded – provided they were prepared to undergo the training. In fact, the advantages of training gentlewomen became apparent at an early stage. In July 1861, Sir Joshua Jebb, a Fund committee member, wrote to Miss

Nightingale, 'The question I am anxious to submit to your better judgment is whether . . . it would not be advisable to adopt the principle applicable to training School-masters, each of whom is educated with the distinct object of *training others*.' He felt that it was not enough merely to train nurses for the wards of St. Thomas's, or to send them out singly to other hospitals where they would mix with the prejudiced old-style nurse and so lose their usefulness. But he also stated that it would not be reasonable 'to expect she should be placed at once in a more commanding position unless her attainments were backed up by her having been *originally in a higher social position* than the ordinary run of nurses.'

The moral was obvious. If nursing reform was to be successful it had to be imposed from the top. Matrons and superintendents must be gentlewomen, with the education to cope with training and administration and the social status to meet hospital managers and boards of guardians on equal terms. Lady or 'special' probationers would have an additional advantage – they could pay for their own training and board. A circular letter written about 1865 by Sir Harry Verney, chairman of the Fund committee and married to Miss Nightingale's sister, Parthenope, stated: 'Applications to the Committee are frequent from Institutions in want of gentlewomen to fill the office of Matron or Superintendent.' The 1875 Regulations for Special Probationers said that the Fund was 'desirous of affording increased opportunities to gentlewomen to qualify themselves in the practice of Hospital Nursing . . . Only those Candidates will at present be admitted who may desire eventually to become qualified for superior situations in public Hospitals or Infirmaries.' The special probationers, who paid £30 for the privilege of undertaking the course, received the same instruction as the nurse probationers and also kept diaries and case notes; but, as time went on, they were given extra lectures and more off-duty time for additional study and reading.

Training in the early years was not of a particularly demanding nature. Mrs. Rebecca Strong, a widow with one child who entered the School in 1867, remembered, 'Very little was expected from us, as progress was slow in regard to organised teaching. Kindness, watchfulness, cleanliness, and guarding against bed-sores were well ingrained. A few stray lectures were given. One I remember especially, I think it was on the Chemistry of Life or some such title . . . There was a dummy on which to practice bandaging, and some lessons were given, also a skeleton and some ancient medical books, one fortunately on Anatomy for those who attempted self-education . . . Temperature taking and chart keeping were medical students' work but became nurses'.' Mrs. Strong was a probationer during the period when St. Thomas's was in temporary residence in the old Surrey Gardens Music Hall from 1862 to 1871. Accommodation and facilities were all stretched. Mrs. Strong reported that the kitchen was used as an operating theatre. 'All the patients had to supply certain articles for themselves, such as a change of bed wear, a garment of some kind, and a towel – toothbrushes were unknown . . . you can readily understand the difficulty with the class of patient dealt with . . . It was exceptional to receive a clean patient and baths being limited there was much washing in bed.'

However, the situation was soon to be improved. In 1871 the new St. Thomas's Hospital was opened by Queen Victoria on its present site opposite the Houses of Parliament. It was built to the pavilion plan favoured by Miss Nightingale. Instead of the traditional long corridors there were self-contained blocks. There were more beds in the new hospital and the number of probationers was increased to thirty-nine. They were accommodated in the Nightingale Home, the first building specially constructed for this purpose.

The move to the new buildings involved Mrs. Wardroper in considerably more work, so in 1872 it was decided to appoint an assistant to take on the duties of Home Sister. She was to take charge of the probationers and the Home, look after their moral and spiritual welfare as well as doing some teaching and overseeing the probationers' lecture notes, case books and diaries. Mrs. Wardroper, however, resented anyone coming between her and her nurses and made life difficult for the first Home Sister, Miss Elizabeth Torrance, who, after two months, chose the less stoney path of marriage. Miss Nightingale wrote to Henry Bonham Carter, her cousin and secretary to the Fund: 'Miss Torrance says that she is doing almost nothing and can do nothing. That all she does is preside at meals, write out tradesmen's orders, make up Washing Bills and count out linen and read prayers. That all she sees of the Probationers is at meals and prayers.' Maria Machin filled the post from 1873 to 1875, when she took a party of nurses to Montreal. She was succeeded by Miss Mary Crossland. Miss Machin had apparently succeeded in reconciling the matron to the new position. On the evening of Miss Crossland's arrival at the Nightingale School as a probationer in 1874, Mrs. Wardroper is reported to have said: 'That probationer will do for the future home sister.' Miss Crossland had been a governess and, though she never worked as a ward sister, she proved herself an excellent instructor.

Miss Nightingale had the deepest respect for Mrs. Wardroper's abilities and high standards but found her unpredictable temper

A view of Florence Nightingale's grave in East Wellow, Hampshire. Beside it stands Private John Keller, whom she nursed for three months in the Crimea. Miss Nightingale had refused the offer of a national funeral and burial in Westminster

during this period worrying. In one exasperated note to Henry Bonham Carter in 1872 she spelled out Mrs. Wardroper's shortcomings: '. . . that she is in the constant and notorious habit of questioning Sisters, Nurses and Probationers about each other . . . that her inconsiderate practice of scolding Sisters before the whole Ward has caused and is causing Sisters to leave . . . that it is notorious that the Matron will unsay all she has said today by tomorrow or even the same day . . . that it is notorious that at the end of a long conversation with her you are at exactly the same point as when you started . . . that she will stop the Sisters or Lady Probationers in the midst of their work or after a hard day's work going to bed say between 9 pm and 10 pm in the Corridor and talk for $1\frac{1}{2}$ hours till they are ready to sink with fatigue . . . that none but Miss Pringle have anything the least like a "filial" feeling for Matron – and even she always speaks of her as "poor matron" . . . that nearly all the present sisters will leave.' Miss Nightingale rather prematurely diagnosed 'senile activity' but, as Mrs. Wardroper remained matron until 1887, this seems to have been a passing phase. On her death, Miss Nightingale wrote a genuinely appreciative obituary.

Mrs. Wardroper was very strict with her probationers. She used to tell them: 'Nursing is a hard, self-sacrificing life, and this is why our training is so very severe. Few can go on with it; it requires great strength and endurance.' Any sentimental ideas were strangled at birth. Some, indeed, felt that the discipline was too severe. One clergyman said, '. . . the training at St. Thomas's was calculated to crush all enthusiasm and spirit in order to force the character to its ideal without making any allowance for natural bent, and was calculated to turn young women into automatic machines – discipline was too severely directed against natural affection.' But those who survived Mrs. Wardroper's autocratic methods developed a deep affection for her and a respect for her judgement. One of her graduates said later: 'Mrs. Wardroper never lectured to the probationers but she trained them more thoroughly, I think, than the highly trained matron of the present day, and certainly maintained a far higher standard of discipline in the hospital and wards. In her time, if a probationer had been found "chatting" to a young medical student or surgeon she would have been dismissed at once.' Miss Nightingale backed her completely in her aim, which seems to have involved not so much knocking the corners off as hammering them on. 'A woman who takes a sentimental view of Nursing (which she calls "ministering", as if she were an Angel), is of course worse than useless,' Miss Nightingale wrote. 'A woman possessed with the idea that she is making a sacrifice will never do . . . Nurses' work means downright work, in a cheery, happy, hopeful, friendly spirit. An earnest, bright, cheerful woman, without that notion of "making sacrifices", etc., perpetually occurring to her mind, is the real Nurse.'

In 1872 Miss Nightingale instituted a thorough investigation into all aspects of the Nightingale School. She found that standards were slipping and immediately set reforms under way. The Home Sister would take on the job of improving the character of the probationers. The school, Miss Nightingale wrote, 'must be a Home – a place of moral, religious and practical training – a place of training of character, habits, and intelligence, as well as of acquiring knowledge.' Acquiring knowledge, however, was not to be overlooked. With one of the surgeons, Mr. Croft, who had replaced Mr. Whitfield as medical instructor, she drew up a carefully planned course of instruction to replace Mrs. Strong's 'few stray lectures'. Doctors gave clinical teaching in the wards. There were lectures on medical and surgical nursing, elementary anatomy and physiology, and demonstrations and examinations from the medical staff. Miss Crossland taught the probationers about topics such as medical terms, burns and scalds, weights and measures, poisons and antidotes, as well as taking classes in reading, writing and spelling for the nurse probationers and voluntary Bible classes for everyone. Lady probationers were given two afternoons off a week to follow a reading course drawn up by Dr. Croft. This system was to remain basically unaltered for twenty years.

The demand for trained nurses and qualified lady superintendents proved to be too great to allow the course to be extended beyond the single year. (St. Thomas's retained the one-year course long after other, younger schools had adopted a two- or even three-year period of training.) Suitable recruits, particularly from the educated classes, were hard to find. Miss Nightingale wrote: 'Women really trained, and capable for good work, can command any wages or salaries. We can't get the women. The remunerative employment is there, and in plenty. The want is the women fit to take it.' In spite of the high moral tone of the school, parents were reluctant to let their daughters undertake work which was physically exhausting, sordid, and could even be dangerous and which, unlike the more genteel profession of the governess, brought them into intimate contact with the most unsavoury sections of society.

From 1872 onwards, Miss Nightingale made a point of meeting and keeping in touch with all her nurses, sisters and probationers. She would have them to tea and make crisp notes on them as soon as they had left: 'As self-comfortable a jackass (or Joan-ass) as ever I saw.' 'Miserable nurse though an interesting woman and can answer questions.' 'Coarse; uneducated; conceited. Hobnobbing with the Nurses or else spiting them.' Sick nurses were sent invalid delicacies or packed off to Lea Hurst or Embley to rest. Nightingale matrons and superintendents received support and advice in a constant stream of correspondence. Starting in 1872, Miss Nightingale sent annual letters to be read aloud to her probationers. They were simple in tone, encouraging here, reproving there, some light-hearted discourses, others amounting almost to a sermon. Nothing was overlooked, but one theme ran through all her addresses. The Nightingale School was training not just nurses but missionaries. The aim was, 'To reform the nursing of all the Hospitals and Workhouse Infirmaries in the world, and to establish District Nursing among the sick poor at home.' Her graduates were her disciples, preaching the word of trained nursing. They were soldiers, marching to battle against dirt and disease, prejudice and ignorance.

Spreading the Word $\boxed{5}$

Everyone wanted Miss Nightingale's 'soldiers' – or, at least, her 'infantry training manual'. Dr. Elizabeth Blackwell, a friend of Miss Nightingale since the Crimean War, heard about the plans for the Nightingale Training School in 1859 and carried the word home to America. The Crown Princess Frederick (Queen Victoria's daughter) was keen to establish similar nurse training in Germany. Hospital managements in Australia and Canada, anxious to improve their own nursing, looked to St. Thomas's Hospital for leadership and inspiration. But before the rest of the world could be satisfied, reform had to begin at home.

Mrs. Wardroper received the first request for trained nurses as early as January 1861. The first call to be answered came from the Liverpool Royal Infirmary. Mr. William Rathbone, eager to extend an experiment in district nursing, had been unable to find trained nurses to do the work. He appealed to Miss Nightingale, who recommended him to start a training school in Liverpool. Rathbone found that the committee of the Royal Infirmary was keen to improve the nursing but that there was another major problem, the shortage of suitable accommodation. He undertook to build a training school and nurses' home and present it to the committee if they, in return, would undertake the training. In 1862 the training school opened under Miss Merryweather, with four trained nurses from St. Thomas's Hospital, London. Probationers were to be trained for the Infirmary, for district nursing and for private nursing.

The first request for a complete nursing staff also came from Mr. Rathbone. He had discovered that the poor were reluctant to enter the workhouse infirmary at Brownlow Hill and, on investigation, found that the main problem was the nursing. The infirmary was gloomy and large but better equipped and built than most of its contemporaries. The guardians were energetic and efficient and the doctors were encouraged to apply for what they needed, but the nursing was in the hands of rough pauper women, supervised by untrained parish officers who wore kid gloves in the wards to protect their hands. At night some of the wards were patrolled by policemen to keep order, others, housing the weakest patients, were kept locked until morning. As expense was the main obstacle to the introduction of trained nurses, Mr. Rathbone, having pointed out that the cheapest way to treat the sick was to cure them, offered to bear the cost of twelve trained nurses and twelve probationers for three years and to pay a small salary to the more promising pauper nurses. The guardians agreed to the proposal and, once again, Mr. Rathbone approached Miss Nightingale.

Deeply interested in the movement for workhouse infirmary reform, Miss Nightingale was delighted by the scheme and proposed Agnes Elizabeth Jones for the post of superintendent. Agnes Jones was then aged thirty-two. The daughter of an army officer, she was well educated and deeply religious, with a tendency to mysticism. She had spent six months at Kaiserswerth and had then worked with Mrs. Ranyard's Bible Women before entering St. Thomas's as a probationer in October 1862. She made an excellent impression there, her record stating: 'Trustworthy, methodical and highly qualified for a position where intelligence and energy are required. In the Superintendence of her nurses her religious, and moral influences would be most valuable.' Miss Jones, then working at the Great Northern Hospital in the Caledonian Road, London, was dismayed at the heavy responsibility of the task proposed to her, but accepted the challenge.

The Fund entered into negotiations with the infirmary on pay and conditions for the nurses, and the authority and responsibilities of the superintendent. Miss Nightingale, Mrs. Wardroper and Mr. Whitfield conferred anxiously on which nurses to select for this exciting development. Miss Jones reached Brownlow Hill in April 1865. After St. Thomas's and the Great Northern Hospital, she was appalled at the conditions she found. There were over a thousand patients, many of them foul mouthed, drunken, vicious, degraded. She compared conditions on the wards to those described in Dante's *Inferno*. The twelve nurses arrived in May and at once took over the male wards. 'I am more afraid of their overworking themselves than of having to urge them on,' Agnes wrote to Miss Nightingale, adding that the surgeons, lady visitors and relatives of the patients were pleased with the improvements that had been achieved in only two weeks. The governor, George Carr, wrote that 'Miss Jones . . . is well qualified to successfully work out the scheme.'

However, there were problems. Miss Jones found it hard to get the necessary supplies. 'Before we began work, sweeping brushes were ordered – and I received seven for thirty-three wards,' she wrote to Miss Nightingale. 'We have often not a drop of water, hot or cold; and as to battles I have had to get the patients' diets and medicines no one could imagine but you.' In common with other hospital officials faced with this new experiment of trained nurses, the governor was not at first prepared to give Miss Jones the full authority the Nightingale system required for a superintendent. On a preliminary visit to Brownlow Hill, Miss Jones had been surprised to be told that all the nurses, including herself, would have to ask the governor's permission before they could leave the infirmary. Many of the probationers, selected against her judgement, were useless, but she was not allowed to dismiss them. Mr. Carr stressed to Miss Nightingale the differences between a wealthy and independent voluntary hospital and a workhouse infirmary, functioning under Poor Law regulations and paid for out of the rates. As he put it, '. . . in Workhouses there can be no authority superior to the Governor's . . . Miss Jones has ample powers and my very best support – but she occasionally appears to me to writhe and feel annoyed when she cannot, according to her own will and desire, dismiss a nurse.' With patience, determination and tact, however, Miss Jones won the co-operation of the governor, though the experiment of using selected pauper nurses was a disaster. They proved to be quite un-trustworthy and had to be watched every second. Thirty-five were dismissed for drunkenness in the first few months and the experiment was abandoned after the first year.

Though Miss Jones often had to work for eighteen hours a day, she found her task both happy and fulfilling. Her nurses were loyal and hard-working and she took great care of them, arranging outings and watching over their general well-being. The wards became clean and orderly. The patients, brutalized by the drunken and thoughtless treatment they had received at the hands of the pauper nurses, mellowed under the skilled and tender care of the Nightingale replacements. Miss Jones's Bible readings in one of the wards were well attended. In 1867, trained nurses took over the female wards and the whole cost was put upon the rates.

The wards were particularly crowded during the winter of 1867–68, with at one point 263 more patients than beds. They were,

Miss Jones wrote, patients of the worst sort – '. . . lost and degraded beyond description and we have scarcely a girl who hasn't been on the town.' On February 1, she wrote a cheerful letter to Miss Nightingale saying she had been ill but only needed rest – and died of typhus seventeen days later. Miss Nightingale entitled her tribute to her, published in the June issue of *Good Words*, 'Una and the Lion'. 'One woman has died – a woman, attractive and rich, and young and witty . . .' Trained nursing had its first martyr. 'Una' inspired many young ladies to join the crusade.

Nightingale nursing had triumphed and in 1869 the St. Pancras guardians followed the example of Liverpool, asking for a superintendent and a staff of trained nurses to run the new infirmary they were building under the Metropolitan Poor Act at Highgate. This was the first London infirmary to apply for nurses and the Nightingale Fund decided to make it a 'daughter' school, where they would finance a number of probationers on the same terms as those in operation at St. Thomas's. Miss Elizabeth Torrance, whom Miss Nightingale described as 'the most capable Superintendent they had yet trained', was selected, together with nine nurses. The first four probationers were admitted on November 1, 1871.

Like all Miss Nightingale's 'soldiers', Miss Torrance kept in close touch with her 'Chief', reporting progress and asking for advice. The Central London Sick Asylum Board (which had taken over from the Poor Law Board) was delighted with the nursing and with Miss Torrance. When Miss Torrance went to St. Thomas's as Home Sister in 1872, she was replaced by Miss Annie Hill. On Miss Hill's death in 1877, the Board appointed an untrained matron and, as this was against the Fund's conditions, it withdrew its pupils and its support. Thirty-one probationers had been admitted to Highgate for training.

In 1866, the Derbyshire General Infirmary was taken over by a Nightingale matron and the Manchester Training Institute was sent staff. In 1868 the Nightingale Fund Council was asked by the War Office to train staff for the Royal Victoria Hospital at Netley, and Mrs. Deeble, a widow with four children, was selected, with seven nurses. In 1872 the Edinburgh Royal Infirmary applied for staff. The Fund Council entered into the usual negotiations (Miss Nightingale insisting on a Home), while Mrs. Wardroper, Miss Nightingale and Henry Bonham Carter corresponded about the selection of superintendent and nurses. Eventually thirteen nurses, with Miss Barclay as superintendent, were chosen. 'I like Miss Barclay exceedingly,' Miss Nightingale wrote. 'She has simplicity, straightforwardness, uncompromising duty, ideas, strong will and

courage and I think sense. (I doubt her knowledge of character . . .)'
After a year, however, Miss Barclay's health broke down and she
was succeeded by her assistant, Angelique Lucille Pringle.

Miss Pringle was one of Miss Nightingale's favourite pupils. After
her first interview Miss Nightingale had written, 'Miss P came. I
have found a pearl of great price.' After that, Miss Pringle was
known as the 'Pearl', or 'little sister'. (She addressed Miss
Nightingale as 'very dearest mother chief'.) She entered the
Nightingale School in 1868 at the age of twenty-two. Her report on
completion of training enthused: 'An active and intelligent
practical nurse particularly in the surgical department – a person of
superior abilities and education, as is apparent from the manner of
reporting her cases and notes of lectures – both highly creditable.'
She went to Edinburgh after three years as sister in the male
accident ward at St. Thomas's. She was reluctant to accept the
responsibility of superintendency but, like a good soldier, obeyed
her general. Although the standard of nursing at Edinburgh was
above average for the time and the atmosphere homely, there were
the usual problems. In 1874, Miss Pringle wrote to Miss
Nightingale, 'we have had a very sad week owing to an outbreak of
drunkenness among the ward assistants – seven having had to be
dismissed.' With the opening of the new infirmary in 1879, the
Nightingale system was firmly established – though without the
lady probationer system – and, in the 1880s, a three-year period of
training was introduced. In 1887, modestly and reluctantly, Miss
Pringle succeeded Mrs. Wardroper as matron of St. Thomas's and
superintendent of the training school. In 1889, to Miss
Nightingale's grief, she joined the Roman Catholic church and a
year later resigned from St. Thomas's.

Miss Pringle's assistant at Edinburgh in the early years was a
woman who held as large a place in Miss Nightingale's heart as Miss
Pringle herself – Rachel Williams, the 'Goddess' or 'goddess baby'.
She was thirty-one when she entered the Nightingale School in
1871, and, until she was placed on Miss Pringle's wards, was
disappointed by the spirit she found. Then, the selfless and
conscientious Miss Pringle became her model. At the end of her
year's training her report said, with moderate enthusiasm: 'A lady
of good abilities, not a great amount of physical power, good and
intelligent nurse.'

In 1876, on Miss Nightingale's recommendation, Miss Williams
applied and was selected for the post of matron at St. Mary's
Hospital, Paddington. There she met some opposition but managed
to improve the nurses' eating arrangements, drew up a plan for

reform of the nursing, which included replacing first- and second-class assistant nurses with staff nurses and probationers, and established a one-year training course. With Miss Alice Fisher she wrote one of the earliest training manuals for nurses. In 1878 a move to increase her salary from £100 to £150 met strong opposition from a section of the board of managers and Miss Williams finally resigned in 1885 after a further financial dispute. Later that year, at the government's request, she took a party out to nurse in the Sudan campaign, returned to England and married in December.

By 1879 eight hospitals were manned by a Nightingale matron or superintendent and staff. The fifty-eight Nightingales in other institutions included twenty-six matrons. The Edinburgh Royal Infirmary and St Mary's, Paddington, had established training schools along Nightingale lines, and the Marylebone Infirmary and the Westminster Hospital were shortly to follow suit. St. John's House sisters were nursing at King's College Hospital and Charing Cross Hospital; All Saints sisters at University College Hospital. The move towards improving the standard of hospital nursing was thus a general one, though what it actually involved was often misunderstood and standards were inconsistent. Evidence for this was produced by Florence Lees, who investigated hospitals for a report on 'Nurses Work and Nurses Training' in 1874–75. The Middlesex, under a lady superintendent trained at UCH, provided its probationers with single bedrooms, a communal dining room and sitting room (lady probationers, who paid one guinea a week, had their own sitting room) and expected probationers to become skilled in the same subjects as St. Thomas's; but no record was kept of their progress, there was no medical instructor, nor were classes given by the superintendent. Guy's Hospital provided no systematic training, no examinations and no certificate. At the Westminster, there was no bathroom and only one portable bath to every six wards and no systematic training or examination. At St. Bartholomew's the sisters were engaged and dismissed by the house committee, not by the matron. Nurses had to cook for the sisters in the ward scullery and sleep three to a room opening off the ward.

Barts began accepting and training probationers in 1877 under the matron, Mrs. Drake, who was herself untrained. The conditions which awaited these first young women were certainly not adequate by Nightingale Fund standards. Twenty-five years later one of the probationers recorded for the *Journal* of St Bartholomew's Nurses' League: 'Mrs. Drake greatly disapproved of such an innovation as "lady nurses", and tried hard to dissuade me from entering.' She shared a room opening off the ward with the staff nurses, 'chiefly women of the charwoman type, frequently of bad character, with little or no education, and few of them with even an elementary knowledge of nursing.' Some of the sisters were of better quality, but few were capable of teaching the probationers. Instruction was unsystematic. 'Mr. Willett used to have in his out-patient children and teach us to bandage, put on splints, to make and apply plasters, bandages, and so on. Sir Dyce [Duckworth] would take us into the wards and give us a lesson on bed-making, poultice-making, or on the contents of the doctor's cupboard, or down to the bath-rooms, where he and old Williams, the bathman, used to show us the best way to get patients in and out of the bath . . . We were known as "Ducky's lambs" . . .'

The arrival of the probationers brought about a general improvement in conditions. A night home was provided for the night nurses, and a separate dining room was improvised for breakfast and dinner – tea was taken in the wards and supper was whatever they cared to get for themselves. 'Of course, nursing as you understand it now was utterly unknown. Patients were not "nursed" then; they were "attended to" . . . What was our life in the home like? There was nothing of the sort. We had breakfast and dinner in the home; otherwise, when off duty, if we did not go out, we sat in the ward kitchens or in our bedrooms . . . There was no one to overlook our behaviour or to see that we went to bed at the right time . . .' At the end of the year examinations were held and certificates awarded. Under the Nightingale-trained Miss Machin, matron from 1879 to 1881, training was increased to two years and to three under her successor, Miss Manson.

In the early years probationers went to work in the wards on their first day in a state of total ignorance, scarcely knowing one end of a patient from the other, and were removed from the wards at irregular and often inconvenient hours to attend lectures. The first preliminary training school was started by Mrs. Rebecca Strong at the Glasgow Royal Infirmary in 1893. After St. Thomas's, Mrs. Strong had gone with the Nightingale nurses to Winchester, then with Mrs. Deeble to Netley, and back to Winchester before becoming matron of the Dundee Royal Infirmary in 1874. The Nightingale system of nursing which she established there was of such a high standard, that, in 1879, she was appointed matron at the Glasgow Royal Infirmary to make similar improvements. 'I am afraid I was a rather troublesome woman, as soon as one step was taken I proposed another; this went on for a few years until it came to my asking for a "Home" for the nurses, which was too much, and I was told quite plainly that I had gone too far.'

Mrs. Strong resigned to run a private nursing home for the next six years and ponder over nursing education. When Glasgow asked her to return as matron, she started her preliminary training school. Candidates, unless they had a leaving certificate of the Scottish Education Department, had to pass an examination in grammar, composition, spelling and arithmetic. Pupils then attended a three-month course at St. Mungo's Medical College, for which they paid a fee and provided their own board and lodging. The course covered elementary anatomy, physiology and hygiene, lectures and demonstrations on medical and surgical cases, and lessons on practical nursing and cookery. At the end of the course, an examination was held and pupils who passed were admitted to the hospital for three years' practical training, during which no further classes were held.

The London was the first hospital to provide its own internal preliminary training. In 1873, the governors had decided to start training nurses and three years later they resolved to build a training school, but the matron at the time, Miss Swift, was untrained, there was little theoretical training and monotonous meals were eaten in the lobby between the wards. In 1880 Miss Eva Lückes became matron. She was well-educated, the daughter of a country gentleman, Westminster-trained and absurdly young – only twenty-four – but she arrived with a well-defined plan. Within a day, she had informed the committee that the nurses were inadequate in numbers and quality. The staff was increased and off-duty periods enforced. She improved the meal arrangements – the House Committee minutes reported: 'Matron complained of the lack of variety in the nurses' food, only one kind of pudding having been given for more than two years.' She employed ward maids in place of an army of charwomen, put the training school on a firm footing, and found better-educated probationers. The first certificates were awarded in 1882. The nurses' home opened in 1886 and a private nursing staff was established. (The voluntary hospitals traditionally augmented their incomes by sending their nurses out to private homes. London nurses nursed Edward VII through the appendicitis that delayed his Coronation.) In 1895, the preliminary training school was opened in Tredegar House because, in Miss Lückes's words, 'a pause on the threshold would give eager beginners time and opportunity to realise the importance of the new life and work on which they are about to enter, work that is taken up far too lightly at the present time by many sadly lacking the necessary vocation.'

Candidates for the six-week course were aged between twenty-three and thirty-three. Twenty-eight at a time entered Tredegar House on a Saturday night. After a 7 am breakfast, the trainees held prayers and did some housework before going to the hospital for lectures on hygiene, anatomy and physiology. A light lunch was served at 11 am and then the pupils returned to the House for teaching in practical nursing, and the demonstration and practice of bandaging. On some mornings there was an ambulance class. Dinner at 1.30 was accompanied by cheerful conversation (shop talk was banned) and the early afternoon filled with cookery classes at the hospital – then back again to Tredegar House for tea. Two hours of classes on hygiene, anatomy and physiology and a study hour were followed by supper and prayers at 9 pm. The pupils went to their rooms at 10 pm with lights out at 10.30. They had two hours off a day and four hours off on Saturdays and Sundays. After six weeks they took an examination and successful pupils went to the hospital. Training then lasted two years – the first for learning, the second to test whether they could practise what they had learned. The nurses were engaged for a further year during which they worked in private homes or in the hospital. They were paid £12 the first year, £20 the second and £25 the third. Discipline was strict and one early probationer reported, 'There was little or no social life with the minimum of opportunity for it. Nurses were strictly forbidden to go out with doctors or medical students and if discovered doing so the penalty was great.'

The most celebrated London graduate was Edith Cavell. A clergyman's daughter born in 1865, she worked as a governess before entering Tredegar House in September 1896. With other London nurses, she worked through the typhoid epidemic at Maidstone before completing her training. Miss Lückes's report on her did not suggest heroic potential: 'somewhat superficial . . . a self sufficient manner which was very apt to prejudice people against her . . . not very much in earnest, not at all punctual, and not a Nurse that could altogether be depended on . . . Her theoretical work was superior to her practical . . .' Edith Cavell spent her third year in private nursing and held several posts around the country before going to Brussels as matron of Belgium's first nurse training school in 1907. The school was a success and work was under way on a new hospital when war broke out in 1914. After the Germans arrived Miss Cavell stayed on from a sense of duty. In November, two wounded British soldiers arrived at the hospital and were taken in and treated. After that the hospital became part of an escape route for soldiers who had been cut off from their units during the retreat – at one time it held thirty-five men. German suspicions were aroused. Miss Cavell was arrested in August and shot on October 12, 1915.

Preliminary training schools were slow to catch on, however. Guy's opened one in 1902. St. Thomas's, where nurse training had lagged seriously behind that of the newer schools, caught up with a rush, extending its lectures to second-year probationers and opening a preliminary training school in 1910. St. Thomas's was the first school to appoint a Sister Tutor.

The first overseas probationer at St. Thomas's arrived from Sweden in 1866, and Germany, too, later sent several young women for training. In the same year the government of New South Wales applied to Miss Nightingale for a staff of nurses for the Sydney Infirmary. The twenty-nine-year-old Miss Lucy Osburn left for Australia in 1867 with five nurses on a three-year contract. The party found poor accommodation, insanitary and inconvenient wards, opposition from some of the medical staff and some slatternly and untrained nurses. Even some of Miss Osburn's own nurses began to conspire against her, and Miss Nightingale came to the conclusion that the experiment had been a failure. At the end of the contract, when Miss Osburn wrote asking for advice, Miss Nightingale wrote to Henry Bonham Carter: 'All I could say . . . would be; God bless her. And for her own sake and the sake of all under her, may she never undertake Hospital Superintendency again.' This was premature. Miss Osburn was asked to stay on; she overcame the opposition and established a nurse training school. Her graduates founded training schools throughout Australia.

The Nightingale system was also established in New Zealand. In fact, the one failure by Nightingale nurses occurred at the General Hospital, Montreal. Maria Machin went there in 1875 with four head nurses. The authorities were antagonistic however, and work on the promised new hospital and nurses' home had not even begun. The party was recalled in 1878 and Miss Machin became matron at St. Bartholomew's.

Nursing in Europe was dominated by the Motherhouse system, with the school maintained by Protestant or Catholic orders or by the Red Cross. The Superior was under the authority of a chaplain or committee and the Sisters usually supported for life and paid only pocket money. But the Nightingale system did make some headway in Scandinavia, Holland and Germany, and even in France. Early attempts were made in Paris to train the nurse attendants, who, as the hospitals were laicized, often provided the only nursing care. Three Paris hospitals – the Salpêtrière, Bicêtre and Pitié – all introduced training in 1878 and the Lariboisière followed suit in

1894. Accommodation, pay, food and pensions were improved in an effort to attract a better class of nurse. In 1901 Dr. Anna Hamilton introduced the Nightingale system into the Maison de Santé Protestante in Bordeaux. She cleaned up the wards, got rid of the bejewelled ladies who were amusing themselves with Red Cross courses and brought in London-hospital trained Catherine Elston to organize the training school. The Mayor of Bordeaux decided to introduce the system to the public hospitals and Miss Elston moved on first to St. André and then to Tondu hospital.

Bordeaux graduates spread the word of the revolution throughout France. Dr. Hamilton said: 'What most surprises the doctors (all more or less prejudiced against lady nurses) is the fact that they do for the patients so many things the nuns would object to do, and they do not discuss and meddle with the doctor's orders.'

In America the Civil War gave the same impetus to nursing reform as the Crimean War had done in Britain. The Women's Hospital, Philadelphia, was anxious to train nurses and opened its doors to pupils in 1861 but training was not properly established for some years. The New England Hospital for Women and Children, one of several to be called the first training school for nurses in America, was founded with the objects of providing for women 'medical aid by competent physicians of their own sex' and 'To assist educated women in the practical study of medicine. To train nurses for the care of the sick.'

Thirty-two nurses were trained between 1862 and 1872 when the hospital moved to Roxbury, Massachusetts, and founded the modern school of nursing there. The year's course was divided into four parts covering medical, surgical, maternity and night nursing experience plus a course of twelve lectures. The first five probationers were so grateful for their training that, when they heard the hospital was short of funds, they donated a quarter of their wages to it. Miss Linda Richards was the first to receive her certificate and earned the title of First Trained Nurse in the United States. Looking back, she wrote of the first class that they were 'very happy, very united, and pretty well instructed.'

When the Civil War was over, the men and women who had devoted their energies to the Sanitary Commission turned their attention to investigating civil institutions. Bellevue nurse training school in New York was established at the instigation of the Bellevue Hospital Visiting Committee, a section of the Hospitals Committee of the State Charities Aid Association. A member of the committee had visited Bellevue and been deeply shocked by the conditions she found there. Some of the nursing was still done by convicts, the patients' dinners were dumped without plates on the bare tables and the laundry had been without soap for six weeks. Improvements were made in the supplies, the laundry and the kitchen and one of the doctors volunteered to go to Europe and report on nursing there. He returned with a detailed report and a letter of encouragement and advice from Miss Nightingale.

The Committee put forward a plan for establishing a nurse training school at Bellevue and eventually received permission to take over five wards for the purpose. A fund was opened, a house rented for a nurses' home and Sister Helen Bowden of the All Saints Sisterhood, who had trained at University College Hospital in London, was appointed superintendent. The school opened in 1873. After a few months Linda Richards joined the staff as night superintendent. The experiment was a success and the school gradually took over the nursing of the whole hospital. The Nightingale principle that, in matters of discipline, the nurses were responsible to the superintendent who was, in turn, answerable to the warden or medical superintendent was accepted in spite of some opposition. Contrary to British custom, however, only better-educated women were admitted for training – women of the domestic servant class who formed the bulk of the nurse probationers (as opposed to the 'special' probationers) in England were excluded. Training was for one year and certificates were awarded after a further year had been spent in the wards. After two years the nurses were not offered employment in the hospital but became independent. Bellevue graduates became pioneers in their turn.

Two other training schools opened in the same year as Bellevue. The Women's Educational Association was responsible for founding one at Massachusetts General hospital in Boston. The hospital was clean and cheerful and already manned by respectable and conscientious women. The medical staff were happy with things as they were and resented the intrusion of the training school nurses into two wards. The first two superintendents lasted only a short while and it looked as if the experiment might have to be abandoned. Then the ubiquitous Miss Richards became superintendent, succeeded in proving that trained nurses were superior to untrained ones, and after a year of her leadership the school took over nursing of the whole hospital. Miss Richards left the school after two and a half years, spent eight weeks in London at St. Thomas's, and went on to organize schools at the Boston City hospital, in Tokyo for Japanese nurses and at the Methodist hospital, Philadelphia. In 1893 she became superintendent at Bellevue.

A lecture on bandaging at the Blockley Training School for Nurses in 1886. Over the forty years after the Crimea the status of nurses was transformed. In Britain in 1861 they were classed as 'domestics'; by 1901 they appeared under the heading 'medicine' in the census

The first four pupils arrived at the Connecticut training school, New Haven, on October 6, 1873 and were at once employed in nursing typhoid cases. By the end of the first year the school had received nearly 100 applications for a place on the course. By the end of the second, graduates were undertaking private nursing and, by the end of the fourth, the Connecticut school was supplying superintendents for other hospitals and nursing the sick poor without charge.

The gigantic task of reforming Blockley Hospital, Philadelphia, fell to a Nightingale nurse, Miss Alice Fisher. She had already reformed nursing in three English hospitals – Addenbrooke's, Cambridge, the Radcliffe Infirmary, Oxford, and the General Hospital, Birmingham, before going to Blockley at the end of 1884 to establish a training school there. The hospital contained about 3,000 beds, the nursing was done by inadequate attendants and the management was poor. Miss Fisher attracted a better class of nurse, introduced lectures and achieved an almost complete reform by her death in 1888.

Most of these early nursing schools followed the Nightingale system, with the independent female head (though this was later modified) and the emphasis on morality and duty. They did not contract, though, for employment after training and trained nurses had to make their own way in the world. By 1890, America had fifteen nurse training schools and by 1900 the number had grown to 432. Waltham Training School was the first to establish a preparatory course. This started in 1895, followed by Johns Hopkins hospital school, Baltimore, which, from its foundation in 1889, gave the most up-to-date nurse training in America. Three-year courses, started by the University Hospital, Philadelphia, in 1893 and Johns Hopkins in 1895, caught on fast, but the eight-hour day, pioneered by the Farrand School in Detroit in 1891, was much slower to get off the ground.

Health in the Home 6

Britain led the world in reforming hospital nursing, but most people sickened – and died – at home, easy victims of filth and infection which loving kindness alone could not defeat. While Miss Nightingale's missionaries were spreading her message throughout the world, the cities at home were welcoming the birth of modern district nursing. The movement was to be as much a force for good in England and throughout the world as the changes that were going on in the institutions and the demands made of its protagonists were to be even more challenging. Such early hospital reformers as Agnes Jones and Rebecca Strong had to face and subdue dirt and drink, ignorance and prejudice once or twice in their careers. District nurses – Mary Robinson in Liverpool, Florence Lees in London, and Lillian Wald in New York being three examples – had to overcome these obstacles in every new home they visited. The rooms, bodies and bedclothes of their poor patients were usually filthy and often verminous, the windows stopped up to prevent dangerous fresh air coming in, sanitation was poor and food inadequate.

Before the nurse could begin to treat her patient she had to put the room into good 'nursing order', cleaning the room, washing the patient, scouring utensils, improving light and air. She had to be a health missionary, teaching the principles of ventilation, sanitation and cleanliness to the patient's family. She had to be a sanitary inspector, reporting blocked drains and unemptied dustbins to the relevant officials. Though in Britain she was usually forbidden to act as a relieving officer, she had to be able to advise her patients which charities or Poor Law bodies might be able to help. A district nurse had to do battle alone. With a doctor rarely to hand she had sometimes to act on her own judgement. With no hospital store cupboard, she often had to improvise the most basic nursing requirements out of a jam jar, a soup plate or a sheet of paper.

The only women capable of carrying off these multiple roles successfully, according to Florence Lees, one of the founders of modern district nursing, was a thoroughly trained gentlewoman. Miss Lees, superintendent of the Metropolitan and National Nursing Association, believed that women of education would be best able to exercise the greater responsibilities of district nursing, and that 'ladies' would have greater influence over their patients. She felt the vocation would attract large numbers of ladies anxious for independent employment and that their higher social position would tend to raise the standing of professional nurses in the public's eyes. Miss Lees's views eventually triumphed.

The Metropolitan and National Nursing Association was by no means the first, or even the first successful, venture into district nursing. Visiting and tending the sick poor had been a sacred or moral duty for centuries before Christianity. It was a particular object of the early deaconesses, while medieval sisterhoods, such as the Béguines and St. Vincent de Paul's Sisters of Charity, counted it as one of their prime duties. In England, the new Protestant orders undertook to visit the sick poor. Later, Mrs. Fry's Institute and St. John's House members nursed them when not engaged on private work. In the large cities, charities distributed religious tracts and warm petticoats. In country districts, benevolent ladies handed out broth and supported the work of a clean and sober village midwife. But, until the Liverpool experiment, there was no organized system of trained home nursing for the poor.

In 1859, Mr. William Rathbone, a well-known Liverpool merchant, Unitarian and philanthropist, was left a widower with five small children. His wife was nursed through her last illness by a trained nurse, Mary Robinson. Mr. Rathbone wrote thirty years later: 'The great comfort and advantage derived from trained nursing, even in a home where everything which unskilled affection could suggest was provided, led to the conclusion that among the less fortunate – the poor – untold misery, lasting disability, and death itself must ensue in cases where these comforts and appliances, as well as skilled nursing, are almost altogether wanting.' Mr. Rathbone employed Mrs. Robinson for three months to nurse poor patients in their own homes and provided her with the necessary medical supplies and appliances. After a month the nurse came to him and begged to be released – she could not endure the misery she had found among the poor – but she was persuaded to stay. After three months, she reported that she had been able to do so much good that she wanted to devote herself entirely to nursing the sick poor. Her skills had not only restored patients to health but had, in some cases, saved whole families from ruin. In two cases a wife's sickness had driven the husband to drink and despair. The nurse showed the husbands what they could do to restore order and the men gave up drinking to do what they could.

Encouraged by this, Rathbone decided to extend his experiment. He applied to the new training school at St. Thomas's and to St. John's House at King's College Hospital for another nurse but neither had one to spare. Finally he consulted Miss Nightingale, who advised him to start a school of nursing in Liverpool. In connection with the Royal Infirmary, the Liverpool Training School and Home for Nurses opened in 1862 to provide trained nurses for the Infirmary, for district nursing among the poor and for private families.

By the end of 1865 Liverpool was divided into eighteen districts (hence 'district' nursing rather than 'visiting' nursing which is the term more commonly used outside Britain), each with a trained nurse and a lady or committee of ladies. The ladies found and paid for lodgings for the nurse, superintended her work, provided through their own or their friends' generosity the necessary medical supplies and comforts, and made contact with local doctors and clergymen who might have cases to recommend. They visited all cases under treatment, examined the nurse's register book and consulted with her on old and new cases. The nurse, whose salary was paid by the training school, was expected to spend five or six hours daily in visiting nursing. She reported any cases where she thought extra food would help recovery or where she felt the patient would be better off in hospital. In addition to nursing, she undertook to teach the patient and his family the basic principles of cleanliness and fresh air and the importance of obeying the doctor's orders.

At first, nurses were tempted to act as relieving officers and distribute more food than was necessary on purely medical grounds. As their skills became known and appreciated, more and more difficult cases calling for genuine nursing rather than ordinary relief were referred to them and, as a consequence, expenditure dropped. The quality of their work was further improved by moving the nurses out of their solitary dwellings and putting them into district homes under trained matrons who supervised the professional side of their work.

The Liverpool experiment was regarded as a success and other towns and cities soon followed suit. In the first year 1,376 cases were dealt with (consumption was the most common complaint, followed by fever). In 1864 the Manchester and Salford Sick Poor and Private Nursing Institute was founded on similar lines to Liverpool. Leicester set its first district nurse to work in 1867 and in 1870 Birmingham began district nursing. Two district nursing societies were founded in London in 1868 – Mrs. Ranyard's Biblewomen nurses and the East London Nursing Association. The Ranyard Mission had been started in 1857, as its founder's response to the appalling misery and degradation she found in the Seven Dials district of London. Knowing that ladies of her own class would make little headway in such conditions, she appointed 'missing links' – Christian women from the same background as those of the district – to undertake the work. Supervised by ladies, they went from door to door selling Bibles on subscription and offering Christian comfort and advice. By the end of 1859 she had thirty-seven Biblewomen, each with her own lady supervisor. From these women Mrs. Ranyard heard how the sick poor suffered and in 1868 she extended the Mission's work to district nursing. The training involved three months working as Biblewomen only, then three months in a hospital or infirmary, spending half the time in medical and half in surgical wards, and then two weeks in a lying-in hospital, followed by a three-month probationary period in district work under a lady supervisor. The nurses lived at home and were paid 15s a week. Comforts and medical supplies were provided from the Mother House. Mrs. Ranyard knew the sort of conditions her nurses would have to face and warned, 'It is possible to be far too clean and respectable for the work that has to be done.' The work of the nurses was valued by doctors and deeply appreciated by the patients. The nurses walked safely through the most dangerous slums and one reported proudly that a Guy's student doctor she had been working with had asked her to escort him back to the main road.

Many clergymen in the poorer areas, however, already had nurses to help them with the work of the parish. The East London Nursing Society, founded with the aim of 'providing nurses for the sick poor in East London', started by taking under its wing three such privately employed nurses. The Society operated on lines similar to those in Liverpool and of the Ranyard Mission.

In 1874, an investigation into existing nursing in London found that the Ranyard Mission with fifty-two Biblewomen nurses and the East London Nursing Society with seven nurses were the only two organizations employing trained nurses to nurse the poor in their own homes. The National Association for Providing Trained Nurses for the Sick Poor, which carried out the investigation, was launched at a public meeting under the auspices of the Order of St. John of Jerusalem. Its declared objects were: 'To inquire into the state and need of district nursing; the training schools already existing capable of training women for nursing the poor in their own homes, and the hospitals suitable for such institutions; the district nursing already at work and the places where the need for nurses is felt.' The sub-committee which investigated district nursing had William Rathbone, by then an MP, as chairman, and Florence Lees as honorary secretary.

Miss Nightingale described Florence Lees as a 'genius of nursing'. A lady by birth, she entered St. Thomas's as a probationer in 1866 at the age of twenty-five. The following year she went to Germany and worked in deaconess institutions in Dresden and Kaiserswerth before going on to visit most of the principal hospitals in Europe. On her return to England, she took charge of the male accident and female surgical wards at King's College Hospital. In 1869 she crossed the Channel again and gained further experience of French civil and military hospitals. When the Franco-Prussian War broke out she served on the German side, taking charge of the second fever station of the 10th Army Corps at Maranque before Metz, and, when that closed, the Crown Princess (Queen Victoria's daughter) made her superintendent of the Royal Reserve Hospital for wounded soldiers at Homburg. After the war she toured hospitals in Canada and the United States.

Miss Lees did most of the investigative work for the sub-committee and was largely responsible for the report which appeared in 1875. Investigations had shown that the existing organizations gave too much relief and provided too little nursing, that too little control and direction led to slovenliness and neglect by the nurse, that there was too little communication between the nurses and the doctors and that not enough instruction was given to the patient's family on such matters as cleanliness and ventilation. It was also found that training schools did not satisfactorily train nurses for district work. The report concluded that nurses should receive a more complete and systematic hospital training, that they should work in close touch with doctors and surgeons and as far as possible under their orders, that the duty of granting relief should be separated as far as possible from nursing and left to other agencies, that in large towns nurses should live in District Homes under a trained superintendent and that such homes should give special training in district work to hospital-trained probationers. The report also contained Miss Lees's recommendation that district nurses should be gentlewomen, a break with the system already operating in some parts of the country. The suggestion met with strong opposition from all of the committee except the Duke of Westminster. Even Miss Nightingale wrote dubiously, 'I don't believe you will find it answer; but try it – try it for a year.' Miss Lees was allowed to try it.

The East London Nursing Society amalgamated with the new body, which was re-named the Metropolitan and National Nursing Association for Providing Trained Nurses for the Sick Poor. Florence Lees was appointed Superintendent General, a Central Home was acquired in Bloomsbury Square and the Nightingale Fund offered to finance the training of probationers at St. Thomas's Hospital. The training and conditions for the new district nurses established a standard and pattern which was later to be enforced nationwide by the Queen's Institute. Candidates spent one month's trial at the Central Home where their vocation was tested. After one year's hospital training they returned to the Home for a further six months' district training. This included advanced lectures on anatomy, physiology and hygiene, maternity care and how to teach mothers a degree of self-help. There were examinations at the end. During these six months the students spent six hours daily on district work, escorted to each new case by the superintendent who taught how to extemporize appliances and how to put the room in good nursing order. If a case of scarlet fever was found, the students were taught how to nurse and disinfect in contagious conditions. Training at an end, the six-hour day was extended to eight hours. Only in exceptional cases were the nurses to do evening or night work. They were uniformed in washable brown holland dresses and dark blue cloaks and bonnets and paid £35 a year plus board and lodging, rising in installments to £50.

Miss Lees crystallized the philosophy and practice of district nursing in her *Guide*, published in 1889 at the request of the Queen's Institute. A district nurse, she wrote, 'must be content to be servant to the sick poor and teacher by turns, and have the tact necessary to win the entire confidence of her patients . . . Her aim must be not only to aid in curing disease and alleviating pain, but also through the illness of one member of a family to gain an influence for good so as to raise the whole family; to teach them how to render brighter and more cheerful, as well as to cleanse, their rooms, and to introduce order, cleanliness, sunshine, and fresh air to rooms or homes where they have been hitherto unknown.' The *Guide* instructed the district nurse in a whole list of duties, ranging from washing the patient and nursing infectious cases to performing the last rites. It explained how to improvise bed-rests, window blinds, bronchial kettles, how to make spittoons out of jam pots, baths out of wash tubs and iced drinks without ice. But above all, Miss Lees stressed, the patient's feelings must come first. Never, for example, should a nurse cut off a patient's hair unless it was diseased: 'Poor women take a great pride in the length of their hair, even when they have taken none in keeping it in good order, and it is better to take *any* trouble rather than lessen a woman's self-respect.'

Recruits of the right calibre flocked in and, though Miss Lees had some initial difficulty in finding work for them to do, she soon drummed up support among local doctors and clergymen, charities and Poor Law authorities. In 1877, district homes were opened in Paddington and Holloway. In 1876 the Association nursed 339 cases; in 1877 the number was 907, and in 1878 it was 1,094. As early as April 1876 Miss Nightingale wrote lyrically to the secretary of the Association: 'As to your success – what is not your success? To raise the homes of your patients so that they never fall back again to dirt and disorder: such is your nurses' influence. To pull through life and death cases – cases which it would be an honour to pull through with all the appurtenances of hospitals, or of the richest in the land, and this without any sickroom appurtenances at all. To keep whole families out of pauperism by preventing the home from being broken up, and nursing the bread-winner back to health . . . District nursing, so solitary, so without the cheer and the stimulus of a big corps of fellow-workers in the bustle of a public hospital, but also without many of its cares and strains, requires what it has with you, the constant supervision and inspiration of a genius of nursing and a common home.'

The Metropolitan and National Nursing Association's reports are a steady record of enlightened skills overcoming dirt and ignorance, as well as disease. One case, quoted by William Rathbone in his *Sketch of the History and Progress of District Nursing*, captures both the strength of the enemy and the sweetness of victory. 'In this instance we were called in by Dr. W. to go to a case of typhoid. On the evening of 11th September we first saw our patient, an ill-nourished lad of sixteen, lying on a bed hardly covered with various rags and old garments, moaning in his delirium, this being already the eighth day of the fever.

'It was a small back room, its narrow window and fireplace both carefully closed (happily one pane in the former being broken, and only patched up ineffectually with paper, some air did make its way in!); the dirty floor, strewn with dirtier bits of oilcloth and ragged carpet; the bed of iron, but broken in the middle, was propped against the wall in the corner and on a box; the iron laths and ropes gave way everywhere, and the boy threatened to slip through. To open the window at the top and have a fire lighted in the grate was the work of a few minutes, and soon made a great change to the close, damp atmosphere of the room, but to get the floor cleaned and washed with carbolic, the bed moved from the wall ... to remove from it every superfluous article of clothing, and replace these by clean sheets and a warm rug, to fill a large water pillow and get the patient on it; all this was not accomplished without some difficulty, though it was done in the course of two visits. But it took many more to alter in any considerable degree a condition of things which was at first a great hindrance to our nursing. Our patient was nearly devoured by vermin, and everything, including his bed, full of them.

'At first sight it did seem almost in vain that the floor and woodwork of the room were daily washed with carbolic, the patient even sponged with a weak solution of it, and everything on it perpetually dusted with the invaluable Keating. But at last our perseverance has been rewarded, and our patient has long laid comfortably on his bed, and he tells his mother she must never let Doll (his little brother) sleep with him again, he finds the present arrangement so much pleasanter. He was dirty enough when we first had him, and cannot remember how we had to scrub him to begin with, for he had gone to bed with all the dirt of his occupation (his is a plasterer's boy) upon him, and laid unwashed till we came, his mother being "afraid to touch him with water". But his returning consciousness first showed itself by his inquiries when nurse was coming to wash him. Hours before the time he would worry his mother to have the fire ready, and the water hot, etc., and when nurse did appear, one thin arm was immediately stretched out from beneath the bedclothes as though to intimate that he was ready for the sponging he liked so much. He has been very ill; at first the head symptoms and the diarrhoea gave much cause for anxiety, but he is now in a fair way towards convalescence.'

In Jubilee Year, 1887, Queen Victoria decided to devote to district nursing the surplus of the Women's Jubilee Offering, which amounted to £70,000. The money was to be used to raise the standard of district nursing throughout the United Kingdom. Queen Victoria's Jubilee Institute for Nurses was founded to develop training schools for district nurses in London, Edinburgh and Dublin, to advise and assist groups starting or carrying on district nursing, to help local associations to affiliate to the Institute and to supply nurses and recommend superintendents for affiliated associations. The new Institute was connected with the wealthy but moribund charity, St. Katharine's Hospital. Interested parties hoped that at least some of the funds would be available to the Institute but, in the end, all that came their way were three rent-free rooms, which served as the administrative headquarters until 1903, and a small house for resting nurses.

In London the new Institute adopted as its nucleus the Metropolitan and National Association whose Home in Blooms-bury Square became the central training school. A Scottish branch and training school were established in Edinburgh in 1891. In Dublin, the Catholic authorities insisted on separate homes and supervision for Catholic and Protestant nurses and the Institute was obliged to accept these conditions. The training standards of the Metropolitan and National Association became the standards of the Institute (later the year's hospital training was extended to two, and then three, years). In addition nurses destined for country districts had to have at least three months' training in midwifery. To be entered on the roll as a Queen's Nurse, the candidate had then to work for eighteen months in a post selected for her by the Institute. Queen's Nurses were entitled to wear a special badge and brassard and, if their association chose, the uniform of dark and light blue striped dress and dark blue cloak. Pay for a Queen's Nurse living in a central Home was about £30. A nurse living in a country district could expect to be provided with two furnished rooms with fuel and light and 12s a week for food and laundry.

In order to qualify for affiliation to the Institute, local associations had to employ nurses trained to Institute standards. In large towns nurses had to live in Homes under trained superin-tendents approved by the Institute's council. The nurses were to work only for the poor and were strictly forbidden to interfere with the religious opinions of their patients or their patients' families. In return for fulfilling these conditions, the affiliated associations were entitled to some financial assistance, they were supplied with trained nurses (whom they paid) and superintendents and their own nurses were eligible to rank as Queen's Nurses.

William Rathbone's niece, Miss Rosalind Paget, London Hospital trained and a qualified midwife, was appointed chief nursing officer and Inspector General of the Institute. Her name was the first to appear on the Roll of Queen's Nurses. To her fell the duty of touring the country inspecting associations who wanted to affiliate. Liverpool, the cradle of district nursing, was invited to join.

The Ranyard Mission applied – but was rejected. Their training, at that time, was inadequate, and their inability to separate religion from nursing was contrary to the Institute's rules. Other associations were turned down for the same reasons, or because they would not provide a Home, or for engaging in private nursing. Some associations did not want to affiliate, feeling themselves quite capable of serving their own communities without interference from London.

The city associations, with their nurses neatly parcelled up into homes, were easy to inspect. The rural scene was enlivened by local peculiarities and eccentricities. One village might have a trained nurse fully employed and supported by local charity, another an experienced but quite unqualified midwife with no reliable means of support. The Rural District Nursing Association was founded to supply trained nurses and midwives for remote rural districts. From its offices flowed a stream of invaluable advice, information and statistics. Hamlets, for instance, were advised to group together under one nurse who could be supplied with a donkey and cart for the trifling weekly expense of 1s or 1s 6d. The RDNA, with three county centres plus forty-three district associations, was accepted for affiliation in 1891.

By 1896 there were 539 Queen's Nurses on the Roll and by 1906, 1,260. Shortly after the Institute was founded, district nurses were drawn into the earliest of their public health roles – school nursing. An 1891–92 enquiry into the feeding of schoolchildren had discovered incidentally that many children suffered from neglected minor ailments. The managers of a school in the Drury Lane area applied to the Metropolitan and National Association for a nurse to visit the children during school hours. Other associations followed suit and in 1898 the London School Nurses Association was founded to spread the work. In Liverpool a trained nurse was employed, at first by Mr. Rathbone's second wife, later by the District Nursing Association, to care for school children's minor ailments. These local efforts were put on a more formal footing by the 1907 Education Act which gave authorities the duty to provide medical inspection of school children, and the authority to provide nursing service. The extent to which education authorities used this authority varied widely.

In America, the development of district nursing in its early years followed a similar pattern to Britain. At first nurses were employed by religious and philanthropic bodies but gradually the city authorities moved in – Los Angeles employed a nurse in 1897. An interesting new approach to caring for the sick poor in their own

One of hundreds of statuettes of Florence Nightingale, the heroine of the Victorian middle-class. A more worthy commemoration is the Nightingale School for Nurses at St. Thomas's Hospital, which she established in 1860 using £45,000 subscribed by the public for her work in the Crimea

homes was tried by Lillian Wald in New York. This New York Hospital trained nurse was giving a course in home nursing to a group of immigrant women. The small daughter of one of them asked Miss Wald to visit her sick mother. Miss Wald was so appalled by the conditions she found in the tenements of the Lower East Side that she said to a friend, Mary Brewster, 'Let us two nurses move into that neighbourhood – let us give our services as nurses – let us contribute our sense of citizenship to what seems an alien community in a so-called democratic country.'

Other nurses and social workers joined them in the Henry Street Settlement. They opened first aid rooms, became involved in the women's battles for trade unions. Lillian Wald became an expert on the problems of the district and achieved semi-official recognition by the Board of Health. Inspired by the English example she carried school nursing into the schools of New York and cut down the absentee rate by ninety per cent. At her suggestion, the Metropolitan Life Insurance Company employed visiting nurses for their policy holders. Miss Wald, who coined the term Public Health Nursing, was influential in forming the Children's Bureau in 1912 as part of the Department of Labor.

District nursing expanded rapidly in the towns and cities but was badly neglected in the rural areas. Again it was Miss Wald who set the ball rolling by suggesting to the Red Cross that they might organize nursing in the country areas. The Rural Nursing Service got under way in 1912. More and more nurses were drawn into public health work as crusades against such infectious diseases as tuberculosis were organized and pure milk programmes to provide fresh and safe milk for babies and children were set up. Public health nursing was particularly valuable in the field of infant welfare. As well as the pure milk programmes many cities opened Babies' Dispensaries. The first industrial nurse was probably employed by Colmans of Norwich, England. In America the Vermont Marble Company followed the same course in 1895 followed shortly by the Frederick Loeser store in Brooklyn and the John Wanamaker Employees' Benefit Association. This branch of public health work, though, was slow to develop.

Getting Organized | 7

B y the end of the century nursing was in a state of chaos. The burgeoning profession was entirely uncontrolled by law, which meant that anyone could call herself (or himself) a nurse. Any hospital could open a training school, subject probationers to two or three years of drudgery and release them upon the world with a certificate. Highly qualified ladies toiled under the same professional umbrella as village women who alternated nursing with domestic service. The public had no ready means of checking on the qualifications of the nurses they employed and were at the mercy of any unscrupulous person who cared to take up the work. British nurses were the first to realize the need for state control of the profession – to protect both their own professional status and the vulnerable public. The first steps were taken as early as 1887 but, largely because the women were so divided, that date was merely the start of a thirty-year war. When British nurses eventually achieved state registration in 1919 a dozen countries had gone before her – including most of the states of America, comparative newcomers in the field.

In Britain, 70,000 people described themselves as nurses, including nearly 6,000 men, most of whom cared for the mentally ill in asylums or their patients' homes. Little over a third of all nurses were trained in the widest sense of the word and the figure included women trained only in such special fields as fever, or nominally trained in workhouse infirmaries or small provincial hospitals. The demand for nurses was enormous. General hospitals took in more patients and improved their staffing levels. Infirmaries added to their beds and replaced the old-style pauper nurse with trained women. The middle and upper classes, who never entered hospitals as patients, looked enviously at the care the poor received from the Queen's Nurses, and sought similar standards for themselves. Women unsuitable in character and training found no difficulty in getting work. There simply were not enough trained nurses to go round. The big voluntary hospitals turned out the same number of graduates as before – nurses' homes were expensive to keep up and extending the training period to two, and then three, years ensured a ready supply of cheap probationary labour. They had no difficulty in attracting the 'right sort' of girl. 'Nursing,' one matron wrote disapprovingly in 1888, 'is fashionable, and there cannot be the slightest doubt that there are large numbers of young women taking it up, not because they have a taste for it, not even because they wish to be useful in this life, not even because they desire to earn their livelihood, but simply because they have an idea that when once their probation is over they will lead a life of much greater freedom than they possibly could if they continued to reside with their friends, and in this they are right.'

Workhouse infirmaries were the chief sufferers from the nurse shortage. Hospital-trained nurses who took up infirmary work, one nurse wrote in 1890, 'feel self-sacrificing'. Infirmary nursing was monotonous – with no medical school there was no excitement attached to the daily rounds, there were no interesting cases and long-stay chronic or semi-convalescent patients predominated. The Poor Law administration often seemed petty and bureaucratic. Nurses either became bored and resigned or saw 'in every Poor Law windmill a castle of abuses to be stormed, and entangles herself in meshes of red tape . . .' Accommodation was often poor, time off unsuitable. Medical supplies were often basic and, particularly in the small infirmaries, relationships with the guardians sometimes proved difficult. The answer seemed to be for the infirmaries to train their own probationers in Poor Law conditions. Many women took the training, only to disappear into the expanding private sector.

'I remember when I was a boy I never saw such a thing as a nurse inside my house. Now my boy has hardly anything the matter with him before in comes a nurse the first thing before we can say "Jack Robinson",' the Society of Apothecaries' spokesman told the Select Committee on Registration in 1905, adding wistfully, 'We were able to get on perfectly well in those days.' About half the women calling themselves nurses were employed in their patients' homes, working for charitable organizations for the poor or as paid nurses in private families. Private patients had no way of checking on the qualifications of the nurse they called in. The major voluntary hospitals saw private nursing as a means of augmenting their income and were not always too scrupulous about whom they sent where. The London Hospital was strongly criticized for sending its second-year probationers to nurse unsupervised in patients' homes – but at least those women had one year's training. Private agencies and nursing institutes mushroomed to fill the ever growing demand. Some were excellent – the British Nurses' Association started two nurses' co-operatives staffed only with registered nurses – but others signed up women with little or no training and felt no compunction in charging for them the same as they would have for a properly trained nurse.

There was no uniformity of standards or training. Nurses holding certificates might have done three years thorough theoretical and practical work in a large general hospital – or a year's probation in a small provincial hospital which gave little or no training and used its students as a source of cheap labour. Women called themselves district nurses after meeting the rigorous standards of the Queen's Institute – or after walking the rounds for six months. Nurses were exploited because they were not organized. A national public register of trained nurses, a group of senior ladies decided, would protect the public from abuses in private nursing and guarantee the profession's reputation for skill and knowledge. Registration would ensure a reasonable standard of training for probationers. Registration would give trained nurses a status quite distinct from that of the mass of women calling themselves nurses. Registration would transform nursing from a job, a calling, a vocation, into a profession equal to medicine and the law. In raising the standing of nurses, registration would raise the standing of women – an ambition in tune with the feminist mood of the age. Mrs. Bedford Fenwick, 'commanding officer' in the battle for registration, said, 'The Nurse question is the Woman question pure and simple. We have run the gauntlet of those historic rotten eggs.'

Mrs. Bedford Fenwick was born Ethel Gordon Manson in 1857. At the age of twenty-one, she went as a paying probationer to the Children's Hospital, Nottingham, and then to the Manchester Royal Infirmary before becoming a Sister at the London Hospital. At twenty-four she was appointed matron at St. Bartholomew's, where she introduced a three-year training period and improved the nurses' food, hours and salaries. She resigned in 1887 to marry Dr. Bedford Fenwick and devoted the rest of her life to the fight for nursing organizations. She was the prime mover in the formation of a number of national and international nurses' groups and in 1893 bought the *Nursing Record* as a platform for her campaign.

The first move towards registration was made in 1887 when Miss Catherine Wood, superintendent of the Great Ormond Street Hospital, wrote to Mr. (later Sir) Henry Burdett of the Hospitals Association and suggested the formation of a nursing section. The Hospitals Association was already interested in setting up a register of trained nurses. A meeting between a group of leading nurses and the Hospitals Association was arranged which culminated in the nurses, led by Mrs. Bedford Fenwick, sweeping off to the Fenwicks' house and forming the British Nurses' Association. The chief issue in dispute seems to have been that Mr. Burdett proposed that registration should be given to nurses with one year's training, while the nurses themselves held out for three years. The Hospitals Association went ahead with their list and Mr. Burdett acquired a bitter enemy in Mrs. Bedford Fenwick, who pursued him with threats of legal action, and hurled abuse and scorn at him in the columns of the *Nursing Record*, where she generally referred to him witheringly as 'an official of the Stock Exchange'. (Mr. Burdett had been a hospital administrator in Birmingham before joining the Stock Exchange and his involvement in hospital administration continued throughout his life.)

The aims of the British Nurses' Association were 'to unite all qualified British nurses in membership of a recognised profession, to provide for their registration on terms satsifactory to surgeons and physicians as evidence of their having received systematic training, and to associate them for mutual help and protection and for advancement in every way of their professional work.' The BNA hoped to achieve a state register of all nurses who had completed a prescribed course of training in a recognized hospital. For the first twelve months, nurses who had worked for three years or more in constant attendance on the sick and who could provide testimonials of professional competence and personal character would be admitted to the register. After this 'period of grace' only nurses with professional certificates of three years' training would be admitted. The names of unworthy nurses would be removed temporarily or permanently from the register. The BNA hoped to achieve state registration by Act of Parliament but, thanks to covert action by the Nightingale faction, this move failed and the Association decided instead to press for a Royal Charter which would authorize them to establish a legal register of trained nurses.

Recruitment swiftly gathered pace. Within eighteen months the Association had enrolled 2,500 nurses, including the matrons of half the large hospitals in England. Many trained nurses favoured registration as a means of raising themselves above their untrained contemporaries. Provincial matrons hoped that registration would give their certificates the same status as those of fashionable London hospitals and so make it easier for them to attract probationers. The British Medical Association came out in favour of registration – wealthy consultants, whose views the BMA was accused of chiefly representing, had seen the benefits that trained nursing brought to their patients in hospitals and at home. Mrs. Bedford Fenwick heartened the troops, harrassed the enemy and assiduously collected and published stories of untrained nurses found guilty of incompetence or criminality.

But there was major opposition to the move. The most disinterested opponents of the registration campaign were the faction led by Miss Nightingale. At her instigation Henry Bonham Carter, secretary of the Nightingale Fund, published in 1888 a pamphlet outlining the case against registration. Nursing training, he wrote, had always aimed at fostering the moral qualities of the nurse – her conduct and behaviour as well as her practical skill. Such qualities could not be assessed by examination. In an effort to be fair to the many respectable women engaged in nursing, the standard would be set too low. The Register would not give up-to-date information. Hospitals might find themselves in legal difficulties for dismissing a probationer without giving cause.

Vigorous support for Miss Nightingale came from the London Hospital. Sydney Holland, the chairman, believed that registration would exclude from the profession many lesser-educated women, who had made excellent nurses in the past, and hence would ultimately reduce the number of nurses available. State registration, he wrote, 'leaves entirely unconsidered those personal qualities upon which her main value depends, such as good temper, manner, tact, discretion, patience and unselfish womanliness . . . No one would engage a governess, or even a domestic servant, simply because her name is on a register, without inquiring into her character as distinct from her ability to perform her specific duties.' Eva Lückes, an ardent vocationalist, was against uniformity. Nearly everyone could get a certificate, but not everyone made a good nurse. The rumour that Miss Lückes had herself been in love with Dr. Bedford Fenwick added piquancy to her opposition.

Country general practitioners feared the competition of trained nurses and knew that their poorer patients would not be able to afford their services. Matrons of small hospitals were afraid that their training would not be approved and that they would find it impossible to recruit probationers. Some matrons of large hospitals resented what they feared would be interference with their own authority. The nurses thought as their matrons told them to. This was a battle of the giants.

The battle, which was not finally resolved until 1919, got under way. Princess Christian, Queen Victoria's daughter, accepted the presidency of the British Nurses' Association and in 1893 the Queen gave the BNA permission to add 'Royal' to its title. The same year the Privy Council granted the RBNA a Royal Charter. Thanks to the opposition, the terms of the Charter were considerably weaker than the RBNA had hoped. They were given the power to maintain and publish a 'list' rather than a 'register' of trained nurses. They went ahead and compiled a voluntary register but it was not a success. The Charter also provided that all members of the RBNA's Council should stand for election every three years, and so deprived Mrs. Bedford Fenwick of her permanent presidency. The following year, too, the Bedford Fenwicks quarrelled with the RBNA, the result being that Mrs. Bedford Fenwick at once founded the Matrons' Council to continue the battle for registration. Two years later, the RBNA resolved that a register was 'inexpedient in principle, injurious to the best interests of nurses, and of doubtful benefit.' The Matrons' Council fought on alone until 1902 when Mrs. Bedford Fenwick launched the Society for State Registration of Nurses. The Midwives Act of that year, which laid down that no woman might practise midwifery habitually and for gain except under the direction of a doctor or unless she was certified by the Central Midwives Board, heartened the pro-registration lobby. The RBNA returned to the cause and in 1903 and 1904 two private members bills were presented to Parliament. Both were rejected but they led to the appointment of a Select Committee on Registration.

All the old protagonists spoke (except Miss Nightingale, then eighty-four) and twenty-year-old arguments were dusted off and given a fresh airing. In 1905, the Select Committee reported in favour of state registration. It recommended that a Register of nurses should be kept by a central body appointed by the state and that no person should be entitled to call herself a registered nurse unless her name was on the register. (This left the door open for untrained women to continue to practise, as long as they did not call themselves 'registered'.) The central body should admit to the register nurses trained at a recognized training school for a certain period and who held a certificate. The central body would decide what the period of training should be and what was a recognized training school. The central body should publish its register annually and make provision for the removal of the names of nurses no longer practising and those guilty of serious misconduct or moral delinquency. A separate register was to be provided for asylum nurses.

It looked like a victory for the pro-registrationists, but the battle had never captured the public's imagination and Parliament still had to be convinced. Every year until 1914, a Bill (or two) was laid before the House of Commons and each year it was rejected. It took a war to pass the recommendations of the Select Committee into law.

The domestic struggle for registration had not monopolized Mrs. Bedford Fenwick's attention. Her hopes for an International Nursing Congress during the 1894 World's Fair at Chicago came to nothing, but she seized her opportunity in 1899, when the International Council of Women met in London. The Matrons' Council met immediately afterwards and she addressed them on the subject of international co-operation. The following day, the officers of the Matrons' Council and some of the overseas nurses who had remained in London met and formed the International Council of Nurses, the first international organization among the health professions, and the first international organization of professional women. Mrs. Bedford Fenwick was elected president, Miss Lavinia Dock of the USA, secretary, and Miss Mary Snively of Canada, treasurer. The ICN held its first Congress in Buffalo in 1901, when between 500 and 600 nurses attended each day. The Congress voted unanimously in favour of registration. It had been decided that each country should be represented on the Council by one national nursing organization. Mrs. Bedford Fenwick formed the National Council of Nurses from the Matrons' Council, the Society for State Registration, the League of St. Bartholomew's Hospital Nurses and the Leicester Royal Infirmary Nurses League. The National Council represented Britain at the ICN in Berlin in 1904.

As the first ICN Congress demonstrated, the battle for registration was being fought worldwide. The Cape Colony in South Africa was the first to achieve national registration in 1891. Nursing there in the early days was of the old order and bad. Then, trained nurses were recruited from Britain and, presumably, many of them held strong views on registration. Indeed, Sister Henrietta of Kimberley, the leading fighter for registration, hoped that legislation in the colony would encourage similar action in Britain, as well as safeguard patients and protect the profession in South Africa. It was largely due to Sister Henrietta's energetic lobbying that the provisions of the Medical and Pharmacy Act were extended to include a register of trained nurses and midwives. Natal soon followed suit, and New Zealand introduced a register of trained nurses in 1901.

In America, as in Britain, hospitals had been quick to realize the cheap labour potential of nursing schools. These had multiplied rapidly and while some gave excellent instruction, many more – particularly the smaller ones – worked their students long hours for little pay and less teaching. In spite of this, the opportunity for independence and a good salary for the trained nurse and the protection and safety of the Home during training made nursing in the United States, as in England, an attractive career.

The first move to organize this rapidly expanding profession came from Isabel Hampton (later Mrs. Robb), the superintendent of Johns Hopkins Hospital Nursing School. She was the moving force behind the Society of Superintendents of Training Schools for Nurses, founded in New York in 1894. This exclusive group soon realized the need to involve a wider section of nurses and two years later was instrumental in founding the Nurses Associated Alumnae, which became the American Nurses Association.

The first target for organized nursing was registration, with particular emphasis on controlling nurse training. Sophia Palmer, first editor-in-chief of the *American Journal of Nursing*, founded in 1900, said in 1899: 'The greatest need in the nursing profession today is a law that shall place training schools for nurses under the supervision of the University of the State of New York' – as other professions were. There was considerable opposition from quarters which had a vested interest in third-rate nurse training. The battle had to be fought state by state and the results were not uniform. North Carolina was the first to introduce registration into law in 1903. The law there allowed a three-month 'period of grace' to allow practising nurses on to the register, but, after that, nurses were certified only after examination by a board. Certified nurses were allowed to put 'RN' after their names. The New Jersey law, passed the same year, imposed less rigorous conditions. There was no state examination and two years training was all that was required. Opposition in New York State concentrated on the nurses' demand for a board of nurse examiners nominated by the State Nurses' Association. The nurses won and New York State also passed a nurse registration law in 1903. By 1910, twenty-seven states had nurse registration Acts.

Call to Arms 8

Military nursing in the Crimea had done so much to establish female nursing as a respectable career that the reformers by no means abandoned the military field when hostilities came to an end. Thanks largely to the efforts of Miss Nightingale and her friends the health of the troops gradually improved. The Army Medical School was created in 1860. New military hospitals were built. Patients moved into the first, the Royal Victoria at Netley, in 1863. Though Netley was completed against strenuous opposition from Miss Nightingale, because it was built to the old corridor pattern, the Herbert Hospital, Woolwich and the Cambridge at Aldershot met her approval as they were constructed in the pavilion style. In 1866, a Royal Warrant authorized the appointment of nursing sisters in any military general hospital and eight lady nurses under Mrs. Shaw Stewart took on day duty at the Herbert Hospital which was completed that year. In 1869 Mrs. Jane Deeble went from St. Thomas's Hospital, London, to Netley with six ward sisters.

Army nursing was still largely in the hands of male orderlies – in theory at least. Mrs. Rebecca Strong, one of Mrs. Deeble's ladies at Netley, wrote: 'There was normally an orderly attached to each ward, but they were often taken away for relief work such as coal carrying, etc. Each sister had from six to eight of these wards under her charge, and speedily found that the nursing must be done by herself . . . A special orderly could be had in emergencies, but the nursing was nil.' The army showed its appreciation of female nursing by dispatching Mrs. Deeble with fourteen nurses to serve in the Zulu War of 1879, but the service was not given any formal structure until 1881, the year the War Office granted the National Aid Society (the British Red Cross organization) permission to train military probationers.

These developments were closely linked with the International Red Cross, founded in 1864 and the inspiration of one man, Jean Henri Dunant. In 1859 Dunant, a Swiss citizen, set out in search of the Emperor Napoleon III of France, to enlist his support for a shaky business venture. His travels took him to Italy where the French and the Sardinians were fighting the Austrians, and to the bloody battlefield of Solferino. The medical services of both sides were overwhelmed, the wounded lying unattended on the ground and filling every building in the nearby village of Castiglione. Dunant was appalled and set to work at once to organize relief. In 1862 he published *A Memory of Solferino* in which he outlined his experiences and appealed for better treatment for the victims of battle. 'Would it not be possible, in time of peace and quiet, to form relief societies for the purpose of having care given to the wounded in wartime by zealous, devoted and thoroughly qualified volunteers,' he wrote, and continued: '. . . There is need . . . for volunteer orderlies and volunteer nurses, zealous, trained and experienced, whose position would be recognised by the commanders or armies in the field, and their mission facilitated and supported.'

The book caused a sensation and an international conference was called at Geneva in October 1863 to discuss Dunant's proposals. Prussia, then other German and Italian states and Spain formed national relief committees. At a second conference in June the following year the Geneva Convention was drawn up. The fundamental principle was to give neutrality and protection to the wounded in war, the official personnel caring for them and medical equipment and supplies. A common emblem, a red cross on a white background (the reverse of the Swiss flag) was adopted to identify hospitals, ambulances and staff. Countries which signed the Convention undertook to found in peacetime National Aid Societies with government sanction which would, in time of war, come under military discipline, and to give permission to the Societies of neutral states to give aid. Twelve states signed the Convention at the Conference and a further eight by 1866. (The United States, otherwise engaged in its Civil War, did not become a signatory until 1882.)

When France and Germany went to war in July 1870, both sides had national aid societies acceptable to government and the military authorities. Although Britain had signed the Geneva

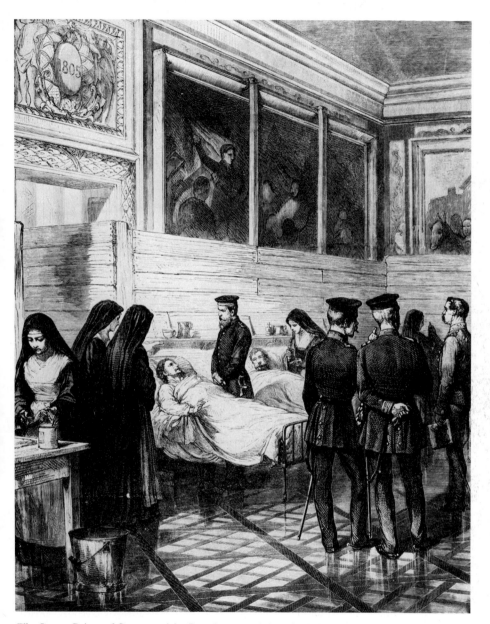

The Crown Prince of Germany visits Prussian wounded at the Palace of Versailles during the Franco-Prussian War of 1870 to 1871. As in most Continental countries, nuns supplied the bulk of the nurses – Britain was the exception

Convention in 1865 she had not organized a national society. Spurred on by the crisis across the Channel, a public meeting was called at Willis's Rooms on August 4 and the National Society for Aid to Sick and Wounded in War was launched. £30,000 had poured into the Society's office by the end of August. By mid-

September the Society employed 110 people including sixty-two surgeons and sixteen nurses who treated the wounded of both sides. The Anglo-American Ambulance was formed, the main section working at Sedan with a section at Belan in the Town Hall to which the All Saints Convent in London sent two trained nurses under a Mother Superior. Dr. Marion Sims, a member of the Ambulance's American contingent wrote, 'As nurses, I would not exchange one woman for a dozen men. From the moment that women were introduced as nurses, the whole aspect of our establishment was changed.' Peace was signed in February 1871.

National aid societies grew rapidly and became involved in all aspects of medical relief work. They were particularly influential in the nursing field in German-speaking countries where they concentrated on training and preparing nurses for war. Within a generation of the war of 1870, the German Society had over 3,000 Sisters employed in between thirty and forty nurses' homes run on similar lines to the deaconess motherhouses. Red Cross nurses were freer, intellectually and socially, than deaconesses and they were at liberty to leave the motherhouse and work elsewhere. This, plus the patriotic appeal of the work, made Red Cross nursing an attractive proposition. As early as 1884 the Austrian Society had 1,754 men and women nurses on its books.

The Japanese Red Cross was also active in nurse training. It joined the International Red Cross in 1887 and shortly after, established a Volunteer Nursing Association. Members were drawn mainly from the upper classes – to set an example to the others – and the ladies met once a month for training in nursing and dressing wounds. From 1890, the Japanese Red Cross also selected and trained nurses who, after graduating, swore to respond to a call from the Red Cross for fifteen years. In the Russo-Japanese War of 1904–05 volunteers helped in base hospitals, established rest stations and made bandages.

In America, the Red Cross was formed in 1881 (the year before the USA signed the Geneva Convention). It was organized chiefly to give relief in times of national disaster and was quite unprepared to organize nursing when the Spanish-American War broke out in April 1898. In fact, since the Civil War, the country had had no organized female military nursing establishment at all. When trained nurses, seeing the crisis ahead, offered their services to the army and navy they were told that the regular orderlies would be able to cope with the expected casualties. Then typhoid and yellow fever swept through the troops and the Surgeon-General was forced to take action. He appointed not a nurse but Dr. Anita Newcomb

McGee as Acting Surgeon-General in charge of army nurses.

Dr. McGee gave devoted service. She established standards of admission and introduced a valuable system of records. But she and the 1,600 nurses who served in the war were working against the odds. The army medical services were in a state of confusion and hygiene was poor. When the war ended after only four months, the battle started for an organized and efficient military nursing service. In 1901, Congress created the Army Nurse Corps and the Navy Nurse Corps followed in 1908. In 1909, the Red Cross undertook to develop an army nursing reserve.

In Britain, where female nursing was already established in military hospitals, the Red Cross did not undertake training school work. But, bearing in mind its responsibilities in case of war, it asked the War Office for permission to finance the training of a group of probationers at Netley and to maintain them for a further two years in military hospitals. The Society hoped to create a pool of trained military nurses whose services would be available to the country in time of war. Advertisements appeared in the newspapers in January 1881 and eight probationers reported for duty on May 1. The Army Nursing Service, with Mrs. Deeble as the first lady superintendent, came into being, though a Code of Regulations was not published until 1884. Netley probationers had to provide evidence of good health and character and be aged between twenty-five and thirty-five, with preference being given to widows and daughters of army officers. During this year's training they were paid £12 by the National Aid Society, rising to £30 a year for the next two years plus board, laundry and travelling expenses. A maid was provided between four or five nurses. At the end of the year's training written, oral and practical examinations were held. Only twelve nurses were trained under the National Society's scheme.

Britain continued to call on its nurses in time of war. Miss Nightingale selected twenty-four under Mrs. Deeble for the Egyptian campaign of 1882. Army nurses served in Cairo and on board hospital ships on the Nile during the Sudan War of 1883, accompanied the expedition to relieve General Gordon at Khartoum in 1884 and served in another Nile campaign in 1889. Miss Nightingale, determined to gain the total acceptance of female nursing as part of the army medical services, cautioned her nurses about to embark for Egypt: 'Remember when you are far away up country, possibly the only Englishwoman there, that these men will note and remember your every action, not only as a nurse but as a woman your life to them will be as rings a pebble makes when thrown into a pond – reaching far and reaching wide, each ripple gone beyond our grasp, yet remembered almost to exaggeration by these soldiers lying helpless in their sickness. See that your every word and act is worthy of your profession and your womanhood. God guard you in His safekeeping and make you worthy of His trust – our soldiers.' Like all her protegées, the sisters were never to forget that they were missionaries.

In 1883, when the Royal Red Cross was instituted by Queen Victoria for ladies 'for special exertions in providing for the nursing of sick and wounded soldiers and sailors in Our Army and Navy', Florence Nightingale and Mrs. Deeble were the first to receive it. Until that year, only Netley and the Herbert Hospital had a female nursing staff but it was then that the War Office decided that sisters should be appointed to every military hospital with 100 or more beds. Mrs. Deeble made it clear to the Army Hospital Inquiry Commission what sort of people these nurses should be: 'A class of women entirely superior to that of the wardmaster and sergeants,' she said, 'because she must be a terror to the wrongdoer. When a Sister comes in it must be, "Oh, here is Sister"; she should be the shadow of the medical officer and she should be superior to all the female relations of the patients if she is to have her proper influence.'

By 1891, it was understood that the army nursing service was to be socially as well as technically a superior force. The *Nursing Record* explained to its readers that an applicant 'must also produce a recommendation from some person of social position – not a member of her own family – to the effect that her family is one of respectability and good standing in society, that she is in every way a desirable person to enter a service composed of ladies, and that she possesses the tact, temper, and ability qualifying her for the appointment.' The Army Nursing Service then comprised three classes of nurse – lady superintendent, senior nursing sisters acting as superintendents and nursing sisters. The lady superintendent received £150 a year rising by £10 annual increments to £200, sisters were paid £30 rising by £2 a year to £50 and sisters acting as superintendents were paid an extra £20.

Women aspiring to the Indian Army Nursing Service had to be even more socially acceptable. Miss Catherine Loch, writing in 1896, believed that it was vital that the sisters should be gentlewomen, as 'those who have not an unquestionable social position are not suited either for the work, or the society into which they are admitted when they join the service; they will be out of their element, and it will be hard both on themselves and on their colleagues.' The Indian Service started in 1888 when eight sisters sailed for the east under Miss Loch and Miss Oxley. Eighteen more sisters followed and in 1891 the total strength was increased to fifty-two nurses, who were settled in small groups in the principal military stations in India and Burma. There were difficulties to start with. Some of the doctors had no idea what lady nurses should or could do. Until then, nursing work had been divided between untrained soldier orderlies and a class of assistant surgeons who were jealous of the new arrivals, but the sisters soon made a place for themselves. Not long after they arrived they set to work with the medical officers on a course of instruction for the orderlies.

The climate could be a killer, with temperatures on the plains reaching into the hundreds and monsoons when, Miss Loch reported, 'one often has to splash courageously through waterfalls and deep mud to reach one's patients.' But there were ample compensations. Pay and leave were generous and accommodation spacious, each nurse having her own bedroom, dressing room and bathroom and sometimes a sitting room as well as a common drawing room and dining room. There were opportunities for tennis, golf, and gardening, while the sisters could keep a pony and trap or a bicycle, as well as take part in the exclusive local social life.

Although naval hospitals had long used women nurses they were, in the early days, ignorant and untrained – chiefly the widows of seamen. From 1834, these women were partly replaced by equally ignorant pensioners. In 1884, however, the navy decided to establish a trained sick berth staff and to employ trained nursing sisters in naval hospitals. Six sisters were appointed to Haslar Hospital which had opened in 1754, and five to Plymouth. A report a year later found that the sisters had wrought such a great improvement in the behaviour of the patients and the standards of nursing that it recommended that they should also serve in Malta, Gibraltar, Hong Kong and the naval colleges at Osborne and Dartmouth.

Princess Christian founded the Army Nursing Reserve in 1897. She took a keen interest in it, personally selecting candidates and asking not only for certificates of training but guarantees of social position, character and education. Applicants had to sign a declaration of willingness to accept service in military hospitals in time of war. When the Boer War broke out in October 1899 the Reserve had about 100 members. The Army Nursing Service then consisted of a lady superintendent, nineteen superintendents and sixty-eight sisters.

Obviously many more nurses would be needed to care for the casualties of the largest army Britain had ever sent abroad. To process and administer all offers of voluntary aid, the National Aid

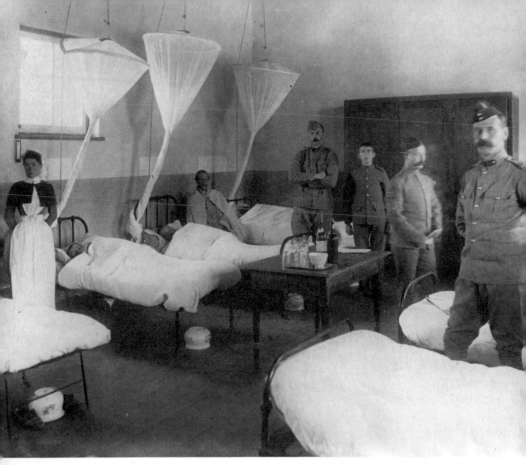

A ward in a British military hospital during the Anglo-Boer War of 1899 to 1902. Twenty-two general hospitals were opened in South Africa by the British to cope with their casualties and about 1,800 nurses served there

Society, the St. John's Ambulance Association and the Army Nursing Service Reserve formed themselves into the Central Red Cross Committee. The Committee delegated to the Army Nursing Service Reserve the job of dealing with offers of help from nurses. Eventually about 1,800 nursing sisters served in South Africa, most of them recruited through the ANSR, with contingents from Canada, Australia and New Zealand and a group selected by the Princess of Wales (later Queen Alexandra) from the London Hospital.

Twenty-two general hospitals were opened in South Africa, each with at least twenty nurses. Four sisters were attached to each base hospital on the lines of communication and two to each of the seven modern and well-equipped hospital trains. Officially, sisters did not serve with the field hospitals, which were set up in tents and moved with the army, but several, in fact, found their way there.

Conditions in the base hospitals were a great improvement on those at Scutari. Nurses were highly qualified, in general the importance of cleanliness was appreciated and anaesthetics were readily available. Thanks to the Army Service Corps, established in 1881, the troops were better fed – and so were the sisters. One nurse found the general hospital food 'excellent, and added to this we received daily quantities of food and dainties sent by the Red Cross Committee of the Colony, besides many medical comforts from England.' Up country she found 'fresh milk was hard to get . . . but of condensed milk, beef tea, champagne and jelly we had plenty.' Such treats were for the patients. Another nurse was posted to a ration station, 'therefore we did not get quite so many "allowances", but "skoff" seems fairly good.'

The efforts of the official medical services in the early days were hampered by the many ladies who were convinced that, though wholly untrained and unused to hard work, they could be of use. Donning the Nightingale mantle, they flooded the hospitals and overwhelmed the poor wounded soldiers with their attentions. One story told of a lady visitor asking, 'What can I do for you, my poor man? Shall I wash your face?' 'Thank you kindly, ma'am,' the man replied, 'but I've already promised fourteen ladies that they shall wash my face.' Another more brusque soldier is reputed to have hung a card on his bed reading, 'I am too ill to be nursed today.' Nursing Sister Laurence, lady superintendent of a privately financed field hospital with 100 beds, wrote: 'There were shoals of letters . . . of nurses and others wishing to go out with us. Some of them were amusing: one was from a viscountess, another from a member of a theatrical troupe; a large proportion of the applicants had no training, but were "willing to learn", some offered to pay their own expenses if I would only act as their chaperon – they seemed to think we were going out for a picnic.' How depressing for the emerging profession to discover that the public's understanding of what nursing involved seemed scarcely to have changed since 1854.

The British delegate to the International Congress of Red Cross Societies in his report to the Secretary of State for War had prophesied just such an emotional and chaotic response: 'Voluntary Aid such as would be forthcoming in abundance in the event of our being involved in an international war, would come upon military authorities in the form of a mass of unorganized and untrained elements, probably so unsuited to the actual requirements of the moment that, for a time at any rate, the administration of the Regular Army Medical Services would be considerably hampered and embarrassed.' But stern action by Lord Kitchener, the British Commander-in-Chief in the field, soon cleared the hospitals of the ladies' unwanted ministrations. Unfortunately, stories which circulated concerning these women and nurses recruited locally in

South Africa without reference to the ANSR and without examination of their qualifications reflected on the army nurses.

This was unfair, as those in the best position to judge testified. 'The nurses employed in this war have shown great devotion, and many have lost their lives in the discharge of their duties,' the Royal Commission appointed to investigate the care and treatment of the sick and wounded in South Africa reported in 1901. It continued: 'Scarcely any complaints have been made during this campaign with regard to the nurses.' The surgeon Sir Frederick Treves wrote: 'Their ministrations to the wounded were invaluable beyond all praise. They did service during those distressful days which none but nurses could have rendered, and they set to all at Chievely an example of unselfishness, self-sacrifice, and indefatigable devotion to duty.'

Nurses' uniforms were specially adapted for the African climate. Sisters were issued with a straw boater with a smart red ribbon round the crown and a white parasol lined with scarlet. They wore the skirts of their grey uniform dresses to just above the ankle – a little shorter than at home. Thus attired, they went nearer to the front line than nurses had ever been before, nursing and living in tents, sometimes within the sound of gunfire, and facing all the hazards of African life – '. . . the adventures of camp life, and the power of an African mid-summer sun together with sand storms, rain-storms, and sometimes a too intimate acquaintance with scorpions and snakes,' as a Canadian army nurse, Georgina Fane Pope, recorded of her time at Rondebosch. At Pinetown, seventeen miles from Durban, Miss Laurence and her nurses wore canvas gaiters as protection against snakes: 'As summer comes on, the creeping and crawling beasts are getting very objectionable; amongst others that come into my room are grasshoppers, locusts, flying beatles (huge beasts), and mosquitos.' One night she nearly died of fright when a furry black creature leapt through her window on to her bed. Fortunately it was only the camp kitten. Later, in a tented hospital on the borders of the Transvaal, she was flooded out: 'I had to paddle about and rescue our goods from the floor, pitching most of them on to Sister's bed, and she was rather amused when she came over to call me, to find me fast asleep under a mackintosh and umbrella, my bed a simple island.'

Nurses were trapped in the sieges of Kimberley, Ladysmith and Mafeking. Sister Henrietta, in charge of a Nurses' Home at Kimberley, wrote: 'One of our great trials during the early part of the siege was that our nurses had so little to do.' As the siege wore on, however, the picture changed. 'After Christmas there was a great strain upon all our resources. Every moment of my time was taken in trying to spin out our wretched scraps of horse-flesh and our few ounces of milk in our own household, and I often had to send nurses to houses where food was so scarce I was terrified for them.' The army entered Kimberley on February 15, 1900, but nursing work only intensified as sick and wounded poured in, filling schools and halls. Sister Henrietta wrote that she and her nurses worked 'through the whole day standing in the furiously hot little operating rooms, or dressing ghastly wounds, almost standing on our heads – for the men were all on the floor. Indeed, the heat of the whole place was indescribable.'

Georgina Fane Pope, like army nurses before and after her, was greatly struck by 'the wonderful pluck of these poor fellows who had jolted over rough veldt in ambulances and then endured the long train journey . . . Tommy made the least of all his woes. A drink first; then, after his wounds had been attended to, a bit of tobacco for a smoke, and a piece of paper to "send a line so they won't be scared at home," were invariably the first requirements.' Miss Pope reported that there was a high success rate among surgical cases and that X-rays were most helpful in saving the men suffering. In the early months of the war almost all the casualties were wounded, but then enteric, typhoid and dysentery took hold and claimed more victims than the enemy. The later casualties were in a far more pitiable state. 'I can't describe the condition of these men,' Miss Laurence wrote, 'they have not had their clothes off for weeks, creeping things are numerous, but we are getting them clean by degrees. Those who have been ill sometimes have sore backs – I can't say "*bed*-sores", as they have had no beds.' Her orderlies were members of the St. John Ambulance Brigade. Some were to become skilled attendants but in the early days they were 'about as useful as an average ward-maid at home, and the sisters have to act as sister, staff nurse and probationer too.'

Even before peace was signed on May 31, 1902, it was decided to reorganize the army nursing service. Queen Alexandra's Imperial Military Nursing Service came into being by Royal Warrant on March 27, 1902. (It had been intended to amalgamate the Indian Army Nursing Service with the home service but it retained its independence for twenty-four years as Queen Alexandra's Military Nursing Service in India.) The new service was bigger and took on

The officers' hospital at Wynberg, again during the Anglo-Boer War. The nurses and wounded both seem comfortable, though some over-enthusiastic nurses provoked aggressive reactions. One soldier hung a card on his bed reading 'I am too ill to be nursed today'

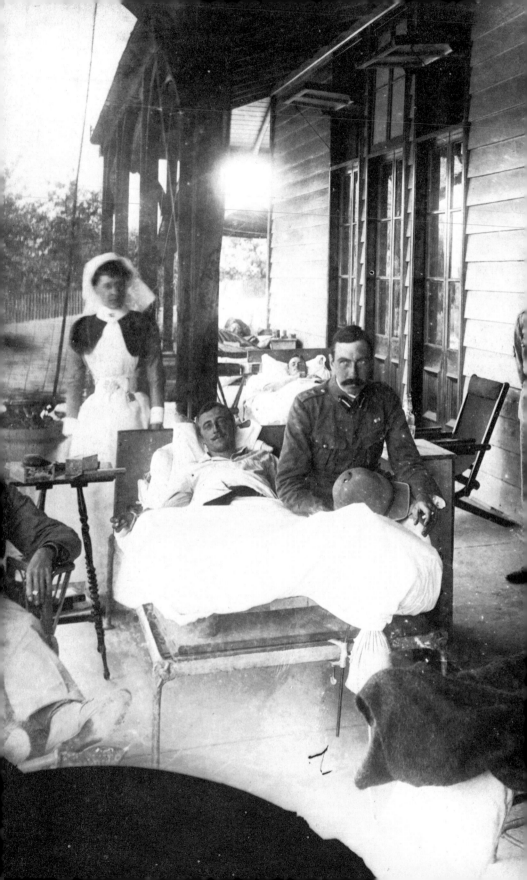

more responsibilities. The establishment was a Matron-in-Chief at the War Office, two Principal Matrons, one in South Africa and the other assisting the Matron-in-Chief, twenty-seven matrons, fifty sisters and 150 staff nurses. The Matron and sisters were in full charge of their own nursing domains and took over the duty of preparing and carrying out a three-year course of instruction for RAMC orderlies on a plan similar to that of probationers in civil hospitals.

Members of the new service were to rank with officers and so had to be of high social and educational standing. They had to have completed at least three years' training in an approved civil hospital and be of good character. Applicants were rejected because they were of 'unsuitable appearance' or 'unsatisfactory social status'. Army nurses were to be an élite. Promotion was on merit, not seniority. Army nurses had the opportunity to serve abroad in Egypt, Gibraltar, Malta, South Africa, Bermuda, Ceylon, Hong Kong and Singapore. Travel, the chance to study diseases they would not come across at home, its social standing and royal patronage all made the service most attractive.

In 1907, the Territorial Force Nursing Service was created to meet the needs of the new Territorial Army, which was organized for home defence. Hospitals were planned and staff recruited for mobilization in the event of war. The same year Princess Christian's Army Nursing Service Reserve became the Queen Alexandra's Imperial Military Nursing Service Reserve, rather to the annoyance of Princess Christian who had spent much time and effort in the cause of army nursing. The two new services wore grey or grey-blue capes with a red border, rather than the QA's distinctive scarlet cape. In 1902, the year the QAIMNSR was created, the Naval Nursing Service became Queen Alexandra's Royal Naval Nursing Service. At the suggestion of the Queen the uniform was a navy blue linen dress with red cuffs, and for outdoors a scarlet hooded and lined navy blue serge cloak and navy straw bonnet with velvet bow and strings.

Britain's position in the International Red Cross community, meanwhile, was mystifying her friends. Instead of just one national association, Britain appeared to have two: the Central British Red Cross Committee, formed in 1899, and the National Aid Society, which had taken to calling itself the British Red Cross Society. Other nations wanted to know which was the official body. After lengthy negotiations the answer turned out to be neither. An entirely new and officially recognized (though independent) Red Cross authority was created with the King as Patron and the Queen as President. The National Aid Society having been persuaded to drop the title, the British Red Cross Society came into being in 1905. The National Aid Society and the Central Committee disbanded themselves.

The new body was officially recognized in Field Service Regulations which laid down that 'all voluntary offers of assistance in aid of the sick and wounded made in the United Kingdom on the outbreak of war or during the outbreak of hostilities other than those coming from the Ambulance Department of the Order of St. John and the St. Andrew's Ambulance Association for the provision of personnel, must be submitted in the first instance to the British Red Cross Society, who will communicate them to the Army Council if they are likely to be of any value.' The British Red Cross Society formed county branches and a War Office memo of 1908 encouraged the new Territorial Army county associations to work with the BRCS branches on medical services.

The Territorial medical services lacked personnel for transport duties and for staffing rest stations and temporary hospitals. The BRCS would fill this gap and so channel into useful outlets the national urge to help in time of war which had sometimes proved such a nuisance in the Boer War. In 1909, a Scheme for the Organization of Voluntary Aid, which was inspired by similar programmes in Germany and Japan, was published. The scheme provided that each Territorial Army county branch 'should through the medium of the local branches of the British Red Cross Society form "Voluntary Aid Detachments." ' Members of the new VADs would have to hold St. John Ambulance Association certificates in first aid and home nursing. Each women's detachment was to consist of a commandant, a quartermaster, a lady superintendent (preferably a trained nurse) and twenty women of whom four should be trained cooks. (The men's detachments were larger.) Once a detachment had reached seventy per cent of its complement it was registered by the War Office. Detachments were expected to make use of local resources to provide goods and dressings for improvised ambulances, trains, make ready rest stations on railway lines, run private hospitals and convalescent homes, prepare schedules of equipment promised for times of emergency, accept discipline and 'set forth to do the lowliest tasks from the highest motives.' To begin with no uniform was planned but when detachments started to improvize their own one was introduced. Members wore an unbecoming light blue overall dress and dark blue serge overcoat and peaked cap. Quartermasters and trained nurses' dresses were in a darker blue and commandants' in red.

The VAD scheme was intended to appeal to all classes but it tended to attract women of the middle and upper classes with nothing much else to do. Eleanor David had left school and was feeling bored. When a friend in the next village suggested that she and her sister join a detachment she asked, 'What is the Red Cross?' but went along, took the examinations and became interested. The detachment in the next village grew too large and she and her sister started their own. 'There was nothing else to do, you see, nothing . . . It was wonderful for us to have something definite to do . . . the Red Cross was something to get away to even for two or three hours.' Some detachments skated along doing the minimum of training and practice to pass the annual inspection. Others became highly proficient, attending summer camps, giving displays and bullying friends into promising a comprehensive list of bedding and equipment for the hospitals and rest rooms which were still only a gleam in the quartermaster's eye.

Recruitment was boosted by a play of the time, 'The Englishman's Home' by Guy du Maurier. The theme was the invasion of Britain by a foreign power and the grief of a family at its hopeless inability to cope with the stream of casualties brought into their home. By October 1910, 202 detachments were registered with a personnel of over 6,000. The play also encouraged young ladies with nursing ambitions to enlist in a rather more dashing project – the First Aid Nursing Yeomanry, founded by Captain Baker in 1907.

After being wounded in the Sudan campaign it occurred to the gallant Captain that there was a missing link in the Ambulance Department. He visualized a band of female nurses attached to field hospitals who would gallop off to attend to the wounded on the battlefield and render first aid there until the horse ambulances arrived. When his plans came to fruition he clothed his ladies in a startling uniform of scarlet tunic with white facings, navy bell-shaped skirt and hard-topped scarlet cap with a shiny black peak, black patent riding boots, white gloves, riding crop and white first aid haversack: 'We were stared at so much that you simply had to have a sense of humour to carry on,' an early FANY admitted. The ladies were trained in first aid and cavalry drill and so impressed the military that one evening the 'Blues' invited ten girls and Captain Baker to one of their smoking dinners. Unfortunately, such a splendid organization was bound to attract attention seekers and one of the founders reported: 'I hunted round for recruits and pestered all my friends to join. That was the first step. The second was to weed out others, among them a soulful lady with peroxide hair, very fat and hearty, who insisted on wearing white drawers with frills under her khaki skirt. She also insisted on falling off at every parade and displaying them.' (Khaki uniforms replaced the colourful ones of the early days.)

Nor was the VAD scheme running entirely smoothly. The St. John Ambulance Association was not happy at being passed over in favour of the BRCS. Some BRCS members found the St. John training too expensive. People holding first aid and home nursing certificates from other bodies objected to having to take the courses again and those other bodies objected to their certificates being unacceptable. Some Territorial Army county associations did not want to delegate their authority to form VADs to the BRCS. In 1910 the BRCS told its branches that they might accept people holding certificates from organizations other than St. John. This annoyed the St. John Ambulance Association. Then the War Office gave the Territorial Army county associations power to raise detachments through organizations other than the Red Cross and this upset the BRCS. So much friction built up that in June 1914 the War Office appointed a committee to inquire into the working and organization of the Voluntary Aid Detachments. Before it could reach any conclusions, war intervened.

9 | First World War
The Home Front

War came to Britain on a hot and sunny day in August 1914. Sons abandoned family holidays at the seaside to rush to the recruiting depots. Fiancés reassured their sweethearts that it would all be over in a month, and left for France. And every woman, it seemed, wanted to nurse the wounded. 'I was working at the Red Cross Centre in Vincent Square,' Violetta Thurstan wrote, 'and all day long there came an endless procession of women wanting to help, some trained nurses, many – far too many – half-trained women, and a great many raw recruits, some anxious for adventure and clamouring "to go to the front at once", others willing and anxious to do the humblest service that would be of use at this time of crisis.'

At the outbreak of war there were nearly three hundred trained Queen Alexandra's nurses, with a reserve of 200 prepared to mobilize at twenty-four-hours' notice and a further 600 available. Two hundred reserve nurses stood by to augment the small number of peacetime Navy nurses. Nearly three thousand nurses, members of the Territorial service, were ready to transfer from civilian work to the twenty-three Territorial Force general hospitals as they opened in schools, universities and institutions – the first was ready to receive patients three days after war was declared. Mobilization of the military medical services ran smoothly and efficiently.

The same could not be said for voluntary aid. The rush of 'uninformed and unorganized sympathy' which the VAD (Voluntary Aid Detachment) scheme had been designed to channel into manageable and useful outlets, once again threatened to get out of control. Some donors scorned the BRCS (British Red Cross

Society), the official channel for offers of voluntary hospitals, and besieged the War Office. A Red Cross official had to be sent there to sort out these offers. Society ladies flaunted themselves in prettily designed matron's uniforms and proclaimed they were ready and willing to care for convalescent officers. The friction which had developed between the St. John's authorities and the Red Cross over the administration of the VAD scheme was aggravated by the decision to pass hospital offers through the BRCS. Officials of the medical services and the War Office were forced to waste precious time trying to reconcile the conflicting interests of various voluntary organizations.

Finally, the Army Council notified the British Red Cross Society, the St. John Ambulance Association and the St. Andrew's Ambulance Association that they all formed part of the Red Cross organization of Great Britain, and were recognized by the British Government as societies authorized to assist the medical services in time of war, under Article 10 of the Geneva Convention. The Joint War Committee first met on October 20, 1914, and did valuable – and united – work throughout the war.

Then there was confusion over the use of the Red Cross name and emblem. Unofficial voluntary workers sported it in France; private individuals flew it over their homes, mistakenly believing that it would give them protection; and clothing and arm bands bearing the Red Cross were on sale, marked 'very smart for present wear'. The War Office had to remind the country that, under the Geneva Convention, the Red Cross was the symbol only of official army medical establishments and personnel and those authorized to assist them – as the BRCS and the Orders of St. John and St. Andrew now were.

Meanwhile, in the counties, the Voluntary Aid Detachments were stirring up trouble. Over-eager to put preparation into practice, some of them invaded local schools, turned out equipment, and converted buildings into hospitals long before they were needed. The Army Council had to restrain its volunteers and placate enraged education authorities.

In November 1914 the *British Journal of Nursing* was commenting bitterly, 'It is regrettable that even now . . . the idea is still prevalent that little more than an impulse of goodwill is necessary to qualify a woman to nurse wounded soldiers.'

'Nursing was the first thing – I might say the only thing – a woman thought of as war service,' a VAD said. When war broke out, over forty-seven thousand women were members of VADs. (Soon the members of voluntary aid detachments were themselves

known as VADs.) Thousands more rushed to register for first aid
and home nursing courses. As it became obvious that the war would
not be over by Christmas, and as the casualty lists of friends and
brothers grew, more and more women began to realize that the war
was, after all, something to do with them, and that it demanded
some kind of commitment.

Girls who had never done anything more strenuous in their lives
than put up their hair and pour the tea in drawing rooms, pleaded
with hospitals to let them scrub wards, feed patients, take
temperatures. Parents, used to keeping their unmarried daughters
in decent subservience at home, had first to be won over. Lady
Diana Cooper's problem was typical. At first, she tried to get to
France, but this came to nothing. She then decided to try nursing at
Guy's Hospital in London: 'This took a stiff fight, but as an
alternative to rape at the Front the civil hospital was relieving to my
poor, poor mother, who knew, as I did, that my emancipation was
at hand.'

In 1915, the novelist Naomi Mitchison 'became more and more
impatient with Oxford and my own non-involvement. Girls I knew
had gone to do "war work" . . . I nagged and nagged and finally
went off to be a VAD at St. Thomas's.' Another literary figure, Vera
Brittain, who had fought so hard and for so long against the
restrictions of her 'provincial young-ladyhood' in order to go to
university, became increasingly restless during her first year at
Somerville College, Oxford. Her brother was in uniform, her fiancé
and other close friends at the front. 'I longed intensely for hard
physical labour which would give me discomfort to endure and
weariness to put mental speculation to sleep.' In June 1915 she
started work at the hospital in her home town in Devon.

One young girl just out of school defied parental disapproval and
went to be interviewed by the matron of the local war hospital. In
an effort to look older she had put up her hair and borrowed her
mother's veil. 'All the veil achieved was to tickle my nose and make
me sneeze, causing the unaccustomed hair pins to drop all over
matron's carpet.' Having assured the matron that she was twenty-
one, she was told to report in thirteen days. 'The fact that I was
going to nurse other ranks and not convalescent officers was spoken
of in hushed whispers and with much head shaking. In those days
teenagers lived . . . very sheltered lives and I'm sure my parents'
reaction was protective and not snobbish.'

*One of a set of postcards produced 'In praise of Nurses' during the First World
War. The nurse is portrayed with a flag brooch showing all the Allied nations of
the time; behind her the Red Cross flag flutters proudly*

ed Cross

Most of the girls had no idea what a hospital was like. 'I doubt if I had ever been inside one,' Naomi Mitchison wrote. 'Our friends and relations would never find themselves in a hospital; they went to a nursing home.' If any of them set out in a spirit of rosy idealism, they were quickly disillusioned. At first they were called on to exercise all sorts of domestic skills that few of them possessed. 'I can see a girl now sitting on the stairs with a duster, wondering what on earth to do with it,' one recalled. Another was asked if she would cook with her friend: 'I'd never cooked a potato in my life.' Naomi Mitchison was told to make tea but failed to realize that tea must be made with boiling water. 'All that had been left to the servants.' Some of the trained nurses welcomed every opportunity to put these flighty young things in their place, though Agatha Christie, a VAD in a Torquay hospital set up in the Town Hall, sympathized with them. 'The poor hospital nurses were driven nearly frantic by the number of willing but completely untrained volunteers under their orders.'

Most girls survived their first encounters with bucket and mop and with real hard work. In Agatha Christie's hospital at first only older women were thought suitable to nurse sick men. This soon changed. 'Many of the middle-aged ladies had done little real nursing at all, and though full of compassion and good works, had not appreciated the fact that nursing consists largely of things like bed-pans, urinals, scrubbing of mackintoshes, the clearing up of vomit, and the odour of suppurating wounds. Their idea of nursing had, I think, been a good deal of pillow-smoothing, and gently murmuring soothing words over our brave men. So the idealists gave up their tasks with alacrity: they had never thought they would have to do anything like *this*, they said. And hardy young girls were brought to the bedside in their places.'

The hardy young girls also survived, with remarkable sang-froid, their first encounters with the most unromantic sight of the wounded. 'For many of the girls it was something of a shock to have so close an experience of naked male bodies, seldom beautiful,' Naomi Mitchison wrote. 'But I don't remember being shocked by the soldiers I had to wash, only pitying, sometimes disgusted, usually matter of fact.' She was harder tried when she first helped with the dressings: 'We VADs were put to help holding dishes and so on during the hideously painful dressings, often with strong stinging antiseptics, when strong men whimpered and cried out . . . Here I disgraced myself once and once only by fainting.' Another VAD reported: 'My first day on the wards and a man had an operation and the nurse told me to hold his arm. The smell of the dressings was terrible. One of the VADs saw I was green and said, "Would you go and get the fomentations?" Directly I was outside I was all right and it never happened again.' Not long after, the same VAD was told by Sister to put a dry dressing on a man's foot. 'The foot was black and one of the toes fell off. I just picked it up. We were young then.'

Enid Bagnold had a particularly horrifying introduction to wartime nursing. Still studying for her VAD certificates she was sent with her detachment to the station to meet a train full of wounded. 'The wounded came just as they were, their bandages soaked in blood . . . Everyone, trained or not, was rushed into the great military hospital, the Royal Herbert Hospital, at the foot of the Hill, to fetch and carry. Operations went on without stopping. I saw legs in baskets outside the theatre doors.' As one VAD remarked, 'You grew up rather suddenly.'

It was for voluntary hospitals that VADs had been recruited and trained and it was in voluntary hospitals – called auxiliary hospitals – that most VADs spent their war service. About sixteen hundred hospitals, mostly selected by the Red Cross, were opened in private houses and schools and any other property enthusiastic volunteers could lay their hands on. They took from six to over two hundred patients. Most were staffed by unpaid VADs – full or part-time – working under trained nurses recruited locally or through the Red Cross. A few, better equipped and with more trained staff, took more seriously sick and wounded but most were intended for convalescent patients. VADs wore the uniform of their detachment – blue for the Red Cross, grey for St. John, with the Red Cross or the St. John emblem on their apron bibs.

Eleanor David was commandant (non-nursing administrator) and her sister quartermaster of the local detachment, Sussex 66, at Ditchling. Their detachment was well prepared, with the members, all aged about twenty, suitably certificated, their trained nurse signed on and their list of articles promised for time of war kept up to date. When war came, their father, terrified that his girls would join the WRNS or escape from him in some other way, rented a house and told them, 'You will get it ready for a hospital', which they did.

Sussex 66 was typical of the smaller auxiliary hospitals. When it was expanded after a year it took about thirty patients in wards with two to six beds. Only the trained nurses lived in. The VADs, who were very keen and stayed throughout the war, lived at home and came in for morning or afternoon shifts. Their patients were convalescing from wounds or sickness and were sent from military hospitals in the Brighton area. Eleanor David submitted monthly

As the casualties from the front poured in, hospitals had to be extemporized from whatever was available. Here nurses work in a temporary hospital at Ashburton, Devon, UK

accounts, the military authorities paid for everything except the rent of the house, and every now and then some colonels would come and tell them they were doing very well. It was a friendly, happy hospital. The VADs put up visiting wives or parents and the men helped in the garden, played billiards and the gramophone and went about the village. Miss David lied to the authorities about this. She assured them that the men were never allowed out un-accompanied: but they were, 'And they were very good.'

Throughout the autumn of 1914 and early 1915 the wounded and sick poured in, mainly through Southampton and, later, Dover. From the ports they were dispersed by train throughout the country. Territorial hospitals expanded from 520 beds to 1,000, 2,000 and finally 3,000. These hospitals were established in huts, asylums and town halls. RAMC orderlies were mobilized for service abroad. Nurses with varying standards of certification and experience rushed to help but it became clear that there simply were not sufficient trained staff to go round. On February 1 the War Office proposed that, 'Members of recognized Voluntary Aid Detachments might advantageously be employed, and so enable us to release a number of fully trained Nurses for duty in new Hospitals.' Two VADs were to replace one nurse.

Applicants had to be aged between twenty-three and thirty-eight (twenty-one and forty-eight by August 1918). They came under military authority, worked under trained nurses, lived in nurses' quarters and were paid a salary of £20. The Joint Women's VAD Department at Devonshire House under Dame Katharine Furse was responsible for postings. The applicant presented herself with application form, references and medical certificate for interview by a matron of a large training school and her papers were then placed before a selection board. If she was accepted she signed on for one year (soon six months) or for the duration of the war. Over seventeen thousand VADs eventually served in military hospitals at home and abroad and auxiliary hospitals had increasingly to rely on those too old or too young for military service and those who could not be spared from their duties at home.

Trained nurses, from Queen Alexandra's matron-in-chief Dame Ethel Becher down, viewed with horror this influx of partially trained and, they feared, undisciplined women into military hospitals. One matron refused to allow her VADs to be addressed as nurse – 'practically impossible to explain this to our patients', a VAD commented ruefully. The nursing press, which sometimes seemed to regard the war as an irritating interruption to the real battle (for registration), eagerly took up stories of VADs taking on work and responsibilities for which they were plainly unqualified, without apparently wondering how hospitals would cope without them. For their part, VADs wrote to Devonshire House complaining that, with two years' experience, they were not allowed to do any nursing. Or, that with no experience at all, they were expected to take charge of wards and assist in operating theatres. Trained nurses complained that VADs were snobs. At least one society lady was accused of accepting the army's capitation payments and the unpaid services of VADs while taking in paying patients. Probationer nurses justifiably resented the fact that VADs were getting paid more than they were.

Relationships at hospital level were often better. A fair-minded nurse who found that a VAD was prepared to work, accepted her help with relief. The matron of one large auxiliary hospital near Eastbourne which often took men straight from the Front, wrote: 'I

A nurse at the wicket captured in action in this view of a nurses versus patients cricket match at a military hospital in 1916. Despite the inevitable jealousies that arose between professional nurses and the volunteers, both were totally dedicated to their tasks

have nothing but praise for the VADs. They were mostly *ladies* who had never done any manual work . . . They cleaned and cooked and nursed and were happy.' Many VADs were grateful for the training

nurses gave them, but at least one found: 'Although VADs had tremendous admiration for their skill and knowledge we were most unpopular with them. Maybe it was some form of professional jealousy, a fear that the VADs might want to detract from their professional status – this was most certainly not the case.' Another wrote: 'People slang nurses for being callous, but I really marvel sometimes that there is not more truth in their accusation. I am beginning to realize more and more what a wonderful set of people nurses are.'

VADs went through their first months of unaccustomed work with aching limbs, swollen feet and numbed senses. Except in those auxiliary hospitals staffed by part-timers, the hours were long. Day nurses would come on duty at about 7.30 am and work through until 8 pm with only two or three hours off in the afternoon and one free half-day a week – 'All of which we gave up willingly enough when a convoy came in or the ward was full of unusually bad cases', Vera Brittain wrote, on behalf of all nurses. Enid Bagnold found: 'The cap wears away my front hair; my feet are widening from the everlasting boards; my hands won't take my rings. I was advised last night on the telephone to marry immediately before it is too late. A desperate remedy. I will try cold cream and hair tonic first.' Louie Johnson was Sister in charge of two thirty-five-bed wards of acute surgical cases at East Leeds War Hospital. 'When the work used to get terribly hard and terribly bad I can remember people saying, "Sister, you shouldn't do so much," I'd say, "Well, it might be my fiancé, it might be my brother, and I can't stop because somebody might be looking after them".' She spoke for most other nurses and VADs.

Convoys of wounded could and did arrive at any hour of the day or night. The Sister, given due notice, would get as many men as possible out into convalescent hospitals to empty beds for an influx of up to one hundred men at a time. 'But when it came to some battles, particularly the first battle of the Somme . . . we'd have two convoys in twenty-four hours and we'd so many in they were laid on floors and in corridors because we couldn't get them into beds,' Louie Johnson remembered.

In strange contrast to peacetime, when a probationer was unlikely to be entrusted with more than a thermometer for the first year of her training, VADs were usually thrown in at the deep end and left to get on with it. It had originally been intended that they should at first do the work of ward orderlies – cleaning, bed making, feeding, blanket baths and temperatures – and then perhaps help with the dressings as they became more experienced. But the shortage of trained staff meant that far more was demanded of them. 'After my first week at Plymouth Military Hospital', one VAD said, 'I was put on night duty, for one whole block of six wards, which was terrifying. I appealed to the under-matron, telling her how ignorant I was, but she said she could do nothing about it . . . Luckily I had excellent RAMC orderlies, one in each ward, who did know what they were doing, and it all worked out in the end.' Another VAD found herself drafted to take sole charge of forty skin cases in a barracks hospital, when all the RAMC orderlies were sent to France. VADs responded magnificently to the demands on them, though most, at some time, were acutely aware of their own inadequacy. 'Being detached to "special" a dying man produced terror, not necessarily of death but one was terrified of somehow failing the patient through ignorance or incompetence.'

Nurses needed a strong stomach as well as a working knowledge of skills now fortunately outdated. Patients often arrived verminous and filthy from weeks in the trenches and exhausted from hours or days of travel. Each man was supposed to be labelled with his name, number, regiment, type of wound and whether or not an anti-tetanus injection had been administered, but sometimes the label read GOK (God only knows). In this pre-antibiotic age, wounds often went septic and the pus had to be drained out through tubes which the VADs cleaned. 'Everything was done by antiseptics, continuous dressings, continuous draining with tubes, hot fomen-tations – it was terribly painful for the men, dreadful,' Louie Johnson said. Ether and chloroform were unpleasant to administer and made the men sick. Pain-killers were distributed sparingly, blood transfusions were in their infancy and there was a constant fear of haemorrhages after amputations. Edith Evans remembered one particularly macabre duty: 'I used to have to go round on night duty with a torch looking under the bedclothes for the first eight or ten days after an operation to make sure nothing had gone wrong.'

Most hospitals were well equipped, though often a shortage of dressings meant that bandages had to be washed and ironed for re-use. Sterilizing equipment was sometimes inadequate. One VAD remembered a single gas ring for seventy beds, another was in charge of 'a tiny sterilizer which used to go off the boil, the gas was so bad; it was a great worry to me because if they dropped an instrument it had got to be boiled again and they couldn't have it till it had had its proper time'. A third, working as a theatre nurse, became so obsessed by her sterilizer that she used to get up in the night and cross to the wards to check that she had not left it on.

Discipline was imposed with pre-war military zeal. 'Punishments were severe,' Lady Diana Cooper found. 'Twice late for closing time at 10 pm would forfeit your long desired week-end, and less serious demeanours would stop your rare theatre-leave.' Agatha Christie wrote: 'I soon learned to spring to attention, to stand, a human towel rail, waiting meekly while the doctor bathed his hands, wiped them with the towel, and, not bothering to return it to me, flung it scornfully on the floor. . . . Actually to speak to a doctor, to show that you recognized him in any way, was horribly presumptuous.' For the rest of her life another VAD found it difficult not to address a doctor as 'Sir'. 'It was difficult to learn that a nurse must hurry but never run. It was difficult to keep one's Sister Dora cap on straight. It was difficult to have to stand, even during sheet hemming (we were cheaper than sewing machines) when a doctor came into the ward,' Naomi Mitchison wrote. 'We were reprimanded for things you wouldn't think mattered the slightest bit', another VAD sighed. When Enid Bagnold fell in love with the patient in bed 11 she recorded, 'I am conspired against; it is not I who make his bed, hand him what he wishes; some accident defeats me every time . . . Last night it was stronger than I. I let him stand near me and talk. I saw the youngest Sister at the far end of the ward, by the door, but I didn't move; she was watching . . .' Next day she found no. 11's bed empty. The *British Journal of Nursing*, reviewing *Diary Without Dates*, in which this story was told, remarked that it would have been more sensible to move the VAD than the patient.

Most VADs accepted discipline as a matter of course. They were, after all, closely guarded at home. In fact Diana Cooper welcomed it: 'To me all this discipline spelt liberty. I had never been allowed to go out alone on foot. My every movement at all times of the day must be known at home. Now, suddenly, my non-working hours up to 10 pm were my very own.'

In their turn, VADs had to impose discipline on the men, but this usually was not too arduous a task. Rules for the wounded were more relaxed than for civilian sick and bed patients were unable to get up to much mischief anyway. However, convalescent patients in search of a drink could be something of a nuisance. All the men wore special hospital blue uniforms which were meant to get them seats on public transport and keep them out of bars but several VADs remember night duty and the eerie sensation that they were not, after all, alone, before spotting one of the men lurching and mumbling down the ward. Agatha Christie sometimes escorted a party across the town. 'One had to watch out for a sudden request to cross the road, "because I've got to buy a pair of bootlaces, Nurse". You would look across the road and see that the bootshop was conveniently placed next to "The George and Dragon".' One VAD found it useful to invent a fiancé but most found the men behaved wonderfully well. 'I think they respected us because we were without a man,' Edith Evans said. 'I thought they were wonderful and I heard very little bad language.' Most of the men thought quite

Royal Consideration for the Wounded.

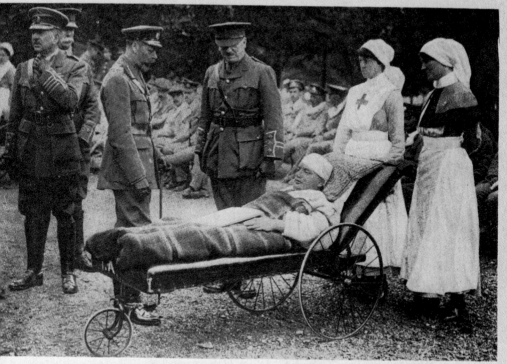

Royal recognition for nurses, as well as consideration for the wounded, was the theme of this visit by Britain's King George V and Queen Mary to three military hospitals in 1917

highly of the VADs too, and willingly contributed to their autograph books such verses as:

> 'The Red Cross Sister so demure
> On any chaps would work a cure:
> To part with you will be a loss,
> For you were never red or cross.'

VADs in military hospitals were meant to share the nurses' quarters, which often meant that nurses and VADs lived in equal degrees of discomfort. Sister Louie Johnson, on night duty, found: 'We slept in a working men's club . . . I had a little tiny room near a little tiny stage which was dreadful because down below the working men's club was still going on and you could hear billiard cues all the time. Up above us was the caretaker's flat and you could hear the patter of tiny feet . . . Outside was a school playground.' A VAD in a military hospital converted from an asylum was quartered with other VADs at the top of a tower which had in the past been reserved for dangerous lunatics: 'To reach the loo or the bathroom we had to go down a flight of stairs and then through a ward full of Tommies – and we must be properly dressed, nothing so informal as a dressing gown.' Her bed was comfortable but the roof leaked. 'We put up umbrellas over our beds and laughed about it.' Bedrooms were unheated – but so they were at home.

Vera Brittain found herself in a cold and comfortless cubicle in a hostel nearly two miles away from her hospital, the 1st London General at Camberwell. VADs and nurses were due at the hospital for breakfast at 7 am and, because the trams were almost always full, they usually had to walk there and back in all weathers. 'At the hostel, to meet the needs of about twenty young women, was one cold bathroom equipped with an ancient and unreliable geyser . . . It still seems to me incredible that medical men and women, of all people, should not have realized how much the efficiency of over-worked and under-trained young women would have been increased by the elimination of avoidable fatigue?'

Food varied according to the efficiency of the matron or commandant and the ability of the cook. Like everyone else, as the war went on, hospital staff suffered from shortages, particularly of sugar and potatoes. Only the patients got full rations. While most nurses found the food adequate, if uninspiring, others were so hungry they resorted to pilfering. One VAD used to take butter pats off the matron's breakfast tray. At another hospital the night staff were fed so poorly that the sister organized nightly raids on the stores and cooked wonderfully filling puddings for everyone.

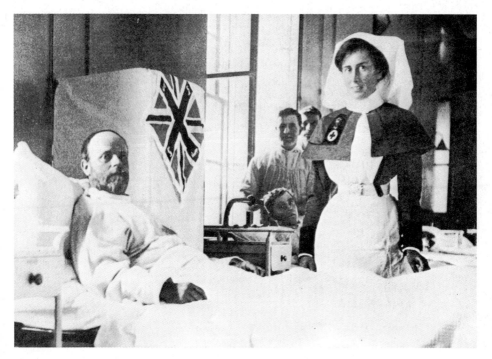

A patient poses proudly with his nurse. This particular man had been torpedoed in three different ships on the same voyage

'Finding was eating,' Diana Cooper reported.

At least the uniform became more comfortable. In September 1915 stiff white collars which chafed the neck gave way to a soft Peter Pan style and handkerchief caps, pinned at the nape of the neck, replaced Sister Doras.

If ever nurses and VADs felt tempted to give up, the courage, stoicism and cheerfulness of the patients and their generosity to each other kept them going. Most of these women were making their first contact with working-class men, other than servants and forelock-tugging labourers. They were impressed by the quality they found. The feeling that the British Tommy was one of nature's gentlemen is implicit in all they said. 'The British Tommy is a marvellous man,' Edith Evans said. 'The worse the conditions the brighter he is. I had the greatest admiration for them, they were so brave.' Another VAD agreed: 'In their own inarticulate and sometimes rough and ready way their kindness to each other was something not to be forgotten and this more than compensated for the long hours, "VAD baiting" by the trained nurses, discipline, etc. and I'm still grateful . . . to have been allowed to share in a very humble way in the comradeship which existed in the hospital.' 'One felt so bitterly sorry for them,' Louie Johnson said, 'You just felt angry – they'd no

143

Christmas on the ward in 1916. The casualty flow at the height of the First World War imposed massive burdens on both the professional and volunteer nursing services

right to be there. They ought to be playing cricket or enjoying themselves with their families.'

'They will take nearly anything from each other,' Enid Bagnold found. 'The only thing that cheered Rees up as he was wheeled away was the voice of Pinker crying, "Jer want white flowers on yer coffin? We'll see to the brass handles!" ' In passing, she wondered why soldiers are always called Tommy. 'I never heard the word "Tommy" in a soldier's mouth: he was a red-coated man. "But every mate's called 'Bill', ain't 'e, Bill?" '

Occasionally a soldier would be caught out trying to fake his condition. One of Agatha Christie's patients warmed his thermometer on the radiator. 'You should be ashamed of yourself!' 'Ah, Nurse, it's all a bit of fun.' Sometimes it could be more serious, as one VAD discovered. 'Some decided they were not going on the draft and undid their bandages. On one I found two matches and a brass screw.' She put an end to that problem by sealing the bandages with wax.

Gramophones blared, patients sat on each other's beds smoking and playing cards. Life in some hospitals was one long social whirl of ladies from the Red Cross, visiting padres and sympathetic locals.

More isolated ones hardly ever saw an outsider. Visits from relatives were rare as patients were often miles from home. Most convalescent hospitals had a billiard table, outings were got up for those fit enough and most patients enjoyed a royal visit. There were concerts, visiting violinists, brass bands playing weekly. 'Concerts twice a week,' one VAD remembers. ' "I'll sing you songs of Araby" till I was sick of it. Matron came to play the piano for us to dance, to encourage the men to get better.' Wards were decked out for Christmas, when even the most Scrooge-like matron managed a special dinner and many patients woke to find Father Christmas had visited them in the night.

As the years dragged by, girls who had joined up for the war that was to be over in a few months found themselves entitled to a scarlet efficiency stripe for one year's military service, then two stripes. Next, one hundred VADs were appointed Assistant Nurses and were officially entitled to undertake the sort of responsibilties most of them had been doing for some time anyway. A few nurses and VADs succumbed to infections, exhaustion and breakdown, but most soldiered on.

Outside, war work had forced a lowering of the standards of chaperonage, but VADs were still stunned to discover how little their families understood their role. One deeply shocked her mother by going into a visiting officer's bedroom to dress his wounded finger. Vera Brittain was summoned from the ward of the 1st London General to nurse her mother who had no urgent need of her. 'Forgetting that parents, who had been brought up by their own forebears to regard young women as perpetually at the disposal of husbands and fathers, could hardly be expected to realize that Army discipline – so demonstrably implacable in the case of men – now operated with the same stern rigidity for daughters as for sons, I gave way to an outburst of intemperate fury.' This sort of parental attitude was common enough for Dr. Flora Murray, administrator of the Women's Hospital Corps which ran the Endell Street Hospital, to sympathize with her girls who had to give up work because, 'Mother is dull at home,' or 'Father likes to have his girls with him in the evening.'

After three years of war, even the supply of VADs began to dry up as other opportunities appeared for girls with enthusiasm and initiative. Dame Katharine Furse, the VAD Commandant, knew where to put the blame. In October 1917 she wrote: 'In our anxiety to "help the sick and wounded" and to prove efficiency, we have, during the last three years, invariably given the hospitals all [the VADs] they asked for. Matrons have taken advantage of this. They have treated VADs any way they pleased and have always said, "Oh! there are plenty of other VADs to be had," and we have let them have other VADs and so the poor discouraged VADs have just thought to themselves that they really did not count.'

In 1918, the nursing service was stretched even further by the 'flu epidemic. As sick soldiers poured into hospital, the nurses themselves fell ill, while many sick families summoned VAD daughters home to their rightful position in the household. Civilian hospitals already suffering from lower staffing levels than military ones found it hard to cope, while doctors complained they could not get nurses for their patients at home. In August 1918 a cartoon caption read: 'Ist VAD: "What! You'll be away next week? But you've had your holiday, darling." 2nd VAD: "Yes, but I haven't had flu yet".' Probably this failed to raise a laugh among the young women who had spent the last three or four years in hospital wards.

One VAD heard the news of the armistice from the family gardener while she was at home nursing her flu-stricken parents and was terrified that the hospital would close before she could get back. With 364,133 beds still to empty there was little chance of that and, while there was some celebrating, most wards just carried on. Medals were distributed at an investiture at Buckingham Palace, and the Army Council thanked VADs for their 'Keenness, self-sacrifice, and devotion to duty'.

Slowly everyone returned to civilian life. Some got married, the fathers of others reasserted their authority and daughters returned to tennis parties and golf with happy memories of independence and comradeship. A few took up nursing as a career. But others were truly liberated by the war. Eleanor David and her sister left for London, no longer intimidated by their father. Two other unmarried VADs adopted children. Like everyone else involved in the war, VADs felt barriers between themselves and girls a few years younger for whom the war was history. It was a terrible way to achieve release from 'provincial young-ladyhood', but it worked.

After all the VADs had endured, it was galling to find that certain sections of the public and the nursing profession were eagerly resurrecting the portrait of a VAD as a flighty young thing. In 1919 the *Edinburgh Evening News* published a letter which indignantly and forcibly (if somewhat incoherently) put the record straight. 'Scrubbing etc. we must do as an Army Order was issued in 1915 saying all nursing orderlies were required in France, and the VAD would perform the following duties: sweep and dust wards, clean brasses, wash patients, crockery, etc. Flowers are arranged when brought to bedridden patients – perhaps annually, the public being sick of the wounded here. Of course our matron once scrubbed, etc. One usually climbs up the ladder by starting at the foot, so it is believed. A VAD's day was eleven hours, with three spent off duty, which I presume may be spent where and in whose company she wishes. Subalterns have been known to have fiancées, sisters and cousins and the VAD perchance is one. Our friend, knowing hotel lounges, etc., will perhaps note the subaltern alone, drinking liqueurs and smoking expensive cigarettes to create an impression. Is it not better for our VAD to lift him out of this degenerative status?'

10 First World War
Service Overseas

The excitement of the nurses and VADs called up for war service at home was nothing compared with the euphoria and impatience to get on with the job that filled those who served overseas. Crossing the Channel was a thrill, but for those who went further afield – British nurses to Egypt, Salonika and Russia, and Canadians, Australians, and New Zealanders to Europe – it was a great adventure. Three years of bloodshed, stench and mud later, the empire nurses observed with war-weary wonder the arrival of the American nurses, fresh as daisies and patriotic as pecan pie. Had they once been as youthful and confident as that?

The British medical units destined for France mobilized quickly and efficiently. The first hospital, complete with personnel, equipment and transport, and accompanied by the matron-in-chief Dame Maud McCarthy, landed on August 12, 1914. Others soon followed, but no sooner had they begun to prepare for duty than a sudden decision by the army threw the medical services into confusion. Hospitals which were opening on the routes to the Channel ports had to pack up and move (mostly by a five-day sea voyage) to Nantes and St. Nazaire where a new line of communication with the Front had been established.

Most sites and buildings suitable for hospitals had already been taken over by the French. Sick and wounded trying to come down and medical units trying to get up the line found themselves competing with troops being rushed to the Front. The staffs of many hospitals were left with nothing to do. At one time, 233 unemployed nurses were squashed into a small seaside resort. Medical equipment was hopelessly muddled in the rapid transfer, and all the equipment for one hospital went back to England by mistake. To make matters worse, the ambulance trains which were being assembled in France were found to be short of stretchers and supplies. For a time the evacuation of casualties was threatened. In October it was decided to move back to the Channel ports. By the end of the year the chief hospital bases were established at Rouen, Boulogne and Le Havre with minor centres at Calais, Abbeville, Le Tréport, Etretat and St. Omer.

The early delays and confusions were infuriating for the nurses who had left England with such speed and with so much excited anticipation – 516 arrived in France in August. One of the early arrivals at Le Havre wrote in her diary on August 26, 'It is absolutely maddening sitting here still with no work yet, when there must be so much to be done.' At the beginning of September the Le Havre base was shipped to Nantes. 'We are in palatial rooms with balconies overlooking the sea . . . Everyone is too sick at the state of affairs to enjoy it all . . . One of the minor errors has been sending 600 sisters out with 600 trunks, 600 holdalls and 600 kitbags! The Sisters' luggage is a byword now.' A month after leaving England she was still unemployed. 'Isn't it absolutely rotten?'

Another nursing sister who had been sent down to St. Nazaire during the retreat from Mons was waiting for new orders at Versailles when a convoy of wounded arrived at the Trianon Palace Hotel. 'It was a curious sight, almost unbelievable – the brightly lighted Hall, scarlet carpeted stairs . . . stretcher after stretcher being carried in with wounded men caked in mud and blood . . . What a night it was! Had we stopped to think, the work would have seemed hopeless.' At the end of October she was posted to Boulogne. 'The place gave us the impression of being a seething mass of ambulances, wounded men, doctors and nurses: there seemed to be an unending stream of each of them. All the hotels were hospitals, which gave one a horrid feeling of disaster.'

Before Casualty Clearing Stations were properly established, the wounded entrained fully dressed and straight from the battlefield. Nurses were assigned to ambulance trains in August 1914 and one of the earliest noted: 'Only those who have experienced it know what it means to undress a heavy man, badly wounded and lying on the narrow seat of a railway carriage. Never before had it been brought home to me what a quantity of clothes a man wears.' The earliest ambulance trains were cobbled together from whatever rolling stock could be found and the coaches rarely interconnected. 'Climbing from coach to coach by way of the footboard was a practice absolutely forbidden, though like more than one other rule, it was more honoured in the breach than in the observance.'

The retreat from Mons and the early confusion following the move from the Channel to Atlantic ports and back gave the impression at home that the organization of medical services had broken down. The War Office was besieged with offers of aid. Voluntary workers and medical teams dashed off to France and Belgium with no official recognition and without the knowledge of the medical authorities. Unprotected by the Geneva Convention, some were captured during the German advance and accused of spying.

Eventually some order was imposed. Official arm bands were issued to voluntary workers who could be accepted into the army medical units. The Joint War Committee took control of the dozen voluntary hospitals eventually accepted for service with the expeditionary forces: they were numbered as Red Cross hospitals. Only the largest, the St. John Ambulance Brigade Hospital at Etaples (like the BRCS hospital at Netley), came directly under the control of its founder. Finally, in February 1915, the Army Council ordered that no voluntary aid organizations other than the Red Cross and St. John should be recognized in France by the Army.

The first detachment of VADs sent to France under military contract arrived on April 17. By the end of the year there were 709, replacing trained nurses in general and stationary hospitals in the ratio of three to two.

Volunteers did not stay meekly at home just because the War Office did not want them. Many immediately offered their services to the French and Belgians while others had gone to them first in any case, feeling their need to be the greater. Several of the units were all-women and were deeply committed to the cause of women's emancipation.

Mrs. St. Clair Stobart's Women's National Service League was turned down by the British Red Cross but invited by the Belgians to open a hospital in Brussels. She was caught up in the German advance and arrested as a spy. After her release and repatriation she returned to Belgium and reopened her hospital in Antwerp but was again forced to retreat and the hospital was finally established in a château near Cherbourg.

The Women's Hospital Corps, led by Dr. Flora Murray and Dr. Louisa Garrett Anderson (daughter of Elizabeth), ran a hospital for the French Red Cross first at the Hôtel Claridge in Paris and then at the Château Mauricien, near Wimereux. They wore suffragette badges and one nurse found herself caring for a wounded ex-policeman who had arrested her during a woman's suffrage

British volunteers came from all social classes. Here the Duchess of Sutherland drinks tea with her patients at her hospital at Calais

demonstration. In 1915 they offered their services to the British who gave them a 500-bed hospital in London.

A unit of the Scottish Women's Hospitals, also rejected at home, ran a hospital for the French military authorities at Royaumont and another at Villiers-Cotterets which had to be evacuated almost in mid-operation as the Germans advanced in the spring of 1918.

In October 1914 the First Aid Nursing Yeomanry opened a hospital at Calais for the Belgians, and found some of the Belgian ways difficult to accommodate. On Sundays when the chaplain held a service in each ward the faces of non-Catholics were covered with newspapers and it was considered etiquette then for probationers to wash up after dressings in a devotional attitude. In June 1915, FANY ambulances were loaned to a British hospital in Calais and from then on FANYs took on all sorts of transport work for the British authorities.

The French needed all the help they could get. Their medical services were far inferior to those of the British and Germans throughout the war. The British Committee of the French Red Cross reported: 'Permanent officers of the French Army Medical Service seriously underestimated the actual scope of their forthcoming work and this left much to be improvised which should have been foreseen.' Although excellent nurse training schools had been established, the idea of nursing as a profession for educated women had not really become established and most nursing was done by religious sisterhoods, volunteer lady nurses who had taken a brief hospital course and women who did work considered menial by the ladies. The French Flag Nursing Corps was set up to send units of trained nurses to help in French military hospitals and the Red Cross appealed for money and supplies.

Nurses who responded to the call had great difficulty with some of the partially-trained helpers. Ladies reported for duty wearing jangling bracelets, high heels and tight skirts. They insisted on helping with the dressings but looked amazed when British nurses started to make the beds. In April 1915 a nurse wrote to the *British Journal of Nursing*: 'French habits and customs, the absence of organized military hospitals and nursing staffs, the shortage of nursing requisites, of dressings, of medicines – in fact, the pitiable lack of cleanliness, of hygiene, and of sanitary arrangements have been hard facts to face.' The French had a much higher ratio of deaths to wounded than the British or the Germans.

The Germans had about 75,000 trained women nurses at the outbreak of war, most of them Roman Catholic sisters or Protestant deaconesses, the rest Red Cross nurses or the new 'free' nurses, and a number of *Helferins*, who came from upper-class families and had had a short hospital training.

The hospitals and hospital trains (only the Red Cross trains carried female nurses) were well equipped and one American Red Cross nurse working in Germany in 1915 wrote that 'every precaution is taken by the Army to keep dysentery, cholera and typhoid from the soldiers'. Towards the end of the war, though, the British blockade led to a serious shortage of medical supplies. A German surgeon in the 1918 advance came across an abandoned British Army Medical Corps depot: 'For months the German doctors had had to use crepe paper bandages, like toilet rolls, to cover wounds . . . Instead of cotton wool, we used a kind of cellulose paper . . . In one corner I found innumerable boxes full of something German Medical Officers could only remember from the distant past, namely surgical rubber gloves.'

All this was far in the future, however. By the end of 1914, the medical services in France had settled down. Nurses were assigned to regular duties, Casualty Clearing Stations set up and ambulance trains evacuated the wounded with reasonable efficiency. The numbers of nurses in France increased as new hospital units opened. In August 1914 there were 516 nurses with the British forces in France. At the Armistice there were 2,500 British trained nurses, 1,729 VADs, 300 nurses and VADs with the voluntary hospitals, 2,000 nurses from the United States and Dominions, and thirty-three members of the Almeric Paget Military Massage Corps.

Troops came from British dominions and colonies all round the world to join the battle – and with them came nurses. The Canadians were the first to arrive – 101 landing at Plymouth in October 1914. Twenty nurses were detached for duty in France. Other units followed with Canadian hospitals and Casualty Clearing Stations, and the numbers in France reached a maximum of 828 in March 1918. Canadian nurses were the only ones to carry military rank. Twenty-eight Australian nurses arrived in Europe in June 1915 to serve with the British Expeditionary forces and completely staffed Australian general hospitals began to arrive in

The essential back-up services at home were not neglected. Here, prominent pillars of American society hard at work making bandages for shipment to France are captured in action by a news cameraman

France from Egypt in 1916. Smaller contingents of South African and New Zealand nurses also arrived in France in 1916 with their hospitals. All these medical services established their own hospitals and convalescent depots in Britain.

As the war went on the medical services adapted themselves to changing conditions, putting the harsh lessons of the early months into practice. Special wards were set aside for chest and abdominal wounds, fractured thighs, ophthalmic, aural and neurological work. In 1918, sixty-seven nurses who had trained as anaesthetists replaced medical officers in hospitals and CCSs. Nurses themselves became war casualties. In 1917 a nurse and two VADs were killed, another nurse died of wounds following an air raid at St. Omer and another nurse was killed by shellfire at a CCS at Brandhoek. Nine nurses, six of them members of the Canadian Army Nurse Corps, were killed in 1918 when No. 1 Canadian General and No. 3 Canadian Stationary Hospitals were bombed. A further seventy-one nurses and VADs were injured by enemy action in the same two years. Thirty-eight nurses died from sickness, and wards and convalescent hospitals were opened for sick and wounded nurses. Ninety-one nurses received the Military Medal for 'bravery and devotion under fire'.

Casualty Clearing Stations (CCSs) received the wounded and sick from field ambulance units, kept for treatment those who were too ill to travel or who would be fit to return to duty in a few days and evacuated the rest by train to base hospitals. They were usually in tents or huts beside or near railway lines. They were planned originally to be mobile but after the first few months of war they took up pretty well permanent positions and so much surgical work was transferred to them from base that they became almost immobile. From time to time CCSs became centres for research into such wartime conditions as trench feet and gas gangrene – which was caused by mud, dirty clothing, and filth being driven deep into wounds and was often fatal unless treated quickly.

At first five and then seven sisters were assigned to each CCS but during battles these were reinforced with extra nurses and surgical teams, each with a surgeon, anaesthetist, sister and orderly. The work was often arduous and distressing. Sister K. E. Luard, in charge of seven different CCSs between October 1915 and August 1918, wrote during the German bombardment of Vimy Ridge: 'It is packed tonight. I have been mostly in a ghastly hut full of head cases (falling off their stretchers), compound fractures, chests, two amputations and five compound fractured femurs. It is only equipped for walking cases and has no beds, but has had to take

Enmity ceases in this photograph of French, British and German troops having their wounds dressed at a casualty clearing station in 1918

these as the rest are full.' Many died. 'We went to the cemetery and counted the graves since Sunday week, fifty in a fortnight died of wounds at this one little CCS,' and, later, 'Still busy with increasing demand for coffins.' It was her job to write to the relatives.

The CCSs often came under fire and most had to evacuate hurriedly before the German advance in 1918. Sister Luard wrote: 'The guns came nearer and soon Field Ambulances were behind us and Archies cracking the sky with their noise. We stopped taking in because no FAs were working and we stopped operating because it was obvious we must evacuate everybody living or dying or all be made prisoners . . . We had about a thousand patients.' But her diary also records picnics on Vimy Ridge, tea with a general and the Battle of Arras was hardly over before she was recording: 'Invitations are descending on us.' The shells were still falling round her CCS at Brandhoek as she wrote: 'Party, supper and concert at the Warwick camp.' Miss Luard well understood the need for

One of the grimmest sights of the First World War – the arrival of a crowded hospital train. In this picture the American Red Cross are hard at work 'somewhere in France' as the official censor had it

relaxation and instituted 'Sunday At Homes'. 'In these Eve-less Edens such harmless socialities are of real value to the trench-worn officers and strung-up surgeons.'

The sick and wounded were transported, four or five hundred at a time, from CCS to base hospital by ambulance train. Forty-one eventually operated in France and Italy and the custom-built ones had accommodation for lying and sitting cases, dispensary and kitchen and comfortable staff accommodation. During battles, when CCSs were evacuating at top speed to empty beds for the freshly wounded pouring in, many of the men were critically ill and deaths on board were common. Trains were often shelled, quite short journeys could take days and in the early months trains often had to wait hours in sidings before they could unload their patients.

A sister who had loaded up at the Front during the Battle of Ypres in 1914 wrote: 'Two were put off dying at St. Omer, but we kept the rest alive to Boulogne.' And, two days before Christmas: 'We loaded up at Lillers late on Monday night with one of the worst loads we've ever taken, all wounded, half Indians and half British . . . [One] was sent on as a sitting-up case. Halfway through the night I found him gasping with double pneumonia; it was no joke nursing him with seven others in the compartment. He only just lived to go off the train . . . Another one I found dead at 5.30.' After her first few weeks of living on board she wrote, comprehensively, 'The worst discomforts of this life are (a) cold; (b) want of drinking water when you're thirsty; (c) the appalling atmosphere of the French dining car; (d) lack of room for a bath, and the difficulty of getting hot water; (e) dirt; (f) eccentricities in the meals; (g) bad (or no) lights; (h) difficulties in getting laundry done; (i) personal capture of various live stock; (j) broken nights; (k) want of exercise on the journey up.' Christmas was celebrated on the train which had loaded at Merville. 'Our great anxiety is to get as many orderlies and NCOs as possible through the day without being run in for drinking.'

Conditions had greatly improved by 1917, when a sister rhapsodized: 'My first impressions were of the extreme cleanliness, order and brightness of everything on the train . . . These railways were the highroads of the war. Wherever we went there were trooptrains, ammunition trains, food supplies, guns, tank stores . . . seldom were two days alike, no one knew where we might be sent next, or what adventure awaited us on the road.' By then, CCSs were well established and the men came on board in good condition. 'When loading was finished, our immediate duties were to inspect all medical cards, diet the patients and take note of all treatment to

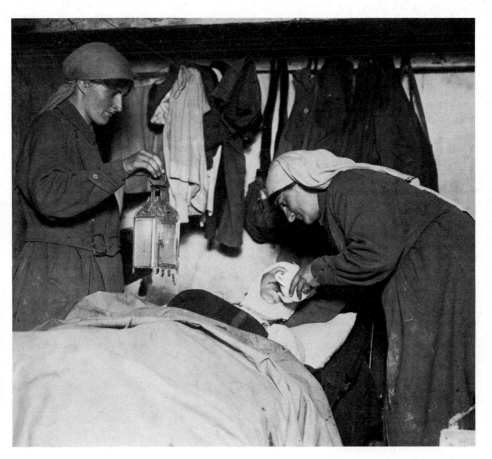

Conditions were frequently primitive. Here Baroness T'Serclaes and Miss Mairi Chisholm (with lamp) care for a wounded Belgian soldier in their cellar dressing station

be given during the journey; after this had been carried out, cigarettes, sweets and books were handed round and the sisters usually had time for a chat with the patients.'

Five ambulance flotillas, each with six barges, were mobilized to evacuate men suffering from head and chest wounds, gunshot fractures of the thigh and other injuries which would benefit from a smooth trip. Each flotilla had a kitchen, dispensary, its own stores and accommodation for thirty patients. The barges often had electric fans and stoves and cheerful striped awnings and the peace of the empty return journey made it a popular posting for sisters, though the rounded top of the barge with only a narrow ledge was a hazard, and several nurses slipped and fell into the water.

General and stationary hospitals were mobilized with 520 and 200 beds but from 1915 these numbers were doubled and when a hospital centre was opened at Trouville in 1917 the three general hospitals there each had 2,500 beds. Hospitals were installed in schools, convents, hotels, tents and huts and conditions varied accordingly. Olive Dent, installed in a tented hospital on a racecourse, reported, 'No hot water, no taps, no sinks, no fires, no gas stoves.' Trying to make an egg flip in February 1917 she found the eggs were frozen solid. 'The normal outfit of a night nurse on winter duty consists of woollen garments piled on cocoon-like under her dress, a jersey over the dress and under the apron or overall, another jersey over the apron, a greatcoat, two pairs of stockings, service boots or gumboots with a pair of woollen soles, a sou-wester, mittens or gloves (perhaps both) and a scarf.' Another VAD, who had been quartered in a hotel at Le Tréport, submitted a report describing good quarters but bad food, 'and there was such a shortage of bed linen that we often had to remake a bed with the sheets some poor fellow had died in – so long as there were no blood stains.'

There were never quite enough nurses to go round, even when VADs were posted in, and the work could be very hard, particularly

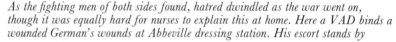

As the fighting men of both sides found, hatred dwindled as the war went on, though it was equally hard for nurses to explain this at home. Here a VAD binds a wounded German's wounds at Abbeville dressing station. His escort stands by

during a 'push', as the offences were termed. Vera Brittain, arriving at No. 24 General, in huts at Etaples, in August 1917, just before the battle of Third Ypres, found that 'the ward staff had passed a self-denying ordinance with regard to half-days, and only took an hour or two off when the work temporarily slackened'. She was particularly impressed by this, as the ward housed wounded German prisoners.

The German offensive in the spring of 1918 brought dark days to the base hospitals, as the enemy came ever nearer and, with CCSs packing up, wounded poured straight in from the front. Vera Brittain came on duty to find in her quiet medical ward 'dishevelled beds, the stretchers on the floor, the scattered boots and piles of muddy khaki, the brown blankets turned back from smashed limbs bound to splints by filthy blood-stained bandages. Beneath each stinking wad of sodden wool and gauze an obscene horror waited me.' For the first time she was afraid the Allies might lose the war: 'We were already becoming a Casualty Clearing Station, with only the advance units at Abbeville between ourselves and the line . . . That night we began to pack our boxes.' A resigned despair settled over the nurses. Then one day going on duty Vera Brittain stopped to let a contingent of troops march by. 'They looked larger than ordinary men; their tall, straight figures were in vivid contrast to the undersized armies of pale recruits to which we had grown accustomed . . . they seemed, as it were, Tommies in heaven . . . Then I heard an excited exclamation from a group of Sisters behind me. "Look! Look! Here are the Americans!" . . . Somehow the necessity of packing in a hurry, the ignominious flight to the coast so long imagined seemed to move further away . . . I found myself beginning to cry.'

Relationships between nurses and VADs were usually good in France and professional jealousy was put to one side for the duration. Vera Brittain was surprised to be greeted by her Matron with a friendly smile and another VAD found that, 'the Sisters were wonderful and seemed pleased to have a little extra help'. Summoned home to marry by her fiancé, she approached Sister reluctantly. 'She said, "Dear child, go home and get married and bear some sons to replace all these brave men who have given their lives for us." '

In the quiet times there were walks and picnics and sightseeing, and many a nurse's heart beat faster at the sight of butter and French meals and French patisserie. Concert parties were got up: one VAD remembers seeing a youthful Flanagan and Allen. Olive Dent described a typically homely event:

PART I
1. We commence.
2. Smith asks Romeo for a row.
3. Brown wants to sing – so let him.
4. Jones bursts into song. The audience will probably burst into tears.
5. Robinson will oblige.
6. Smithson insists and won't be kept back.
7. Sketch – some lorry inspection.

PART II
1. Robinson with a smile and a kitbag.
2. The Animated Forceps throws things about – including himself.
3. Encore Smith.
4. Jones tours an old-fashioned town.
5. Brown gives pathetic recitation about four 'C.O.' sparking plugs.
6. Smithson refuses to wait any longer.
7. We must be patriotic to conclude.

The sick and wounded were evacuated home from France and the Mediterranean bases by hospital ship. At one time there were 836 nurses serving on 100 hospital ships and ambulance transports. Some were converted luxury liners and one Sister on the Britannic said: 'The stewards and the food were as they would be going to America. We even had olives for breakfast.' Conditions on others were appalling. A naval nurse working between France and England remembers overcrowding and having to dress wounds by the light of a hurricane lamp held by another wounded soldier. Ships evacuating men from the Dardanelles, where conditions made it impossible to set up hospitals, were fully equipped medically. One Sister wrote: 'Surgical operations commenced and were continued for thirty-six hours without pause ... The poor maimed suffering boys lie in rows on the deck outside the operating theatre, just as they are taken from the lighter.'

Torpedo and mine attacks were common – so much so that, in the Channel, the distinguishing marks were removed and the ships armed. In the Mediterranean, hospital ships were given naval escorts. Sixteen hospital ships were sunk and one nurse lost her life.

To the overstretched and overworked British medical teams the Americans appeared in the light of the Sixth Cavalry. The USA declared war on April 6, 1917, and sanctioned the immediate dispatch to England of six base hospitals, complete with medical and nursing personnel, and arranged for more nurses and doctors to follow. By mid-June all units had arrived in France and taken over British general hospitals.

These, however, were by no means the first American nurses to arrive in Europe. The American Red Cross had already sent ten units, each with twelve nurses, and divided them with admirable impartiality between the various warring nations. In July 1915 two complete medical units, from Harvard and Chicago, were assigned to the British Expeditionary Force.

The first American nurses were agreeably surprised by the conditions they found in France. Emma Quandt, with the Chicago unit at Etaples, encountered 'sweet-faced English sisters', beds, hot and cold water, baths and lavatories. 'All these modern conveniences came as a surprise to us as these necessary luxuries were not expected on active service,' she reported to the *American Journal of Nursing*. Katherine McMahon was with the Harvard unit in a tented hospital at Danne Camiers. 'Each nurse, when assigned her respective tent, was given three army blankets and a large canvas bag, in which she was told she would find everything needed for comfort. We were incredulous of finding *everything*, but what was our surprise, on opening this Pandora box, to find a folding cot, a cork mattress, a washstand, a small table, chair, canvas pail in which to carry water, a lantern, an enamelled plate, a drinking cup, a knife, fork and teaspoon. Truly they had not exaggerated.'

The breathless enthusiasm and naive idealism of the American nurses in 1917 even surpassed that shown by their British counterparts three years before. Julia Stimson, chief nurse with the St. Louis unit which took over No. 12 General on the racecourse at Rouen, wrote to her parents: 'It is wonderful beyond belief... to be in the first group of women ever called out for duty with the United States Army, and in the first part of the army ever sent off on an expeditionary affair of this sort, it is all too much good fortune for any one person like me.' Shirley Millard, just out of school and with no nursing experience, felt the same. 'I wanted to help save France from the marauding enemy. Banners streamed in my blood, drums beat in my brain; bugles sounded in my ears. I wanted to go overseas.'

By June 11, Julia Stimson's unit was in France and she was writing delirious descriptions of the hospital, her own rooms, the birds chirping, the food – and getting used to being called Matron

'The Yanks are coming!' Here a party of American nurses arrives at Brest in May 1918, as welcome a reinforcement as the American Army itself

by her VADs – 'We are mighty glad to have them, they are splendid.' Even the bitter winter of 1917–18 did not get her down. As ink froze in the pens and toothbrushes had to be yanked out of glasses she wrote, 'It is awfully funny and doesn't hurt us a bit.'

In the middle of the German advance, Shirley Millard's introduction to a makeshift French hospital was brutal. 'Our first lesson in nursing was to begin nursing, whether we knew how or not ... Someone thrust a huge hypodermic needle and a packet of something into my hands and told me hurriedly that every man who came in must have a shot of tetanus ... After that I was to "get them ready" for the operating table ... I looked about helplessly.' Julia Stimson wrote at about the same time: 'We are having a great number of the most pitiful cases these last few nights, gassed men in terrible condition ... Ambulance load after ambulance load of stretcher cases with bandaged eyes and burning lungs.'

In December her nurses had made up a thousand Christmas stockings out of presents sent from America and she got a wounded soldier to write and thank one lady who had sent gifts. 'I saw the soldier's letter. It was quite typical and was full of such expressions as "fed up with", "carry on", "stick it", "Blighty", etc., and I am sure will be a real object of interest and curiosity at the Old Ladies' Home.'

In America there was the same conflict of interests within the nursing profession as in England, as rival sections called for more and more nurses. Families were reluctant to let their daughters go abroad, doctors emphasized the shortages at home. Civilian hospitals exerted pressure to keep their staff, patients demanded the same standard of care as they got in peacetime, Army camps needed more nurses but nurses were reluctant to accept cantonment service. But somehow, by the Armistice, there were 21,480 members of the Army Nurse Corps, compared with 403 when war was declared.

Although the hospitals in France could use all the nurses they could coax away from home, some had to be spared for the mounting casualties elsewhere. The Mediterranean war zones were slow off the mark but with the Gallipoli landings in 1915 they were soon making up for lost time. The sick and wounded were pouring out as fast as new troops were rushed in and nowhere was quite ready to receive them. New hospitals were opened on the island of Lemnos, while Egypt and Malta woke abruptly from their peacetime doze.

There were only seventeen Queen Alexandra's nurses in Egypt at the start of the war but as the first casualties started to pour in from

An operation in progress at Calais in 1917. Nurses were now totally irreplaceable even in the operating theatre, where for so long male dressers had reigned supreme

Another new involvement. A nurse at work in the laboratory of the Twenty-Fifth Stationary Hospital, Rouen

Gallipoli – 16,000 in the first ten days – nurses were rushed to Cairo and Alexandria. In the end more nurses served in Egypt than in any other war zone apart from France – 2,605 sisters and VADs were posted there, as well as Red Cross nurses who staffed a hospital and ambulance train, and large contingents from Australia, Canada and New Zealand.

Once the nurses and VADs got over their disappointment at not being sent to France, which was what most of them had hoped for, they found Egypt a pleasant posting. There were trips to the pyramids and mosques, camel rides, picnics on the Nile and afternoon tea in the tea gardens. But the heat and the wildlife were real drawbacks. 'Bed bugs and fleas,' Mary Schofield remembered. 'They used to drop from the ceiling onto my table. The men used to have a game at night . . . they used to see who could get the most bugs on a pin.' 'The sweat poured down without any movement', another VAD said. 'There were also flies, fleas and mosquitos. We had to work during the hottest part of the day when even the natives went to sleep. The relief at sunset was terrific.'

Discipline was strict, perhaps to counteract the seductive effect of the Nile at sunset. 'But we managed to break rules without detection,' a VAD confessed. 'We were not allowed to go out alone with a man, and that was why I was on the carpet before Miss Oram (the principal matron). I told her, "I thought it was all right when I had two of them." She was human and couldn't keep a straight face.'

Conditions were much worse at the new hospital sites at Mudros on Lemnos. One Canadian hospital opened on a site previously occupied by Egyptian labourers with no idea of sanitation, while another was sited at an old Turkish camp, where for two months the water supply was dependent on one cart, and the food scarce and unsuitable for sick men. The climate was terrible and the flies so bad that one nurse was employed in keeping them away while another dressed wounds.

The Gallipoli campaign led to a massive increase in the number of nurses on Malta – from twelve at the outbreak of war to 913 by the beginning of 1916. Following the evacuation of the Dardanelles the numbers were more than halved, and Vera Brittain, arriving at St. George's hospital in late 1916, found it a pleasant posting. 'After the fatiguing stuffiness of the hot wards in Camberwell, this open air life in the warm sun beside a sparkling sea sent me tripping up and down the block with a renewed vigour.' She wrote to her mother, 'They even give lectures – good ones – on nursing to VADs here.'

Malta reverted to near peacetime quiet, but Egypt continued to absorb casualties, and as General Allenby advanced against the Turks through Palestine the medical services followed up the line and established hospitals in tents and huts. 'We generally had plenty of water but occasionally there was a sandstorm and the taps seemed to run sand,' a VAD remembered. 'It was hard to see or breathe and very distressing for patients with breathing troubles . . . There were jackals about round the camp and a few people were rather nervous on night duty but the creatures only made horrid noises and slunk away.'

Conditions at Amara and Basra, where hospital centres were established for the campaign in Mesopotamia, made those at Mudros and Palestine seem quite resort-like. The climate was dreadful – indeed, it had been doubted if women would stand it – and the discomforts intense. One nurse in a tented hospital as Basra remembered: 'We had to nurse in topees and sunglasses with a handkerchief tied round the neck to catch the drips, and with sore patches on our arms. We had mosquito nets but still got bitten', but with true stoicism she added, 'The only thing that really frightened me was finding two plague rats in the tents.'

Conditions in the rainy season were no better, as the matron of a hospital up river from Amara found: 'One lived in gumboots, wore topees and sluiced about in mud all day long. Fleas plague everyone at this time of year, but sandflies and flies come later.' There were two 'rather alarming' cholera outbreaks. Many nurses went home sick, but the Red Cross came to the rescue with ice and soda water and gallons of lime juice, and, on the whole, the Sisters stood the climate better than the men. When the army advanced to Baghdad in 1917 the medical services went too, releasing French nuns who had been nursing there in civil and military hospitals.

'Brave little Serbia' attracted a number of voluntary units to its aid, particularly during the 1915 typhus epidemic. Lady Paget twice took out a group, the Scottish Women's Hospitals sent five units altogether, Mrs. St. Clair Stobart escorted a group of twenty-five, and the Joint War Committee sent two units. The conditions were generally bad, the buildings inadequate, equipment lacking and the work overwhelming. One of the Scottish Women's units and one from the Joint War Committee were trapped during the Austro-German offensive in the autumn of 1915, but were released the following February. At the age of fifty-three, Mrs. Stobart escaped by marching her column 800 miles over snow-covered mountains to Scutari. She was the only leader to bring her column intact through the retreat.

The official medical services were based at Salonika in

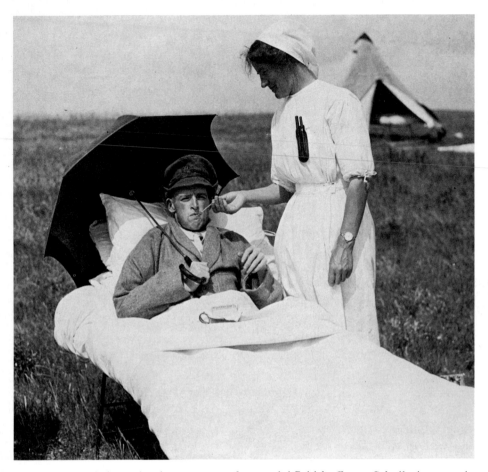

A sister takes the temperature of a wounded British officer at Salonika in 1917. As the war spread, so the work of nurses increased on all its many fronts

Macedonia, forty miles from the border of land-locked Serbia. By August 1917 there were 1,066 nurses and 224 VADs there, including Australian and Canadian army nurses. Bitter winters were followed by intense summer heat, lice and flies. Sisters wore mosquito veils, mosquito gloves and thick puttees to protect themselves from malaria in the summer. But in spite of these precautions, and taking quinine, sixty per cent of the staff of one Canadian hospital went down with the disease.

Considering these disadvantages, one nurse arriving in August 1917 was impressed by what she found. 'The four General Hospitals at the base were in huts . . . while many of the tented hospitals had good huts for operating theatres, bath huts for patients, and most were supplied with huts for sisters' mess, bath huts, etc., a real luxury on active service greatly appreciated by the staff.'

The Red Cross sent five medical units to Italy, but military medical units did not start arriving until 1917. Eventually 682 Queen Alexandra's nurses and VADs were posted there. Conditions during the 1917–18 winter were poor, with shortages of fuel and food. One nurse reported a particularly dreary New Year's Eve at Padova, which had three meatless days a week and December 31 was unfortunately one of them. After dinner, 'we were politely informed that as they had only one charcoal fire for everything, we could not be supplied with both coffee for breakfast and hot water to wash in . . . We chose the coffee, hoping to wash in the water that was in our hot water bottles – this hope, however, had to be abandoned as on pouring out the water it was evident it had been used for washing the dishes in from the previous night's dinner.'

The hospital ship *Kalyan* with accommodation for 900 patients spent the 1918–19 winter at Archangel in northern Russia, nursing sisters and ship suitably clad against the arctic conditions. They treated the sick and wounded and returned to Leith in June. The Joint War Committee had earlier dispatched two field hospitals to Russia and a unit to Romania. In addition, a number of individual women were caught up in helping the Russians. Florence Farmborough was in Moscow when war broke out, visiting the family which had employed her as its governess. She took a Red Cross course and was posted to a front line 'Flying Column' which advanced and retreated – mainly retreated – with the army. Violetta Thurstan was not impressed by the 'war course' which was all that most Russian nurses at the Front had been given: 'They are apt to think that bandaging is the beginning and the end of the art of nursing.' She, too, after working in hospitals, was attached to a Russian Red Cross 'Flying Column' and was engaged in hurriedly opening dressing stations, treating as many wounded as possible, then even more speedily evacuating them as the guns got nearer: 'The never-ending processions of wounded men being brought in on those horrible blood-stained stretchers, suffering unimagined tortures, the filth, the cold, the stench, the hunger, the vermin, the squalor of it all' were among her memories.

And yet, in spite of all this, she wrote elatedly: 'War would be the most glorious game in the world if it were not for the killing and wounding. In it one tastes the joy of comradeship to the full, the taking and giving, the helping and being helped, in a way that would be impossible to conceive in the ordinary world.'

With the Armistice the nurses celebrated – at least the end of the slaughter. Five nurses from CCSs attended the official entry into Mons on November 15, while others caught up on long-deferred leave. In London there was a great luncheon for matrons-in-chief and a commemorative service was held in St. Paul's for nurses who had fallen during the war. In the Christmas fortnight, dancing, hitherto forbidden, was allowed in nurses' and RAMC officers' messes, provided the patients were not disturbed.

Demobilization was ordered on March 9, 1919, when the nursing staff was reduced by half. VADs who had served in France and wanted to take up nursing were allowed to dispense with one year of their hospital training, but not many took up the offer. Sluices and bed-pans had lost their glamour.

‘Who’d be a Nurse? 11

The demand for nurses after the war was enormous. Hospitals as well as the public health field needed more and more. The trend was away from care in the home to treatment in hospitals, as advanced surgical and medical skills were developed. Officers’ hospitals during the war had accustomed the middle and upper classes to the idea of institutional care. The traditional fear of hospitals had almost disappeared and everyone wanted to take advantage of the most up-to-date facilities. New techniques such as X-rays and heat therapy made greater demands on nurses.

The nursing profession anxiously examined itself and sought ways to improve recruitment to satisfy all demands. In America the discovery that ‘flaming youth’ – the name conferred on the emancipated women of the 1920s – was deterred from entering training schools by poor accommodation and lack of educational facilities led to a flurry of building and reform. While searching for other ways to polish up its image the profession in America also found, to its astonishment, that far from being short staffed, there was a real danger of unemployment among nurses, particularly those on private duty. American hospitals then employed almost no trained nurses except in administration and teaching tasks. All ward work, including the jobs, which, in Britain, were done by staff nurses and sisters, was in the hands of the students who, on graduating, went out into the world to fend for themselves, generally in private work. It was a simple case of over-production and poor quality. As the Committee on the Grading of Nursing Schools put it in 1928, ‘Too many but too few’; the unemployed private duty nurses were inadequately prepared for the public health fields which were crying out for more recruits. It was an alarming situation.

When the Depression struck, private duty nurses, largely self-employed, were particularly hard hit. Patients at home could not afford them while the numbers of inmates in voluntary hospitals, who usually employed special duty nurses, declined. Small hospitals were encouraged to close their training schools and employ graduate labour. This led not only to an improvement in training but to a gradual shift from private duty to hospital work. By 1941, nearly half of all nurses were employed in institutions and only about a quarter were still on private duty. The state also intervened in the crisis and set up public health programmes administered through the US Public Health Service and the Children's Bureau. The Depression caused most nurses to become employees.

In Britain the situation nurses faced was the reverse of that in America. Far from fearing a nurse shortage, the profession was afraid of a surplus and consequent unemployment among its trained members. The war united most of the profession behind two aims – to form a legal register of trained nurses and to keep VADs off it. The demands of war had drawn thousands of women with limited training and experience into hospital wards. Trained nurses, anticipating competition from these women when the war was over, became increasingly anxious that their own status should be recognized. In 1916, the College of Nursing Ltd. (later the Royal College of Nursing) was founded to promote better education and training of nurses and uniformity of curriculum, to work for state registration and to promote the advancement of the profession through legislation, post-graduate study and scholarships. In two years the College had recruited 8,000 members.

The College had hoped to amalgamate with the Royal British Nurses' Association but squabbles, both personal and professional, made unity impossible. The petty bickering, fascinatingly detailed by Brian Abel-Smith in *A History of the Nursing Profession*, naturally involved that redoubtable pair Mrs. Bedford Fenwick and Mr. Burdett. Mrs. Fenwick objected to too much lay control of the College of Nursing. (She and Dr. Fenwick founded the British College of Nurses in 1926 in opposition to the earlier foundation.) The Central Committee for State Registration attacked the College's Bill. Mr. Burdett leapt in and attacked Mrs. Fenwick, comparing the war in the nursing profession with the World War: 'Demonstrably both wars had their origin in the overmastering desire for supreme power, possessed, in each case, by a single individual.' The RBNA agreed to amalgamation in principle but the College grew tired of waiting and arrogantly informed the

RBNA that 'as the College of Nursing has now become well known ... the advantage to the College of amalgamation becomes less obvious'. In 1919 two separate Bills, one from the RBNA and one from the College, were presented to Parliament. The Minister of Health, failing to reconcile the two bodies, stepped in with his own Bill. The Nurses Registration Act became law in December 1919.

The Act provided for the setting up of a general register plus supplementary ones for male nurses, mental nurses and children's nurses. Fever and mental deficiency nursing sections were added later. A General Nursing Council was appointed to start the Register (after two and a half years a new Council was to be elected by the registered nurses), to approve training schools and to draw up a syllabus of training for state examinations, the first of which were held in 1925. Until July 1923 people without formal training were to be admitted to the Register provided they were of good character, had adequate knowledge and experience and had been engaged in *bona fide* practice for at least three years prior to November 1919.

It was left to the Council to decide what constituted *bona fide* practice and adequate knowledge and experience. In its eagerness to exclude VADs, it at first tried to insist on one year's training but opposition forced it to propose an ingenious additional method of entry. Women would be admitted to the Register who had been engaged in practice on November 1, 1919, and before January 1, 1900 – a rule calling for twenty years' practice. Parliament intervened and insisted that the Council admit to the Register any applicant who presented a testimonial of good character and certificates stating that she had been nursing the sick for at least three years before November 1, 1919, had adequate knowledge and experience and was competent to attend the sick. For twenty years after the Register closed to practising nurses in 1923 there was only one way into the profession, and that was by state examination and state registration.

Opportunities for nurses increased greatly in the twenty years between the wars. Women aiming for higher administrative and teaching posts (St. Thomas's Hospital, London, had appointed the first Sister Tutor in 1914) could equip themselves with the necessary qualifications by attending post-graduate and diploma courses. Nurses wanting to specialize could take further training.

In these first tentative steps towards forging university and college connections Britain fell a long way behind America. Teachers College, Columbia University in New York, had started a course in hospital economics as early as 1899. Ten years later the

University of Minnesota began the first nurse training course to be affiliated with a university. Though applicants had to meet the university admission standards, the three-year course did not differ greatly from those offered by other good nurse training schools and at the end graduates were awarded a diploma, not a degree.

The Cincinnati medical school set up a degree option in 1916; the next year five-year degree courses were launched by the Presbyterian Hospital, New York, in conjunction with Teachers College and by the University of California. Students spent two years studying basic sciences, two years in hospital work and the last year training in a special field. Collegiate education became quite the vogue and developed rapidly – in name, at any rate. In fact, few of the so-called collegiate schools which sprang up were anything more than hospital schools loosely affiliated with colleges. Hospital managements were often against proper collegiate schemes because they meant sacrificing the staffing needs of the wards to the educational requirements of the students. American hospitals relied as heavily on probationary labour as British ones. Three experimental programmes – at Yale, Vanderbilt and the Western Reserve – did manage successfully to integrate the social and health aspects of nursing in a basic course. A post-graduate course for teachers and administrators was launched by the University of Chicago in 1926 and six years later the Catholic University of America began post-graduate courses in nursing.

Special courses were set up for nurses moving into the fast-growing public health fields, where the emphasis was more on prevention than cure. Public health became so important that in 1925 the British Ministry of Health had to issue regulations governing the training of health visitors. Candidates for the Health Visitor's certificate could either take a three-year hospital training, gain the certificate of the Central Midwives Board and take an approved six-month public health course, or they could do six months' hospital training, plus the midwives certificate and take an approved two-year public health course. The Royal Sanitary Institute was approved as the only examining body.

Special clinics were set up for tuberculosis and venereal diseases, and industrial nursing expanded, boosted by the war when munitions workers were given extra protection. But most public health work was concerned with the welfare of infants and children. France led the field when it established the first crèche in 1844 to help mothers working in the factories in the Industrial Revolution. The modern infant welfare movement originated in Paris. At the turn of the century, centres were opened where mothers could have

Post-war womanhood might be questioning its role but these nursing sisters, pictured on their way to Baghdad, seem confident of their vocation

their babies weighed and receive instruction in correct feeding. America developed pure milk programmes to ensure safe feeds for babies. The Mothercraft Training Society, based on the precepts of Dr. Truby King of New Zealand, started in England in 1918. This movement, which laid great emphasis on breast feeding, correct clothing and the open air life, became very popular. Most towns in Britain opened infant welfare centres and every new born baby was automatically visited by a health visitor. The Education Act of 1921 ensured that healthy babies did not become sick children by obliging local authorities to employ adequate school nursing services.

The League of Nations internationalized public health care by setting up two committees to give technical help to governments on special health problems. To begin with, they were chiefly concerned with infectious and social diseases and teaching public health but they later expanded their work to include the maintenance of good health by hygiene, health insurance and medical care.

But these reforms did nothing to solve the problem of shortage – in Britain at any rate. Supporters of the Nurses Registration Act had claimed that it would attract into the profession more well-educated women. The number of women practising as trained nurses certainly increased considerably – twice as many nurses were admitted to the Register in 1937 as in 1926. The General Register in December 1937 contained 73,849 names, 44,268 of whom had been admitted by state examination which called for a reasonable educational background. But demand was increasing considerably faster than supply. Nurses who had feared competition from the specially recruited wartime nurses found instead that they could pick and choose their jobs, as almost all the emergency nurses returned to their peacetime occupations.

Hospitals responded to the shortage as best they could. The major London voluntary hospitals were scarcely aware it existed. (St. Thomas's training school prospectus made it clear that all important social invitations would be considered. It obviously expected no lack of the 'right sort' of applicant.) Other less fortunate institutions made increasing use of ward orderlies to do the domestic work. Desperate matrons accepted girls as probationers who had not a hope of passing the examinations. The London County Council tried to attract more recruits by improving staffing levels and shortening hours. Like other local authorities, and the Poor Law Boards before them, the LCC paid higher salaries to tempt girls from the more glamorous voluntary hospitals. A class of 'assistant nurse' – untrained or partially trained and with recognized status – appeared, and was particularly useful in the large local authority institutions for the chronic sick. Some counties even started to run two-year courses for these new 'nurses'. The College of Nursing, which had always insisted that there should be only one entry to the profession, was by 1936 forced to admit that there was a need for this special grade of nurse.

Everyone was worried about the nurse shortage. Between the wars, the profession was investigated time and time again to find out why recruitment fell short of need. Time and again the conclusions drawn were similar to those of the Labour Party Report of 1927: 'It is undoubtedly the case that the nursing profession, consisting of nurses who have undergone a course of long technical training, is relatively worse off with regard to remuneration, hours, and general conditions of labour than any other similar group of workers.' The Report ambitiously recommended a salary of at least £40 a year during training, a 48-hour week with an eight-hour day to include lectures, one full day off a week and at least one weekend a month and a minimum of three weeks' holiday a year – and advised the profession to unionize to fight for these conditions.

Would-be recruits, naturally enough, were put off by the low pay and long hours. The Labour Party reported that Poor Law infirmaries paid probationers during training £30 the first year rising to £35 and £40 while general hospitals paid an average of £10 less. Nurses in London Poor Law infirmaries received on average £65 to £75 a year and sisters £80 to £95 while those in London general hospitals were again paid about £10 less. The *Lancet* Commission on Nursing, reporting in 1932, found little improvement, but, by 1937, though probationers' pay had risen scarcely at all, nurses were receiving on average about £10 more. The College of Nursing was against boosting recruitment by paying students (as they were coming to be known) more, 'as it is believed that this does not attract the most suitable type of candidate,' it told the Inter-Departmental Committee on Nursing Services (the Athlone Committee) which published its Interim Report in 1939. If probationers had really been students in training then free board, lodging and laundry plus a salary, however small, would indeed have seemed generous recompense, but in fact they made up the bulk of a hospital's nursing staff, outnumbering trained nurses two to one. Guy's Hospital, London, estimated that, if it did away with its probationers and staffed the wards with trained nurses and domestic workers, it would result in a forty-seven per cent increase in costs. As the *Lancet* Commission pointed out, students were in fact paying indirectly for their training.

No one disputed that the hours were too long. The *Lancet* Commission found that in a quarter of hospitals nurses worked between ten and eleven hours daily, with meals reckoned as off duty, and in sixty per cent of hospitals they worked between nine and ten hours daily. More annoying than the number of hours worked was the span of time they covered. Including the three-hour off-duty period, a nurse's working day could last as long as fourteen and a half hours. In nearly half the hospitals the day spanned thirteen or thirteen and a quarter hours. Another aggravation was the lack of advance notice of off-duty time – fifty-four per cent of hospitals only told the nurses that they had time off on the morning of the same day. Probationers often had to attend lectures in their off-duty time and were generally not given time off before examinations to revise. The *Lancet* Commission recommended at least one day off before exams but the Athlone Committee was still receiving complaints that such time off was not being given and that some probationers had to go into exams straight after night duty. Investigators constantly criticized the double burden of long and arduous hours of ward work plus the mental strain of lectures and study.

A group of Air Force sisters pictured outside their mess in India in 1930. On the civilian front, however, the profession was in a considerable state of flux during the inter-war years, as the return of emergency nurses to their peace-time occupations led to a severe shortage of nurses in the hospitals

Hospitals increasingly provided single rooms, but the *Lancet* Commission still found that, in some cases, probationers shared ill-lit and cold rooms and ate in damp basements. It recommended that each girl should have her own simply but comfortably furnished room adequately warmed, a bath and lavatory for every six rooms and enough hot water for each nurse to have a daily bath, attractive common rooms, a well-appointed dining room, class room, and, if possible, a study room. Conditions improved, but in many cases still fell short of the *Lancet* Commission's cosy suggestions by the time the Athlone Committee came to report.

Food was usually adequate, but often monotonous, carelessly prepared and inappropriate. Uniforms had failed to follow the simpler post-war styles. A nurse's mother wrote: 'At one good London hospital a probationer's dress, apart from the putting on of cap and apron, needs 18 buttons, 6 hooks, and 5 studs to be done up. If she wishes to change, this seriously shortens her off-duty time and increases the mending of buttons and hooks crushed by the laundry.' Many nurses, however, would have been reluctant to part with their traditional and picturesque dress.

The majority of the profession still liked to think of nursing as a vocation, but far more nurses were needed than could be realistically expected to feel a 'call'. An uncommitted girl, coolly surveying the opportunities open to her, was more likely to choose the better pay and hours of an office or school and the freedom of life at home. The *Lancet* Commission reported: 'There is still a widespread belief that nurses in training are worked excessively hard, are allowed no freedom, are subject to unduly severe discipline, and are neither fed well nor lodged comfortably. A girl to whom nursing is proposed as a career envisages a period of three years at least of drudgery during which time she will be cut off from her friends, her games, and her social amusements, will be always overtired physically, and often snubbed and reproved.'

It was ironic that nursing, which was the first profession to offer women trained, paid and independent employment, should have come to be popularly regarded as a cross between life in a convent and a prison. The *Lancet* Commission described these views as 'misconceptions' and they certainly were exaggerated – as many nurses of the period, happily and usefully employed, indignantly testified – but it was true that nursing had failed to adapt to the relaxed social behaviour of the post-war era. Girls who might have been prepared to accept poor pay and long hours in return for the satisfaction of a valuable and interesting job were deterred by the excessive discipline, petty tyrannies and lack of privacy which were widely reported in the press by the disaffected, and which continually surprised investigators from outside the profession.

The hierarchy within hospitals was still enforced with military rigidity, and probationers were expected to pay exaggerated respect to their seniors and to doctors. Cynthia Nolan, in *A Bride for St. Thomas*, recalled: 'A Second [nurse] learned to avoid Night Sister or either of the two Night Assistants . . . but to anticipate, by rapidly rolling down her sleeves and slipping the starched cuffs from pocket to wrists, the rare occasions when one of the trio spoke to her. And she must keep away from the middle table, the territory of the First, when the housemen made their nightly round.' 'Nurse,' a sister said to Monica Dickens, when she was training during the Second World War, 'you must never, never do such a thing again.' The nurse expressing incomprehension, the sister went on, '. . . you mean to stand there and tell me that you don't know that you may not address a member of the medical staff directly, but only through the medium of someone senior to yourself.' The Athlone Committee was distressed to learn that there was no 'friendly intercourse' between probationers and trained nurses.

Anxious though the profession was to attract well-educated girls, it had little idea how to treat them once they had joined it. 'Girls go from an atmosphere of trust at school to being treated as irresponsible children,' reported the Athlone Committee, which had heard of late leave being cancelled because a nurse was three minutes late for breakfast. Girls who were prepared to accept the necessity for discipline in hospital wards found it anomalous that, while they often had to accept responsibility in their work, they had none over their personal affairs. Probationers generally had to be in their bedrooms by 10 pm with lights out at 10.30 and often had to get permission to go out between coming off duty at 8 pm and bedtime. Attendance at meals, even if they fell within off-duty periods, was often compulsory and in many hospitals girls were not allowed to receive male guests. 'The reasons generally given for such restrictions are that the matron is responsible to the probationer's parents for seeing that she gets sufficient rest and food, and that her evenings are devoted to study,' the *Lancet* Commission reported. It continued: 'This degree of supervision was doubtless welcomed by parents when it corresponded closely with that exercised in middle-class homes, but we have ample evidence that it can no longer be held to reflect their wishes.' As one nurse wrote: 'What girl nowadays wants to feel she can't go out unless she shows a pink slip to about six people, on her way probably to buy a stamp or post a letter.' The *Lancet* Commission sensibly recommended that the nurses' home should be run as a hostel under a Warden and that smoking (which seems to have been a contentious issue) should be permitted.

Supervision of the probationers' private life sometimes amounted to prying. Home Sisters regarded it as a duty to check drawers and cupboards for tidiness. Monica Dickens, for example, found her drawers half-open and the contents disturbed after matron's rounds. 'I could never get used to this absence of privacy. You were given a room of your own, but it was not your own. The authorities considered themselves responsible for us and made that an excuse for snooping.' 'Nurse . . . you have been seen leaving the hospital grounds without wearing a hat,' a sister rebuked Cynthia Nolan. 'It isn't done, Nurse, not in London.'

Trained nurses – grown women – were sometimes as restricted in their private lives as probationers. Generally speaking their opportunities for social life outside hospitals were no greater than a student's and they were not as a rule free to spend their evenings as they chose. The Athlone Committee felt that permission to live out should be granted more widely, and welcomed the recent London

County Council's regulations which not only gave nurses better hours but actually treated trained nurses as adults and allowed them to come and go as they pleased when they were off duty. They even allowed smoking in bedrooms and sitting rooms. St. Thomas's had also granted this dispensation and Cynthia Nolan reported that '. . . you were certain to find several prospective Nightingales in a small study where, after they had changed their uniforms, they were permitted to smoke. This tremendous innovation was not really approved of by some of the True Nightingales.' Considerably to the surprise of some of the more traditional members of the profession, all these relaxations of rules did not cause a collapse of hospital discipline.

The nursing profession did not leave the battle for better conditions to outside bodies. The College of Nursing, the leading professional organization, pressed for better pay and shorter hours, but its enthusiasm was dampened by the knowledge that most voluntary hospitals simply could not afford to pay up. The more militant nurses joined trades unions. The National Association of Local Government Officers, the National Union of County Officers, the National Union of Public Employees, the Transport and General Workers' Union and many others all lobbied for recruits from this untapped source. Opposition to strike action, rapid turnover of staff and the influence of the matron's stern presence made recruitment difficult. Nonetheless trade union activity was strong enough and made enough noise to worry the College of Nursing and the Ministry of Health and was one of the chief reasons for the setting-up of the Athlone Committee to investigate conditions in the profession.

The Athlone Committee's Interim Report not only recommended better pay, shorter hours and improved conditions but suggested that public grants should be made to voluntary hospitals to pay for carrying out these proposals. In addition it advised that assistant nurses should be given a recognized status and placed on a Roll, after producing evidence of character and suitability and of two years' training in an approved institute, plus a certificate that they were competent in the work. The Athlone Committee never published a final report because, at this cross-roads in the history of the nursing profession, war once again intervened.

12 | Sisters in Battledress

lad in battledress or army fatigues nurses dug foxholes on the
Anzio beachhead and waded ashore in North Africa and
Normandy. With tin helmets clapped firmly on their heads,
they learned how to dodge bullets and when to throw themselves to
the ground. They were captured in the Philippines, Hong Kong and
Singapore. They went up in the air and down with their ships. US
army nurses snugly dressed in sheepskin-lined flying suits flew in air
ambulances right up to the front line. Some even learned to
parachute. They did without clean clothes and beds, went short of
water and food – though rarely of medical supplies and personnel.
They served in every war zone and in every campaign. Everywhere
the troops went, the nurses went too. Nothing cheered up the
casualties more than the sight of a female nurse – even in trousers –
so, like the men, the nurses learned to 'take it'.

Air raids made it total war. Gas masks hung from stretchers in
civilian hospitals. Babies were born in bomb shelters and operations
performed by hurricane lamp. Frightened probationers smiled and
tried to inspire confidence in their patients as windows were blasted
in and incendiaries lit up the wards. Men and women went to Red
Cross and St. John's Ambulance classes and registered for duty at
first aid posts and in the shelters. No one was safe.

Medicine had come a long way since the First World War. Blood
transfusion units draped every hospital and hospital ship. (The
British Army developed a sophisticated system of central blood

*Nurses of 1939 take cover in a slit trench as a precaution against air raids. The
age of total war had arrived and, with it, the demands on nurses grew
correspondingly greater*

banks which was copied by the Americans.) Sulphonamide drugs helped in the treatment of such diseases as dysentery. Penicillin, the miracle antibiotic, was introduced, with amazing results. DDT was effective in eliminating such insect and rodent-born diseases as malaria and typhus. The troops were instructed in hygiene and such preventative measures as covering arms and legs after dusk in malaria country. Unfortunately these were not the only technological advances; medical units had to develop new methods for treating the burnt victims of tank or aircraft disasters.

Britain went to war on September 3, 1939, and a week later the first six army sisters landed at Cherbourg. The same night they were at work in a wing of a French naval hospital. Base hospitals, casualty clearing stations and hospital trains crossed the Channel and took up their positions. General Hospitals were established round Le Havre, Dieppe, Le Tréport, Etaples, Camiers and Boulogne. The medical services, like the British Expeditionary Force itself, settled down to fight the First World War all over again.

Nobody had much to do for the next eight months. Casualty clearing stations nursed local sick. One hospital, on a First World War site near Le Touquet, had only one appendix – a member of the unit – and one soldier with a bad foot to treat between arriving and evacuating. Then, on May 10, Germany invaded neutral Belgium, Holland and Luxembourg and began the race for the sea. Holland capitulated on May 14, and Belgium followed thirteen days later. Medical units which had rushed to the Belgian front retreated with equal speed. Incredulous sisters were ordered to pack up and run without having set eyes on a war victim. Others had to abandon everything and flee before the advancing Germans.

Everyone rushed for the coast, through burning towns, along machine-gunned roads clogged with refugees, down jammed and damaged railways, to ports that were being bombed out of existence. 'Refugees were pouring through the town in a never-ending procession, poor bewildered children, old men and women carrying large bundles and pushing pathetically overloaded prams and hand-carts. As was now becoming normal, sirens wailed almost ceaselessly, and aerial battles between our own and enemy aircraft were taking place over our heads at very frequent intervals,' an ambulance train sister wrote. Her train left Lille, loaded with wounded, just hours before the Germans marched in, and crawled through St. Omer to Calais. 'The congestion on the line was terrific, continuous dogfights were going on overhead and bombs bursting close by.' The train moved on to Etaples. 'On arrival we were met by very harassed French railway officials who informed us that the

Germans were only eight miles away and that the railway station was to be blown up . . . At about 19.30 we moved slowly along to Boulogne, which was being very heavily attacked from the air.'

The Belgian driver of one ambulance train, which had loaded up at Ninove with the Germans only a couple of miles away, could be induced only at gunpoint to take the train into France. All the signals were against him and the commanding officer had to get down and change every one. Another train arrived at Albert to find the town was being evacuated. Soon everyone except some drunken French infantrymen had fled, but the train was marooned as the line on either side of Albert had been bombed. Ambulances evacuated the train's wounded and at 11 pm, with the Germans only eight miles away, the sisters were ordered to leave the town. They tramped along the crowded roads and hitched a lift on a farm wagon as far as Doullens where they picked up a truck to Abbeville. Their train crawled out of town then stopped and the sisters had a ring-side view of the town being blitzed. They finished their journey in a Salvation Army canteen, the inside of which was saturated with blood from Abbeville wounded.

'We were subjected to raids daily and most of the day,' a sister stationed at a Casualty Clearing Station at Krouhelse reported. 'Our supply of blood had run out . . . The Officer Commanding of the advanced medical stores gave us all the equipment he possibly could to help facilitate work and still it never seemed possible to get through the amount of operations necessary.' The sisters were ordered out on May 29. Nurses evacuating a CCS at Béthune in two ambulances nearly fell into enemy hands. The driver of the second ambulance went over to a group of soldiers to ask their position and the sisters watched in horror as the soldiers motioned the man to put his hands up. They were Germans. The sisters escaped in the first ambulance.

Italy declared war on June 10 and Marshal Pétain, the new head of the French government, asked for an armistice on June 16, while hospitals were still evacuating. Sisters at the military hospital at Marseilles were warned that evacuation was imminent. 'We filled our own and the patients' pockets with everything they could hold that might be useful – soap, stores, clean linen, rolls of gauze, bandages, safety pins, medicine glasses. (Each sister also tied a pillow across her shoulders. She already had a case, gas mask, tin hat, bag of food and rug to carry).' They slipped out of harbour on June 18 on board a packed cargo boat and headed for Gibraltar, hugging the Spanish coast to avoid submarines. 'When we were near any large town or lookout, we were asked to keep all uniforms out of sight. The men in khaki sat down with blankets over them, the sisters took off their capes and hats, and the Naval Officers never wore uniform from Marseilles to Gibraltar.'

One of the last hospitals to evacuate left La Baule after France had capitulated. 'The little railway to St. Nazaire was supposed to take 20 minutes. Matron went ahead with the walking cases and I took the stretcher cases. The journey took six and a half hours with the Germans dive bombing and no food. The patients were restless wanting food and so I got a wounded officer up and combed his hair and he came and spoke to the men. Then we found the doors had been locked. We were terrified of fire.' Eventually they reached the ship. 'As I got to the top of the gangplank matron said, "Wherever have you been?" I thought it was such a silly remark I said, "I thought I wouldn't be back in France for a long time so I'd have a look round".' Thirteen hundred army sisters got out safely, though often with no more than the clothes they stood up in. Many felt they had run away and one sister was so ashamed that she could not bear to show her face outdoors for days.

While the little boats shuttled to and from the Dunkirk beaches taking off the troops, hospital ships and carriers tried to get in close enough to carry the wounded to safety. 'We reached Dunkirk (the two piers were burning and one broken in two) but were signalled to go and stand by,' one sister wrote of her June 9 sailing. 'We waited about four hours, expecting to be sent away as things looked hopeless, but finally we were signalled right into the inner harbour, past both piers, passing many burning ships and much debris. All ships' lights and torches were forbidden, but the burning piers etc. gave all the light we needed except on the stairs. Medical officers, ships' officers and crew helped to load and many, even those who had been stretcher cases, clambered over the side. Patients were packed in all available space and a number of non-wounded had managed to scramble onto the deck. Only one bomb fell near during actual loading. We moved out with nearly six hundred on board, past a destroyer just hit.'

The troops and nurses were home again, but not out of danger. Britain was now in the front line. The Battle of Britain raged overhead and the Blitz was shortly to get under way. One nurse who later served in the front line in both Egypt and Italy considered that she was never in greater danger than when she was training in Cardiff during the air raids. Military targets had already been bombed and adjacent hospitals had inevitably suffered. One of the first, in January 1940, was a small naval hospital by the submarine detector base at Portland. 'There was no warning because we were

In the winter of 1940 everyone in Britain was in the front line. Here, nurses of the Royal Infirmary, Cardiff, salvage what they can from the ruins of the hospital dispensary. The Nurses' Home was also hit in the raid

right on the Channel,' a sister said. 'Another nurse and I were playing tennis with two doctors and we heard the planes go over. One of the doctors said, "Ours I hope" and we looked up as sticks of bombs came down. We lay on the ground. The oil tanks nearby were hit but we weren't hurt. When we went back to the Mess the other sisters said, "We thought we were going to have to hold a memorial service".' Bombing became a regular feature of life at Portland and the sisters got used to nursing in tin hats. 'We had to stay in the wards with the ill patients who couldn't be moved. I wasn't frightened there. It was the beginning of the war and there was a lot of excitement attached to it.' The hospital was so badly damaged that, shortly after Dunkirk, the sisters were moved out.

Lucilla Andrews was a VAD in a military hospital in a permanent army camp on Salisbury Plain. Shortly after she started work in the Military Families Hospital the night raids began. Night after night she and the sisters moved women and babies down to the basement shelter. ' "Blast Jerry! He'll wake Mrs. Y and I hate cold scrambled eggs!" Sister General hauled off her cap, slammed on her tin hat and vanished. Sister Maternity damned all Germans. "My poor kid in first-stage is scared enough without Jerry." She flung her cap on the desk, grabbed her tin hat and fled for her women. I cursed under my breath, kicked off the electric fire switch, slapped the empty side plates over the three plates of scrambled eggs and fled for my babies . . . In the shelter Sister General was fixing cushions behind and spreading rugs over the women sitting on the floor. She had to go back to her floor as neither Mrs. H nor Mrs. Y could be moved.' That night Lucilla Andrews was summoned up to the labour ward on the top floor to help in an emergency. The baby was born safely. 'Instantly, the worst hell of that, or any other night for me that summer, was let loose. Impossible to differentiate between ack-ack shells, tracers, aircraft engines and explosions, but we all heard the small shrill whistle of one falling bomb. Every instinct I possessed demanded that I dived under Mrs. N's labour bed' – but she was too busy.

When the Blitz started in the late summer of 1940 practically every hospital was in danger of being hit by a falling bomb. Gladys Hardy, matron of a small hospital in vulnerable Battersea, had been lulled into a state of false security by the months of phoney war. She was snatching a weekend in Surrey when she heard about the first bombings, and rushed back to London. 'Never, as long as I live, shall I forget the sight which met my eyes as I stepped back into my little hospital, which I had left barely eighteen hours before. Where all had been peace, there was now chaos. Badly-injured patients lay helplessly everywhere. Mattresses had been hastily made up and were occupying all available space in the corridors, the hall, and even between the beds in the wards. The operating theatre could not cope with the many casualties, and there was a sickly odour everywhere. The mortuary was overflowing.'

Miss Hardy was frightened but she took it like a trooper, investing in a siren suit of a similar pattern to Churchill's and wearing it for the next eighty-nine nights. On the tenth day, the whole hospital had

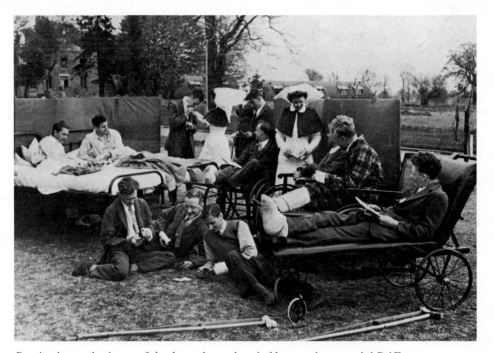

Despite the popular image of the cheery, brave, boys in blue, nursing wounded RAF air crew was not so romantic in reality. Here, nursing sisters pictured with their convalescent patients at an RAF hospital in the UK in 1943

to be evacuated because there was an unexploded bomb in the garden. The staff returned to 'a scene of utter desolation', but soon had the hospital functioning again. 'With grim regularity the Germans returned with the darkness, and the fearful din and inferno started all over again. Casualties were admitted in the first hour; blood transfusions were given and operations begun. Our electricity again failed, the cardboards were blown from the window-frames; flares and torches came back, and we worked, shivering and thirsty, for the gas was still off. It was a dreadful homecoming ... Our patients were mostly air-raid casualties, suffering from broken limbs, or with head or spinal injuries, etc. Some were straightforward surgical cases, with big stitches in their tummies. They were unable to help themselves, or to get out of bed by themselves, so that they just had to "stay put" and stick it out, whatever might be coming to them. Their courage and high spirits were remarkable to a degree . . .'

A tag about the three leading London teaching hospitals ran 'Guy's to flirt, Bart's to work, Thomas's if you're a lady.' When Lucilla Andrews applied to train at St. Thomas's in 1941 she found that the hospital itself was a very battered old lady indeed. 'It was the first time I had seen St. Thomas's. At first sight that morning it did not look like a hospital. It looked like parts of the City after the fire . . . I saw a jumble of three blocks standing close together and one of these looked less than intact.' St. Thomas's had started the war with nine buildings. 'All three had bricks instead of glass in the upper windows and their ground floors were hidden by anti-blast walls and stacks of sandbags. On either side of the standing blocks were the now omnipresent in London blackened roofless buildings, jagged walls, gaping glassless windows, piles of rubble and grime, and one semi-ruined block was still smouldering.'

While sisters were being driven out of France and nursing in tin hats in bomb-torn Britain, the peace-time way of life persisted in the Pacific and the Far East. A US navy nurse stationed on Guam reported tennis, golf, badminton, swimming, sailing and deep-sea fishing. Singapore boasted tennis, swimming and dancing. Then, on December 7, 1941, something happened on another island which not only put an end to all that but brought death and imprisonment to many nurses. The Japanese bombed Pearl Harbor.

'At 7.55 am as I was making out the reports, I heard a roar of planes, very close, and remarked, "Sounds like a plane falling." Then a great explosion – I said, "It crashed." The patients and I ran out on the third-floor porch overlooking Pearl Harbor and saw numerous planes diving – an explosion with each dive, then a great mass of black smoke; startled, I said, "Ye gods! It's the Japanese!" (But I still could not believe it.) . . . Shortly, the first casualties began to come in. I cannot describe the condition some of the cases were in. Everyone was still in a "daze". Phrases registered in my mind that I had never heard used, "All walking casualties in these trucks to Tripler," then I wondered what "shrapnel" and what "strafing" was . . . Then we heard the roar of the planes again – *the second attack* – someone yelled "DOWN", and we fell flat on the floor, and the planes were louder, louder; the bombs – nearer, nearer . . .'

Guam, the Philippines, Hong Kong and Singapore, all with their complement of nurses, fell in quick succession. 'It was a strange sensation to look upon ourselves reacting automatically to situations, keeping quiet voices in the midst of consternation, making rounds in the same manner, checking treatment and the administration of medications, supervising nursing care of the patients,' a US navy nurse wrote of the period after the fall of Guam. In the Philippines US nurses worked in the jungle hospitals of Bataan and the tunnel hospital in Corregidor. Some were evacuated by submarine, others were captured by the Japanese. One of the lucky ones wrote: 'After the first bombs fell there was so much work to do. We were annoyed because of the precious time we lost when we had to abandon the hospital and go into the trenches. The question of uniforms arose. White was too good a target and besides our uniforms were dirty after the first trip to the ground. Our blues would have been more serviceable, but our enemy was also wearing that colour. The final decision was khaki. As the days progressed and the raids were heavier, we were ordered into coveralls. This proved to be the only way to meet existing conditions.'

The first ever British nurses to become prisoners of war were captured when Hong Kong fell on Christmas Day 1941. After a period of intense anxiety with food, water and medical supply shortages, the sisters were removed to Stanley civilian internment camp where they stayed until victory in 1945. Singapore was even less prepared than Hong Kong but, as the Japanese made a lightning advance down the Malay peninsula and news of the fate of the Hong Kong nurses filtered through, belated attempts were made to evacuate women and children, and nurses from the four military hospitals.

A sister with the First Malayan General, which had evacuated Johore for Changi on Singapore Island, wrote: 'The situation now became desperate; we were in the direct line of fire from the enemy's heavy guns on the Johore coast, and in front of our own front line troops. The noise was terrific and the hospital postively rocked at times.' After two days of this the Japanese landed on Changi beach. 'They were so near we could hear their rifle fire.' They evacuated to Alexandra hospital. 'Another sleepless night. We were too exhausted to sleep and the guns kept up their incessant din. Morning came and constant air raids. The Principal Matron sent a message to say eighty of us were to be ready to go to the docks, with hand luggage only. Before we had time to move off, another message came. "Everybody is to go to the hospital at once as the enemy has advanced and is almost at the hospital gates." We went over, dodging machine-gun bullets en route. We were now experts at throwing ourselves prone on the ground. We sat and waited to be handed over to the Japs, but our troops pushed them back four miles and so gave us another chance to escape.' Two thousand five hundred passengers scrambled aboard the *Empire Star*, including fifty Australian sisters and eighty British nurses and VADs. The boat sailed in convoy on February 11. It was bombed for six hours and received several direct hits, causing many casualties, before reaching the safety of Java.

The fifty or so remaining sisters, including the principal matron, three matrons and a home sister, boarded the *Kuala* on Friday,

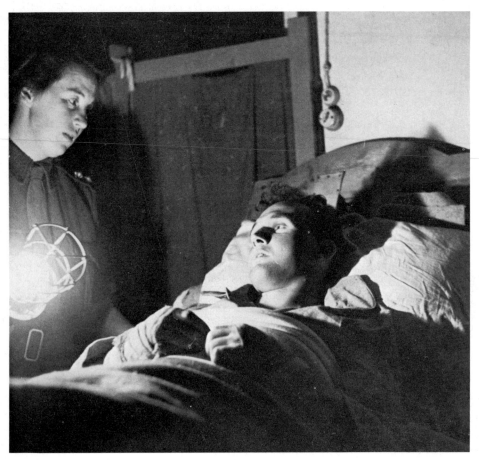

'Lady with the Lamp' – 1943 version

February 13. The vessel sailed that evening and next morning anchored off the small island of Pompong. 'A Japanese reconnaissance plane came over about 7 am and then a flight of six planes came over about 9.30 and bombed and sank a boat about a mile away from us . . . We were bombed at 10.45 am and got a direct hit through the Captain's Bridge, through to the boiler rooms, which burst the boilers. The ship was already on fire from the first raid . . . We had three raids on the ship, and they came over four times while we were swimming in the sea and dive bombed and machine gunned us.' The principal matron, two matrons and the home sister were never seen again. Some survivors eventually made their way to Sumatra and thence to Bombay, but others fell into Japanese hands when Sumatra fell.

This was not the first ill-organized evacuation in which British nurses had taken part. Just under a year after the fall of France, the same experience had occurred in Greece. 'The beauty of the mountains, the fields, the flowers, the lovely pinewoods running down to the sea, the clear sunny atmosphere, the laughing hospitality of the people, the spirit of freedom,' one sister wrote lyrically of the military hospital at Kephissia. In April Germany invaded Greece and soon 'The day came when there was a complete silence from our guns; there wasn't a plane of ours to be seen; we knew then they had gone and didn't like it much.' The nurses liked it even less as the Germans advanced nearer and nearer and more and more British personnel were withdrawn. 'Well, that's the limit. They now took away the British Guards and there was I alone on the top of Olympus with three tiny little Greek Guards who were scared stiff.' Constant bombing had made evacuation more dangerous than staying put, but on April 26 the remaining Australian and British sisters managed to scramble out and reach safety via Crete.

With British and American nurses packing up and fleeing from all parts of the world it seemed odd to talk about a nurse shortage, but the vastly increased demands of the services and, in Britain, the needs of civilian air raid casualties, caused just that. America had started making preparations to cope while still officially neutral. As early as 1940, national nursing organizations and federal agencies had formed the Nursing Council of National Defense (later the National Nursing Council for War Service), which made a national survey of registered nurses. The survey found that, in war, there would not be enough nursing staff to go round, as the demands of the army and navy would leave civilian nursing seriously understaffed. For the first time, the government stepped in to support civilian nurse training. Between July 1, 1941, and June 30, 1943, the government financed refresher courses, awarded grants to teachers and nursing personnel preparing for advanced positions in nursing and encouraged women to enrol for nurse training. In 1940 the Red Cross had started to train nurses' aides and a year later the Office of Civilian Defense asked the Red Cross to train 100,000 aides a year. The course covered eighty hours of instruction over a seven-week period and was intended to fit the aides to do basic nursing work similar to that done by the British Civil Nursing Reserve nursing auxiliaries and the members of Voluntary Aid Detachments. By the end of 1945, 212,000 women had been certified. The government also sponsored the Cadet Nurse Corps. Under the Nurse Training Act, students were given financial aid, books, uniform, tuition fees and were paid a small allowance. In return they pledged themselves to join the services or do essential civilian nursing. For their part, schools had to accelerate their rate of training, reducing the length of their courses from thirty-six months to thirty. Between July 1943 and October 15, 1945, 170,000 cadets had entered training and two-thirds had graduated.

In Britain, instead of the great Territorial force general hospitals and hundreds of auxiliary hospitals of the First World War, the government had planned emergency hospitals which would take military wounded and sick as well as civilian and Civil Defence casualties. A Civil Nursing Reserve was recruited to staff the new emergency hospitals, to replace nurses from civilian hospitals who joined the services, to man first aid posts and evacuation trains and to undertake district nursing in areas receiving evacuees. Trained nurses and assistant nurses were recruited and nursing auxiliaries enrolled for a course of hospital training. The Joint War Organization of the British Red Cross Society and the Order of St. John was at first asked by the War Office to provide only six convalescent homes for officers. These were not found to be enough and from 1940 the War Organization established convalescent homes and auxiliary hospitals for other ranks, civilian air raid casualties among patients, and in general the 'parent' hospital VADs were released in the hope that they would join the Civil Nursing Reserve. The rest continued to work in military, naval, RAF and auxiliary hospitals. Thousands of Red Cross and St. John volunteers were employed in Civil Defence first aid posts. Hospitals in big cities were dispersed to surrounding areas to reduce the risk of casualties among patients and in general the 'parent' hospital received only local cases which it evacuated whenever possible.

The recruitment of assistant nurses to the Civil Nursing Reserve gave a boost to official recognition of a second class of nurse. The Nurses Act of 1943 gave the General Nursing Council power to set up a roll of assistant nurses. *Bona fide* practising nurses would be admitted at first, but future enrolment would follow a two-year course of instruction. There was still a serious shortage of nurses, particularly for tuberculosis, mental and chronic hospitals. The government launched a publicity campaign which had some success, as conscription of women was being introduced and nursing held a far greater attraction for middle-class girls than most of the alternatives. Various other attempts were made to control and direct the movement of nurses, but these resulted only in improvements in the maternity field.

The services had no trouble with recruitment. The Queen Alexandra's Nurses increased their establishment from 550 pre-war to 11,024 by September 1945, including Reserve and TANS. (From 1940 the TANS were absorbed into the QAs.) In 1941 QAs were granted emergency commissions in the Army and these became regular commissions two years later. Queen Alexandra's Royal Naval Nursing Service grew from eighty-five sisters plus fifty-five Reservists when war broke out to a total of 1,129 in April 1945. Princess Mary's Royal Air Force Nursing Service, created in 1918, started the war with 184 regular members and sixty-nine Reservists. By March 1944, the service numbered 1,024. About 70,500 nurses had been assigned for duty in the US army and navy by the end of the war. Although there were always enough nurses to go round, so many experienced nurses left to get married that both America and Britain dropped the marriage bar during the war.

Before the war, nursing in the services was exclusive, selection rigorous and training careful. As a pre-war navy nurse remembered: 'The Mess was very rank-conscious – the laundry matron used to hang out our dresses in order of rank.' When war broke out the urgent need for nurses made such careful preparation out of the question. One QA called up in October 1939 reported to Everleigh Manor, Tidworth, for basic training. 'We were nearly all reservists who hadn't done any military nursing, and a few Territorials who'd taken a few weeks' course. About ten of the older ones were sent to the military hospital so they could learn and come back and teach the rest of us.' The uniforms, hurriedly made up in London, were so mixed up in the packing that they took days to sort out. 'We were issued with tin hats which we called "battle bowlers", which we had to trim with leaves for camouflage and which we painted sand colour when we got to the Middle East, and with our field kit – bed, collapsible wash basin and so on. None of us had ever been to war and didn't know what to do with it. The RAMC men showed us.' Another QA, recruited in 1943, remembered, 'We had one hilarious half hour being taught how to salute.' Everything else they just had to pick up as they went along. 'We suddenly found we didn't have nurses, but RAMC other ranks, usually ex-bricklayers or butchers. It was all very different to a young sister just beginning. We were starting three or four new ways of life at the same time.'

Some of the nurses flung out of France found themselves temporarily unemployed, but first the demands of the Western Desert and then of the Far East brought instant action. India served as a vast military hospital for casualties from Burma, Malaya, Iraq and North Africa – it was safer to ship them there than back to Britain. But, until Japan entered the war, the work was mostly of a peacetime nature, carried out in permanent military hospitals. One regular QA spent a very quiet time in Bangalore and Poona before being posted to Kohima on the border between Assam and Burma.

'The climate was cold in winter. It was an isolated place, one road up and one down. All supplies had to come up the road, and we lived on tinned stuff with meat on the hoof once a month – the poor little beasts were driven up the road and then slaughtered.' The hospital was in huts with earth floors and coconut matting. 'Rats were the worst thing there – they came up through the floors and ran along the top of the mosquito nets. You'd lose a cake of soap and find it half eaten blocking the hole where the rat had tried to take it away.' As the Japanese overran Burma, the hospital got busier. 'Imphal was overrun and they started coming up the road towards us. At three hours notice we upped and packed. We were furious at being sent away, furious before we'd heard a shot fired. We may have felt different if we had.'

This nurse was posted next to a hutted hospital set in the tea plantations at Dibrughar, where she continued to nurse the men from Burma. 'Many were not wounded, more exhausted. Some hadn't had their boots off for months and we had to scrape their socks off.' The place, she said, was swarming with Americans. 'They were a great trial. They hadn't seen a woman for ages. We lived in bamboo huts, two to a hut, and an American face would appear at the window. "Do you want to come out?" They were pretty good really.'

The unexpected extremes of climate were a greater trial than the soldiers. A US nurse in an evacuation hospital set up in virgin jungle reported: 'The winter of 1943 was very cold, a damp, chilly coldness that left one almost paralysed. Our Sibley [belly] stoves were not issued till quite late in the year, one to a ward. They were practically useless for heating purposes because they were so small and the woven bamboo walls were so open. We didn't bathe the patients till around 11 o'clock after the sun took the chill out of the air . . . The fuel situation was desperate. There was no coal and no saws to cut the wood.' The monsoon season was no better. 'The continual rains, oppressive heat, and heavy mud were exhausting. Sometimes the wards were inches deep in water.' But the beauty of the surroundings made up for all discomforts. 'After a rain the foliage shines with freshness. At night the stars and the moon appear at their best through the towering trees overhung with vines . . . We awaken in the early morning to the music of birds or the noise of a band of monkeys.'

While islands in the Far East tumbled like skittles to the Japanese, those in the Mediterranean were made of sterner stuff. Crete had fallen at the end of May 1941 but Cyprus, Gibraltar and Malta held out. Cyprus, in fact, suffered scarcely any enemy action. Gibraltar,

Off duty, but still in battledress. Nurses were sent to every theatre of war – from France to Burma

where a hospital had been installed in a huge underground cavern, was always busy but never had to endure the punishment meted out to Malta, where the naval hospital and the military hospitals were all sited near military targets and suffered accordingly. The first Italian air raids were in June 1940, but the bombing did not become serious until the Germans took over in December 1941. The naval hospital was so badly hit that the sisters were transferred to the military hospital at Imtarfa. They did not escape the bombing there, though, as the hospital was right next to the aerodrome. The Grand Harbour lay in ruins, the civilian population retreated to the underground shelters and an emergency operating theatre was cut out of the rock. Everything ran out – food, fuel, theatre supplies. Gloves were worn only for major operations. The sisters went around bare-legged as the last of their stockings fell apart. There was rarely fresh meat, bacon or fruit and not much of anything else.

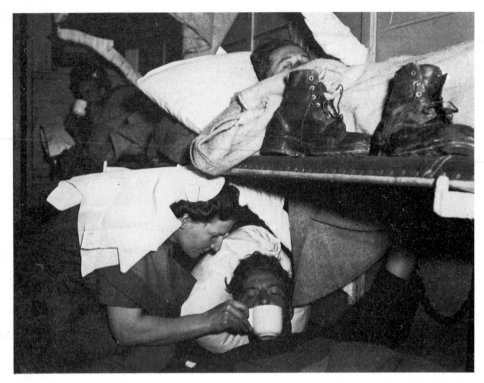

Treatment on a hospital train. Though the conditions look the same, the standard of treatment had risen immeasurably since the First World War, largely thanks to the discovery of drugs such as penicillin

In November 1942, in one of the last raids, the Sisters' Mess was hit and two sisters badly hurt. The others were amused to notice that from the damaged wall of matron's office a sign still hung, slightly askew: 'Don't worry, it may never happen.'

One of the first hospitals on active service in Africa was situated in a college building just down the Nile from Khartoum. The sisters received casualties from the battles with the Italians, and fought their own battles with the desert climate. 'Bed-making in the wards merely consisted of rearranging two sheets. The heat was so intense that sisters have been known to heat an iron in the sun to press handkerchiefs ... The sand-storms are indescribable, and thoroughly disheartening. A nice clean ward could be reduced to a sand-covered horror in ten minutes. The few times we had rain, which was always preceded by a sand-storm, the downfall was so heavy that we felt we would be washed away.'

In 1941 this unit moved forward to an Italian hospital on the road to the port of Massawa in newly recaptured Eritrea. 'When we arrived many of our first patients were South and East African troops. It was here that we first began to see many tropical diseases such as bilharzia, kala-azar and amoebic hepatitis. We also had hundreds of cases of malaria and many types of dysentery.' Each ward was in a separate bungalow. 'Being on night duty was rather an eerie experience, especially if one had to go from ward to ward, as out of the dark would come strange noises from the baboons and hyenas in the surrounding hills. The camp was encircled by barbed wire, but people frequently swore they saw wild animals in the grounds.' The site was isolated, the only recreation was the twice-weekly cinema which often broke down, but one of the medical officers ran Italian classes and the staff organized their own dramatic society.

Nurses' experiences in the Middle East ranged from the peace and quiet – indeed the boredom – of base hospitals, often established in huts in the desert away from all amusements and with the inevitable accompanying sand-storms, to the dangers and elation of Tobruk under siege and a mobile military hospital right behind the front line. The sight of the sisters inspired Robert Liddell to write:

'Where once Lot's wife looked back in horror
To see God's judgment blast Gomorrah,
Today the Sodom sunshine blisters
Queen Alexandra's nursing sisters.'

Palestine was a popular spot for nurses on holiday.

Nurses started arriving in the Middle East in significant numbers at the end of 1939. At this stage it was still possible to travel through the Mediterranean – later, convoys had to go round the Cape. As usual, the nurses did not know where they were going until they got there. One nurse arriving after Christmas 1939 only knew she was in Haifa by a sign on a hotel. From Haifa the unit was posted to Jerusalem, to the Kaiser's Palace in an empty shell of a monastery on the Mount of Olives. The first few weeks were spent fitting up the hospital and being given lectures on military discipline, 'How you can't ask an NCO to scrub floors and so on.' Their first war casualties were members of the rival Vichy and Free French forces. 'One night there was a hell of a row in the corridor and I went to find out what was happening. A man who'd just been operated on would be put into the next empty bed, and two patients had started fighting. I heard from the Sergeant that they'd put a Vichy and a Free French next to each other.' As the Western Desert campaign escalated, patients of all nationalities poured in. In October 1941 the hospital was handed over to the Australians. Half the unit went to India, the other half to Geneifa, halfway down the Suez Canal, where they were kept on forty-eight-hour standby for months.

Tobruk and its garrison had an adventurous war. Besieged by Rommel from April 1941 to December when the Germans withdrew, it again came under attack as the Allies retreated westward and eventually fell in June 1942, to be relieved yet again as the Allies advanced after El Alamein. The matron and three sisters of the hospital ship *Somersetshire* were the first women to go ashore after the siege was first lifted in December 1941: 'Everyone was very pleased to see us and on our way back to the jetty a lad of the Royal Tank Corps ran out of a shattered building and, touching me on the shoulder, said in a bewildered voice, "You are a woman then; you are real." He then stepped back and saluted, saying, "Pardon, but I thought I must have had 'one over the eight' last night; I haven't seen a woman for over ten months".'

Perhaps it was this sort of reception that kept the authorities dithering for so long before finally sending sisters 'up the desert', to join the men of their unit at Tobruk. But finally in early 1942 the sisters twiddling their thumbs at Geneifa received the good news. 'No sooner had we arrived than we saw our first bombing and had to take cover.' There was just one hospital in a bomb-blasted Italian

Japanese nurses pictured at work in the Far East. The nurses seen here were the equivalent of Britain's VADs and are continuing their work under British supervision after Japan's surrender in 1945

barracks for a garrison of 30,000 men. 'It was a real field hospital – patients' beds were stretchers on the floors and there were no sheets or anything.' Soon after the sisters arrived casualties started to pour in. 'Patients were often without beds and the accommodation became inadequate as the raids took toll of the "wards". They were nursed on the concrete floor on stretchers or blankets. The stench from wounds was indescribable. We all worked day and night. "Time off" became a joke. We assisted the team of surgeons in shifts but soon this procedure had to be abandoned and one worked until one became so weary that a rest on a blanket in the Sisters' Mess became the only respite.'

The shelling and bombing continued day and night. The hospital was hit time and again but, amazingly, no sister was hurt. 'The men were marvellous. They could be almost dead and not ask for something because they knew others were worse off. The German troops were really heroic, very tough. The stretcher bearers brought in everyone. We didn't know who we were operating on half the time. There was no question of the Germans being held back till the Allies had been treated. Worst cases first.'

The water ration went down to three-quarters of a pint per person a day. 'So no one got bathed or washed. In the beginning we thought, how ghastly, but at the end we hadn't washed for so long we didn't want to. When our clothes got too filthy to wear we just threw them away. I was bug ridden. Medical supplies were not very good. We were doing so many operations that the instruments were getting blunt and we hadn't water for sterilization. One of the orderlies suggested we try lemonade. Of course, when we heated it, it fizzed up. We had no packs of sterile dressings. We could tell things were getting worse. We would patch people up and as long as they could hold a gun they went back to the line. In the beginning we sent them down to base.'

It became increasingly obvious that the town must fall and, to the sisters' distress, they were ordered to leave. 'To say *au revoir* to the officers and men who were our colleagues seemed ludicrous! They would soon be made prisoners of war and put into the cages behind the wire which had been prepared by our troops for the enemy. I'll never forget leaving. It felt like scuttling.' Going up to Tobruk, this sister had left a suit at a cleaners in Alexandria run by a most civil Greek. Retreating, she went to collect it and met a very different attitude. 'He had my suit and panama hat brought out and placed on the floor at his feet, whereupon he stamped on them in rage and spat in my face.' Perhaps this Greek was an exception, or maybe attitudes changed with the tide of battle, because a sister arriving later in the Canal Zone reported that the Greek manager of the officers' club 'always brought very sticky confits round for the sisters, and bottles of perfume'.

Hospitals took in patients of all nationalities and had to adapt to customs which seemed strange. A sister visiting the Indian section of a hospital at Kirkuk saw the patients squatting on the desert to eat their meal. 'Sister asked me not to approach them lest my Christian shadow should pollute their food.' A desert hospital sister wrote of her first batch of prisoners of war: '245 strange and unfamiliar names we tried to sort out that night, and as over half the patients were native troops, language and customs presented quite a difficulty. The night staff willingly coped with the situation, but what a wealth of pantomime and gesticulation must have been expended by the orderly to convince a patient wrapped in his blankets with pyjamas round his head that such was not our idea of suitable hospital attire.' It transpired that for religious reasons the man could not appear bare headed, so turbans were improvised out of towels.

Foreign climes and patients of all nationalities brought exciting cases for the nurse. A navy sister at the combined army and navy hospital at Alexandria came across smallpox, anthrax and the plague as well as an epidemic of bad diphtheria. Another sister posted to the Canal Zone, which she found 'desperately boring', said, 'The only thing about Suez was that it was a transit area for India and most of the intake had tropical diseases which were interesting. Lots of malaria and dysentery – not much surgery. Suez could be out of bounds every now and then because of smallpox or bubonic plague. We had one or two cases of the plague among the troops which were fatal and one or two of smallpox.'

The battle raged to and fro across the Western Desert until July 1942, when the Allies took up their last-ditch position in a line from El Alamein, sixty miles west of Alexandria. It was a trying time for the sisters at the Army and Navy hospital, who were within hearing of the guns. The city was subjected to terrific bombing and shelling – 'And that's when we discovered that the laundry staff were spies. They were signalling to the pilots.' Ambulances brought back casualties right from the front line and all but the most dangerously ill were evacuated to Cairo. 'The navy and the WRNS left us and the big army people left us until there was just the hospital. The head chap of the Italian prisoners of war went to our Colonel and asked if the PoWs could be moved inland because they didn't want to be captured by the Germans. The names of nurses who were to be evacuated were down on a list but we didn't go because the turning point came before we left.' (Many Italian PoWs had settled happily and satisfactorily into the congenial work of mess waiting.)

In the autumn of 1942, the Allies began to drive Rommel east across the desert, hotly pursued by the sisters and staff of the mobile military hospitals, and American and British forces landed in North Africa. Immediately behind the troops came the nurses. One ship carrying both British and American nurses was torpedoed (eight QAs were lost) and the principal matron at once set about launching a campaign for more practical clothing than grey cotton dresses for her sisters. 'The ordnance has not yet received any women's clothing, but I went and saw them at once, and have arranged for battle dress, men's underclothing, brush and comb, etc., to be issued to each sister,' she wrote to the matron-in-chief, following it up with, 'I do wish we could be allowed to wear khaki. The living conditions for most of the sisters out here are very primitive, almost all are living in tents in ankle-deep mud and with very primitive sanitary arrangements, and smart grey and scarlet suits are most unsuitable and will hardly ever be worn.' She was delighted to learn that khaki uniform as worn by the women of the Auxiliary Territorial Service was on its way.

The US nurses who waded ashore in North Africa were the first of their nation to go into desert duty. 'Army nurses at the front line live the lives of soldiers,' one reported. 'They are used to digging and diving into slit trenches . . . they stay awake and on duty as many hours as necessary; and in a matter of a few hours they can take down a tent city housing hundreds of men.' 'There are girls here who never washed their own clothes, when they were in the States,' a nurse wrote, 'and who now take a bath in a helmet full of water and then wash their clothes in it.'

Sisters in several battle areas were changing from scarlet and grey to the more practical battledress. Geraldine Edge and Mary Johnston, reporting to the Hospital Carrier *Leinster*, were pleased to find that, 'we were fortunately all of the same mind and considered slacks were the only suitable wear for women as well as men; flimsy grey cotton frocks and Army modesty capes and floating veils do not go well with a wind on the boat deck, bending over stretchers, or climbing up to the top bunks.' From January 1944 khaki was generally adopted for nurses overseas, largely because of the difficulty in getting scarlet and grey cloth. In spite of the preferences of nurses in the field, the Nursing Board had greeted the proposals for change from the Board of Trade with displeasure, viewing 'with great disquiet any alterations', and being prepared 'to accept such a change only as a most urgent wartime measure'. American nurses in

Nurses found themselves in widely varying conditions all over the world. Here three sisters watch work in progress on a new ward in Gibraltar's underground hospital.

the Pacific had early adopted soldiers' fatigues and coveralls as the only practical dress for leaping in and out of foxholes and tramping through the jungle. In 1944 white uniforms, the sign of the trained nurse, were abandoned in favour of a more easily laundered brown and white stripe for overseas wear.

Following the Sicily landings in the summer of 1943, the Italian campaign began in the autumn, and hospital ships started a shuttle to ferry casualties across the Mediterranean to North African ports. The *Leinster* was loaned to the Americans and set off for Sicily to load up. 'As soon as the boats were hoisted up to the deck with their precious loads, the stretcher bearers stepped forward, and by the light of shaded torches were guided to the reception room. Here one of the Medical Officers received and sorted the patients, while a sister stood by to give injections of serum or morphia, and an orderly gave them some fruit juice or water to drink; then the same bearers once more picked up the stretcher and took the patients to the selected ward. There were intermittent air raids, but none had time to take them seriously.' In September the *Leinster* was once more in British hands. 'It was lovely to be dealing with Tommies once more. They always seem so pleased to see us and it was grand to hear their caustic humour again. Their grumbles, too, we understood, as doubtless the American nurses understood the humour and grumbles of their own men folk. Many of them were badly wounded, but so brave about it all . . .' Not that the sisters on the *Leinster* had spotted any weaknesses in the attitude of their American patients.

Hospital ships which could not complete loading in one day were often sent out to sea to cruise round for the night. This was meant to be for their own protection as they could then put on all their lights without illuminating their warlike neighbours, and claim full rights under the Geneva Convention. The *Leinster* was ordered out to sea with four other hospital vessels during the Salerno landings. All ships had their lights on but they were bombed. Fires started aboard the *Leinster* and the *Newfoundland* was hit. Later the *Leinster* and two other hospital ships were night cruising off the Anzio beachhead when they got mixed up with a convoy and the *St. David* was sunk. On another occasion a sister on the *Oxfordshire* who had been working on the lower deck surfaced to learn that the Germans had actually been on board. 'We were Red Cross and had the Red Cross on the ship but they came on board to look round in case we were gun running. The only gun on the ship was one the captain had in case of mutiny and he kept that under glass.' But her most unnerving moment had been when she first joined the ship. 'We were told that there were lifeboats for only half of us and the rest would go down.'

Medical units advanced through Italy in the desperately cold winter of 1943–44. A sister who arrived at Andria near Bari in September 1943 remembered: 'We didn't have any warm clothes. Officer shops came round and we stood in the snow and bought long woolly knickers. Then we were issued with battledress. The tents had concrete floors and we sterilized over a primus. Parties would go round knocking the snow off the roofs of tents. On night duty once we had bedded down the patients we had nothing to do so we sat still in tents in the snow wearing everything we could get on. We had Valor heating stoves and hopefully put three down the centre of the tents but the gale blew straight through. Patients had their blankets right over their heads to keep warm.'

Life in Italy was rather grim and serious after post-crisis Egypt.

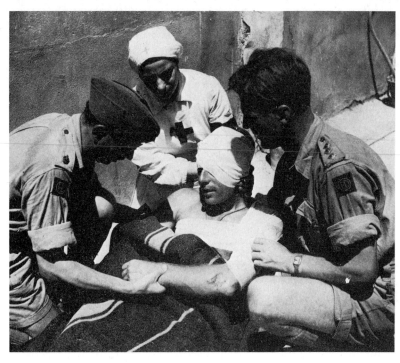

Even in the age of total war, the bonds of the Red Cross proved international. Nurse Yolanda Girasole, of the Italian Red Cross, helps care for a wounded British soldier after her own capture during the invasion of Sicily in 1943

The patients had reasonable food but, 'We didn't have any fresh meat at all, only Spam. We had dehydrated meat which was rather like eating tobacco and dehydrated potato in small cubes which were very tough and American tinned so-called chicken for a treat. It was nutritionally adequate but no place for a gourmet.' Her patients were Yugoslav partisans flown out by the RAF. 'Churchill had promised medical aid and we were it.' Many had old wounds which had not received hospital treatment when they were first received in case the Germans had found out that the patient was a partisan. 'A lot were so emaciated they were like Belsen victims.' The Yugoslav doctors and the British unit got on excellently. 'Medical discipline crossed all frontiers.' The patients had better food than the sisters with fresh meat and tomatoes daily. In spite of this, suspicion grew that the British were 'taking Yugoslav money and using it for Imperialistic purposes, so we brought British casualties into the wards to show they were treated exactly the same as the Yugoslavs'.

The American and British nurses at the Anzio beachhead were as near to the fighting as they could be. The beachhead was under constant bombardment, the nurses slept in slit trenches they had dug themselves and waded through a sea of mud into which the legs of the stretchers sunk. Hospitals were hit time and time again but nurses stayed by their patients. During one particularly nasty night attack, which knocked out the electricity and blasted the medical personnel off their feet with concussion, one American nurse admitted, 'I wanted to jump under the operating table but before I could yield to the impulse I had to help lower litter cases to the floor. Then I noticed that a patient on the operating table had his helmet near him, so I put it over his head to give him that much protection. Two of our enlisted medical men were hit and I just did not have time to stop working.'

In Western Europe, D-Day was approaching. In Britain nurses were preparing for the great invasion. Some American nurses took a fourteen-week course to equip them for combat activities. QAs practised gas drill, climbing nets and pitching tents. Within days of the Normandy landings on June 6, 1944, nurses were leaping from landing craft onto the beaches, to the amazement and delight of the watching troops, some of whom marked the event with a chorus of 'Nursie, come over here and hold my hand.' Hospitals were assembled in fields, only to be leapfrogged by later units who followed the armies forward, passing through towns where flags celebrating liberation still festooned the streets. Residents rushed out to press fruit and flowers onto these liberators. Forward general hospitals found themselves operating as field hospitals or casualty clearing stations. The first eleven US army nurses crossed the Rhine on March 13, 1945, six days after their troops had secured a bridgehead. Montgomery followed on March 23 and British nurses followed. Pushing deeper into Germany the Allied nurses found themselves caring for the German civilian sick and undertaking stomach-churning work in the liberated concentration camps – duties which continued after Germany surrendered on May 7, 1945.

Meanwhile the Americans had re-conquered the Pacific. In the mid-summer of 1944 the marines invaded Guam and a base hospital was set up for the Iwo Jima and Okinawa battles. The casualties were almost overwhelming. The following year the first contingent of army nurses to return to the Philippines got to work on Leyte. Twenty-eight navy nurses, the first white women seen on that particular Pacific island, landed at Tinian in the Marianas – and were delighted to find flush toilets and baths with hot water. Prisoners of war were freed and nursed back to health. Japan surrendered on August 14.

13 | Equal but Different

Nurses have come a long way. In little more than a hundred years they have progressed from being considered drunken, ignorant, promiscuous ward servants to rank as professionals, highly skilled and academically qualified – an achievement unequalled in any comparable field. Yet, in the public eye, nursing has never reached the status of other professions. Traditionally, their sex alone has told against nurses. Historically, two trends in their advance have militated against the appearance of equal rank: the apprenticeship system of on-the-job training, and their subordination to another profession – medicine.

Both these developments were justified in the early years. Doctors, nervous of their own status and incomes, had to be reassured that these new trained women would not be in competition with them. This was particularly true in America where, in the early years, many nurses were being as well educated as doctors. The determination of highly trained nurses to accept a subordinate position led to the 'nurse-doctor game', the rules for which state that it is perfectly all right for doctors to accept help and advice from nurses, so long as nobody knows about it and everyone agrees that medicine is superior to nursing. This farce was reinforced by the American nurse practice acts, which defined and therefore restricted the work nurses could do. To militant feminists, the doctor-nurse relationship epitomizes all that is worst in man-woman role playing.

On-the-job training ensured that basic skills were learned by constant practice and observation under supervision. Unfortunately hospitals came to rely so heavily on student labour that class work was often sacrificed to the staffing needs of the wards. Women who wanted to take a broader view of their patients' welfare, beyond the hospital walls, had either to take courses after completing their basic training or stay out of nursing altogether and move into the expanding field of social work.

An increasing recognition that nursing skills are different from, and not just junior to, medical skills, has led to more independent and academically demanding roles for nurses. American nurses became concerned about the status of their profession during the Second World War, and the years since have seen a steady move away from hospital training schools towards a college education. Three separate routes towards nurse registration developed. Community colleges began offering a two-year associate degree course in the 1950s and by 1972 they were graduating thirty-seven per cent of all nurses. A declining number of hospital training schools continued to run diploma programmes. Baccalaureate degree courses, in which students take regular college courses in sciences and humanities and major in nursing, are increasing. The profession has been further stratified by the introduction of a second grade, the licensed practical or vocational nurse, similar to the British enrolled nurse, and by the increasing recognition of nursing aides and orderlies.

These developments, while strengthening the academic achievements of nurses, have created their own different problems. In the early days of college education, graduate nurses moved quickly into top administrative or teaching posts. Now those jobs are increasingly filled by holders of masters' or doctors' degrees. Associate degree programmes in community colleges were originally intended to train technical nurses capable of understanding how machines as well as people worked. In practice this distinction has not often been made. Holders of baccalaureate degrees, associate degrees and hospital diplomas found themselves after the same jobs. As far as hospital administrators were concerned, a registered nurse was a registered nurse and they were not going to pay more for a liberal education.

One of the results of improved academic standards has been the separation of registered nurse from patient. With the growth of the licensed practical nurse and ancillary workers the registered nurse has increasingly found herself supervising a team. This is particularly true of the baccalaureate degree nurse who is more likely to move into administrative or teaching duties. To reach the top of the nursing hierarchy may be good for a nurse's status, but it deprives her of the satisfaction of caring for sick people – the reason

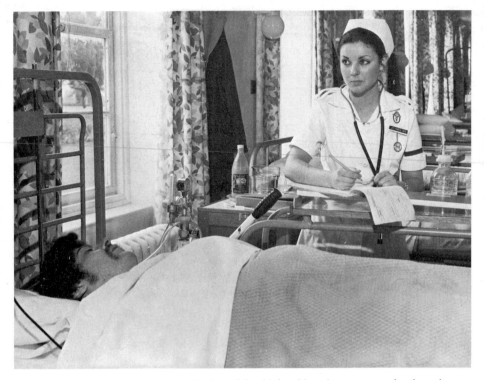

A student nurse at work. One of the chief problems in recent years has been the conservatism of many parts of the nursing profession, especially when contrasted with some of its rivals. It is now no longer the only respectable career that women can follow

she joined the profession in the first place. A movement grew in the 1960s to bring the best-qualified nurses back to the bedside without wasting their superior education and training. One of the most interesting results of this trend was the development of the nurse practitioner.

The idea of the nurse practitioner was pioneered in Canada as a way of using registered nurses more efficiently and the concept soon spread to the United States. The nurse practitioner has taken over many of the functions in primary health care of the medical practitioner. She may take medical histories, make physical examination and order such back-ups as X-rays and laboratory tests, make diagnoses, recommend treatment, teach and counsel and co-ordinate care programmes and make referrals to doctors when necessary for more specific treatment. Patients attending a team practice make an appointment with doctor or nurse according to need. Nurse practitioners have set up on their own or grouped together in clinics, or specialized in, for example, paediatrics, obstetrics and gynaecology, psychiatry and mental

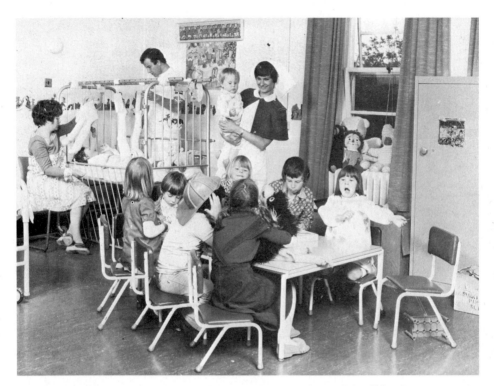

A sister in a children's ward. Nursing's future is today uncertain, as the traditional dedication battles with increasing awareness of exploitation. However, many countries have realized that times have changed and that more opportunities have to be provided to meet this challenge

health. The functions of the nurse practitioner and the relationship between nurse and doctor are still evolving, but the basis is collaboration rather than subordination. Where doctor and nurse work as a team the doctor refers patients to the nurse as well as the other way round.

Basic nurse training programmes did not initially include many of the skills the nurse practitioner needed, so experimental courses were established. A British nurse who attended a six-month programme at Indiana University reported that during the first three months there were lectures on physical diagnosis, paediatrics, obstetrics, medicine, surgery and specialized subjects including infectious diseases, orthopaedics and skin diseases. Students also spent at least thirty-two hours in maternal clinics learning such techniques as taking cervical smears and fitting IUDs, and being instructed in physical diagnoses, history taking and physical examinations. The second three months were the clinical period, during which the students worked under the direct instruction of a family doctor, an internist and a paediatrician. The British nurse told the *Nursing Mirror*, 'I felt I had learned to approach my patient with more understanding and was better equipped to deal with any kind of medical problem.' Recently the trend has been towards including such nurse practitioner skills as physical and psychological diagnosis in the baccalaureate degree programme while more advanced training is given a masters' degree level.

While American and Canadian nurses have taken giant strides forward towards an equal but different status with medicine, the profession in Britain, the cradle of modern nursing, has lagged behind both in attitude and attainment. The Briggs Committee on Nursing, which reported in 1972, found students still complaining about poor living conditions, silly rules, too much harshness over trivia and lack of perspective, exhausting training and too long a day. Turning to personal accounts, it stated that 'Almost all emphasise the shifts in responsibility associated with daily work – at one moment independence, sometimes frightening independence, at another subordination, sometimes oppressive subordination.' One nurse wrote: 'Training tends to destroy initiative, discretion, common sense and dampens the enthusiasm which most nurses have to get to know and look after ill people.' Five years later, critics of the system were still complaining that junior nurses were left in charge of wards, educational programmes were interrupted as nurses were moved in response to staff shortages, night duty might come too early and too often and that theory and practice were unlikely to coincide.

In spite of these depressing reports, which sound as if little has changed for student nurses since the *Lancet* and Athlone committee reports, there have been advances in nurse education in the last few years. As well as a great increase in specialist post-training courses, universities and hospital training schools have combined to provide four- to five-year courses leading to state registration and a degree. These attract into the profession girls with university entrance qualifications and equip them academically for higher teaching and administrative posts and intellectually to take a broad view of patients' needs.

The training period is divided between hospital and college and the development of this sort of course, with its conflicting philosophies of education, has not been without its teething troubles. A General Nursing Council research unit study reported many in 1975. Universities teach students to take a questioning approach while hospitals insist on discipline, teamwork and obedience. Universities have preconceived ideas about nurses as diligent and conscientious students while hospitals assume under-graduates are idle, precocious and unable to make good clinical nurses because they are lacking in necessary experience, application and humility. Universities accept undergraduates' opinions as arguable rather than right or wrong, whilst hospitals see opinions as the prerogative of the experienced. Also, undergraduates in hospitals are spared some of the trials facing orthodox students – their training is shorter and career prospects brighter. This naturally arouses hostility among orthodox students, many of whom are intellectually and educationally equipped to take a degree course. One fourth-year student at Manchester University reported: 'I found myself working harder than other nurses often, because I so much wanted to be part of the ward team, to show them that I *wanted* to do the bedpan rounds, not just the glamorous techniques.' To begin with, the trained staff in hospitals were not adequately informed about undergraduate courses and did not know what to expect of the college students. As they became more used to them, many came to appreciate the undergraduates' inquiring minds and more open-minded approach to the profession they had chosen.

British universities are now making their first move towards higher degrees for nurses. Edinburgh University, the first in the United Kingdom to develop nursing courses, now offers MSc courses in Nursing Education and Nursing Administration. In 1978 the School of Health and Applied Sciences at Leeds Polytechnic was authorized to launch the first European degree course in nursing designed for registered nurses.

Nurses have come a long way – in spite of the century-old traditions of self-sacrifice, obedience, discipline and devotion which have made aggressive techniques alien to them. But now, as so often in the past, nursing is in a state of turmoil. This ever-changing profession still has a long way to go.

BIBLIOGRAPHY

Abel-Smith, Brian, *A History of the Nursing Profession*. Heinemann, 1960

Alcott, Louisa May, *Hospital Sketches*. Harvard University Press, 1960

Andrews, Lucilla, *No Time for Romance*. George G. Harrap, 1977

Bagnold, Enid, *A Diary Without Dates*. Heinemann, 1918; *Autobiography*. Heinemann, 1969

Bolster, Evelyn, *The Sisters of Mercy in the Crimean War*. Mercier Press, 1964

Bowden, Jean, *Grey Touched with Scarlet*. Robert Hale, 1959

British Red Cross Society and the Order of St John of Jerusalem, *War Organisation Official History 1939–1947*

Brittain, Vera, *Testament of Youth*. Gollancz, 1933

Bullough, Vern L., and Bullough, Bonnie, *The Care of the Sick*. Prodist, 1978

Cameron, H. C., *Mr Guy's Hospital 1726–1948*. Longmans, 1954

Christie, Agatha, *An Autobiography*. Collins, 1977

Clark-Kennedy, A. E., *The London*. Pitman Medical Publishing, 1962

Cobbe, Frances Power, *Life, by Herself*. Richard Bentley, 1894

Cook, Sir Edward, *The Life of Florence Nightingale*. Macmillan, 1914

Cooper, Diana, *The Rainbow Comes and Goes*. Rupert Hart-Davis, 1958

Cope, Zachary, *Six Disciples of Florence Nightingale*. Pitman Medical Publishing, 1961

Coulter, Surgeon-General J. L. S., *History of the Second World War: The Royal Naval Medical Services—Administration*. HMSO, 1954

Craven, Mrs Dacre (Florence Lees), *A Guide to District Nurses and Home Nursing*. Macmillan, 1894

Crew, F. A. E., *History of the Second World War: The Army Medical Services—Administration*. HMSO, 1953 and 1955

Davis, Elizabeth, *Autobiography*. Hurst and Blackett, 1857

Deloughery, Grace L., *History and Trends of Professional Nursing*. The C. V. Mosby Company, 1977

Dent, Olive, *A VAD in France*. Grant Richards, 1917

Diary of a Nursing Sister on the Western Front 1914–15. William Blackwood, 1915

Dickens, Monica, *One Pair of Feet*. Michael Joseph, 1942

Dietz, Lena Dixon, *History and Modern Nursing*. F. A. Davis, 1963

Dolan, Josephine A., *History of Nursing*. W. B. Saunders, 1968

Dunn, Lieut-Colonel C. L., *History of the Second World War: The Emergency Medical Services*. HMSO, 1952

East London Nursing Society 1869–1968, *The History of a Hundred Years*

Edge, Geraldine, and Johnston, Mary E., *The Ships of Youth*. Hodder and Stoughton, 1945

Farmborough, Florence, *Nurse at the Russian Front—A Diary 1914–18*. Constable, 1974

Gaskell, Mrs, *The Letters of*. Edited by J. A. Chapple and Arthur Pollard. Manchester University Press, 1966

Goodman, Margaret, *Experiences of an English Sister of Mercy*. Smith Elder, 1857

Haldane, Elizabeth, *The British Nurse in Peace and War*. John Murray, 1923

Hampton, Isabel, and others, *Nursing the Sick 1893*. International Congress, Chicago

Hardy, Gladys M., *Yes, Matron*. Edward O. Beck, 1951

Harrison, Ada, Editor, *Grey and Scarlet: Letters from the War Areas by Army Sisters on Active Service*. Hodder and Stoughton, 1944

Hay, Ian, *One Hundred Years of Army Nursing*. Cassell, 1953

Hector, Winifred, *The Work of Mrs Bedford Fenwick and the Rise of Professional Nursing*. RCN and the National Council of Nurses, 1973

Huxley, Elspeth, *Florence Nightingale*. Weidenfeld and Nicolson, 1975

Jones, Agnes Elizabeth, *Memorials by her Sister*. Strahan, 1871

Kelly, Lucie Young, *Dimensions of Professional Nursing*. Macmillan, 1975

Kinglake, A. W., *The Invasion of the Crimea*. William Blackwood, 1863–1888

Laurence, E. C., *A Nurse's Life in War and Peace*. Smith Elder, 1912

Longmate, Norman, *The Workhouse*. Temple Smith, 1974

Loyd, A. K., *An Outline of the History of the British Red Cross 1870–1914*

Luard, K. E., *Unknown Warriors*. Chatto & Windus, 1930

Macpherson, Major-General W. G., *Official History of the War: Medical Services, General History*. HMSO, 1921

Members of Her Majesty Queen Alexandra's Imperial Military Nursing Service, *Reminiscent Sketches 1914–19*. John Bale Sons and Danielson, 1922

Merrington, W. R., *University College Hospital and its Medical School*. Heinemann, 1976

Millard, Shirley, *I Saw Them Die*. George G. Harrap, 1936

Mitchell, David, *Women on the Warpath*. Jonathan Cape, 1966

Mitchison, Naomi, *All Change Here*. The Bodley Head, 1975

Moore, Norman, *The History of St Bartholomew's Hospital*. C. Arthur Pearson, 1918

Nightingale, Florence, *Notes on Matters Affecting the Health of the British Army* 1858; *Notes on Nursing.* Harrison, 1860; *Subsidiary Notes as to the Introduction of Female Nursing into Military Hospitals.* Harrison, 1858; *To Her Nurses.* Macmillan, 1914

Nicholson, G. W. L., *Canada's Nursing Sisters.* Samuel Stevens Hakkert, 1975

Nolan, Cynthia, *A Bride for St Thomas's.* Constable, 1970

Nutting, Adelaide, and Dock, Lavinia, *A History of Nursing.* G. P. Putnam's Sons, 1907

Oliver, Dame Beryl, *The British Red Cross In Action.* Faber, 1966

Oman, Carola, *An Oxford Childhood.* Hodder & Stoughton, 1976

Osborne, The Hon and Rev Sydney Godolphin, *Scutari and its Hospitals.* Dickinson Brothers, 1855

Parsons, F. G., *A History of St Thomas's Hospital.* Methuen, 1932

Piggott, Juliet, *Queen Alexandra's Royal Army Nursing Corps.* Leo Cooper, 1975

Platt, Elspeth, *The Story of the Ranyard Mission 1857–1937.* Hodder & Stoughton, 1937

Ranyard, L. N., *Nurses for the Needy.* James Nisbet, 1875

Rathbone, Eleanor, *William Rathbone—A Memoir.* Macmillan, 1905

Rathbone, William, *Sketch of the History and Progress of District Nursing.* Macmillan, 1890

Rexford-Welch, Squadron-Leader S. C., *History of the Second World War: The Royal Air Force Medical Services—Administration.* HMSO, 1954

Roberts, Mary R., *The Army Nurse Corps: Yesterday and Today.* 1959; *American Nursing. History and Interpretation.* The Macmillan Co, 1954

Rogers, Joseph, *Reminiscences of a Workhouse Medical Officer.* T. Fisher Unwin, 1889

Ryder, Rowland, *Edith Cavell.* Hamish Hamilton, 1975

Seymer, Lucy Ridgely, *Florence Nightingale's Nurses.* Pitman Medical Publishing, 1960; *A General History of Nursing.* Faber, 1956

Stewart, Isabel, and Austin, Anne L., *A History of Nursing.* G. P. Putnam's Sons, 1962

Stimson, Julia C., *Finding Themselves.* Macmillan, 1918

Stocks, Mary, *A Hundred Years of District Nursing.* George Allen & Unwin, 1960

Strong, Rebecca, *Reminiscences.* Privately Printed, 1935

Taylor, Fanny, *Eastern Hospitals and English Nurses.* Hurst and Blackett, 1856

Thurstan, Violetta, *Field Hospital and Flying Column.* G. P. Putnam's Sons, 1915

Tooley, Sarah A., *A History of Nursing in the British Empire.* S. H. Bonsfield, 1906

Twining, Louisa, *Recollections of Life and Work.* Edward Arnold, 1893; *Recollections of Workhouse Visiting and Management.* Egan Paul, 1880

Ward, Irene, *F.A.N.Y. Invicta*. Hutchinson, 1955
Westman, Stephen, *Surgeon with the Kaiser's Army*. William Kimber, 1968
Woodham-Smith, Cecil, *Florence Nightingale*. Constable, 1951

Periodicals and Reports

American Journal of Nursing
Athlone Committee on Nursing Services. Interim Report, 1939
Briggs Committee on Nursing. Report. HMSO, 1972
British Journal of Nursing
College of Nursing. Memorandum Relating to Conditions in the
    Nursing Profession, 1939
Jubilee Congress of District Nursing 1909. Report and Proceedings.
Labour Party and the Nursing Profession, 1927
Lancet Commission on Nursing, 1932
Lancet Commission on Workhouse Infirmaries, 1865
Nursing Mirror
Nursing Outlook
Nursing Record
Nursing Times
Select Committee on Registration, 1904–05

ACKNOWLEDGEMENTS

The author has made every effort to contact the owners of all copyright material included in this book, and apologizes for any omissions caused through difficulty in tracing such sources.

Acknowledgement is made for kind permission to use material from the following sources:
The Nightingale Collection, the Nightingale Fund Council Records, the St Thomas's Hospital Records and the Greater London Council Records Office, in chapters 4 and 5; the Imperial War Museum, London, for David, Eleanor Millicent, oral history interview 641/06, on pp 126, 133–4, 146; Evans, Edith Cecily, oral history interview 508/06 on pp 139, 140, 143; Johnson, Louie, oral history interview 330/11 on pp 138, 139, 142, 143–4; Schofield, Mary, oral history interview 690/04 on p 168; *Testament of Youth* by Vera Brittain (Paul Berry and Victor Gollancz Ltd) on pp 130, 138, 142, 145, 161, 168; *An Autobiography* by Agatha Christie (William Collins Sons and Co Ltd) on pp 132, 139–40, 144; *No Time for Romance* by Lucilla Andrews (George G. Harrap & Company Ltd and John Farquharson Ltd) on pp 190, 191–2; *Grey and Scarlet* edited by Ada Harrison (Hodder & Stoughton Limited) on pp 186, 187, 188, 193, 194, 195, 200, 201, 202, 204, 205; *American Journal of Nursing*, April 1942 ('At 7.55 am . . .') on p 192; June 1942 ('After the first bombs . . .') on pp 192–3; November 1942 ('It was a strange . . .') on p 192; June 1943 ('Army nurses at . . .') on p 205; December 1943 ('There are girls here . . .') on p 205; April 1944 ('I wanted to jump . . .') on p 209; September 1945 ('The winter of 1943 . . .') on p 198; *Dead Sea Plage, 1941* by Robert Liddell on p 201.

The author would like to thank the Royal College of Nursing Library, Queen Alexandra's Royal Army Nursing Corps Museum, the British Red Cross Society, the British Museum Manuscript Room, and retired members of Queen Alexandra's Imperial Military Nursing Service, Queen Alexandra's Royal Naval Nursing Service and Voluntary Aid Detachments who kindly agreed to be interviewed about their wartime experiences.

Picture Acknowledgements

The following organizations kindly supplied the illustrations in this book. They are listed alphabetically.

Illustrated London News, p 54

Imperial War Museum, pp 134, 144, 151, 159, 160, 164/165, 167 (both), 170, 185, 194, 199, 200, 202, 206, 208

Mansell Collection, pp 59, 60/61, 136/137, 141, 143, 153, 189

Mary Evans Picture Library, pp 58, 156/157

QARANC Museum, pp 35, 41, 45, 50, 68/69, 74, 101, 177, 180, 191, 212, 213

Radio Times Hulton Picture Library, pp 113, 118, 122/123

Sylvia Marie Haynes Museum of Cards, p 131

Wellcome Trustees, pp 6, 12/13, 15, 18, 20, 24, 30, 89

INDEX

(Italic figures refer to illustrations)

Index